The Language of Leaders

How top CEOs communicate to inspire, influence and achieve results

Kevin Murray

KoganPage

LONDON PHILADELPHIA NEW DELHI

First published in Great Britain and the United States in 2012 by Kogan Page Limited

120 Pentonville Road	1518 Walnut Street, Suite 1100	4737/23 Ansari Road
London N1 9JN	Philadelphia PA 19102	Daryaganj
United Kingdom	USA	New Delhi 110002
www.koganpage.com		India

© Kevin Murray, 2012

ISBN   978 0 7494 6396 0
E-ISBN   978 0 7494 6439 4

British Library Cataloguing-in-Publication Data

A CIP record for this book is available from the British Library.

Library of Congress Cataloging-in-Publication Data

Murray, Kevin, 1928-
    The language of leaders : how top CEOs communicate to inspire, influence and achieve results / Kevin Murray.
        p. cm.
    ISBN 978-0-7494-6396-0 – ISBN 978-0-7494-6439-4   1. Leadership.   2. Chief executive officers.   3. Communication in management.   I. Title.
    HD57.7.M868 2011
    658.4'5–dc23
                                                                                    2011025427

Typeset by Graphicraft Limited, Hong Kong
Print production managed by Jellyfish
Printed and bound by CPI Group (UK) Ltd, Croydon, CR0 4YY

To my wife, who inspires our family

CONTENTS

PART THREE Communicate, communicate, communicate 111

13   Watch out for the undermining signals beyond the words   151

14   Prepare properly for public platforms   160

PART FOUR Conclusion   175

15   Learn, rehearse, review, improve; become fluent in the language of leaders   177

16   If you remember nothing else...   182

Meet the leaders interviewed for this book   187

Introduction: communicate to inspire

Inspiring leaders make us want to achieve more. They persuade us to their cause, win our active support, help us to work better together and make us feel proud to be part of the communities they create. They communicate tirelessly, and it is their skill at listening and talking that keeps us passionately connected to their vision.

If need be, great leaders get us to face ugly reality, and then they give us a new sense of direction and optimism. Along the way, they help us to see how what we do makes a difference. They listen to us and they respect us. We feel involved and committed. We watch them for cues, and we feel great when they recognize our efforts – and then we try even harder.

We follow leaders because of how they make us feel.

So, if we want to be better leaders ourselves, how do we communicate in a way that inspires? What do we need to think about when framing our own leadership communication? Is there a system that experienced leaders use, a framework for thinking? These were the questions I had in mind when I set out to interview people at the helm of many well-known organizations – leaders who had faced significant challenges and been through times of dramatic change.

The idea for this book had been at the back of my mind for ages, born of the coaching work I do with leaders. One day, instead of just thinking about it, I started voicing the idea to friends and colleagues. In the main I wanted to concentrate on business leaders, not politicians or public sector leaders. My career has been in business communication, and it was there I wanted to focus. My colleagues thought it was a great idea, encouraged me to do it, and opened their contact books. Together with my own contacts, we soon had a dozen meetings in the diary, then two dozen, then three.

By the time we closed off the interviews to start writing, I had been privileged to speak to 54 people who were chairmen and CEOs of businesses, charities and non-governmental organizations (NGOs), as well as three military generals, a former police commissioner, a university vice-chancellor and a rugby world cup-winning coach. The list of leaders involved is at the end of this introduction, and their biographies appear at the end of this book.

Between them, these leaders are responsible for well over two million employees in a wide range of organizations, from airlines to water companies, from manufacturing businesses to service firms, from mining multinationals to global pharmaceutical companies, from banks to charities. The book includes views from the heads of huge global businesses and small local enterprises.

Few leaders we approached for an interview turned us down. We achieved a 95 per cent strike rate with our requests. Why? Because all of the people interviewed were intrigued and keen to share their thinking on communication. For many, it was a subject they had not been grilled on before, and they all enjoyed the chance to articulate their views.

Sir Richard Branson was one who got away. When I asked him for an interview, he looked dubious and said: 'There are a lot of books on leadership. What will make yours any different?' Clearly, my answer wasn't compelling enough at the time, because I never got the interview. But it was a *great* question. It forced me to be crystal clear about my mission.

To manage your expectations, let me be explicit: this is not a book on leadership in general, and there are many aspects of leadership that are not dealt with in these chapters. My spotlight is on leadership communication, and my mission is to help you become a better and more effective leader, by helping you to be a better, more inspiring communicator.

Why is that important? Because good communication can make the difference between poor performance and great performance. Leaders who can inspire others to great things can do so much good. They create great places to work. They enable the people they work with to be better than they thought possible, to achieve more than they dreamed. They enable innovation. They help businesses to grow and prosper. They help to create the wealth of nations. They build better businesses, and better businesses are good for everyone.

On the other hand, leaders who cannot communicate well, who lack the human touch, can create organizations which are toxic to work in, filled with turmoil and conflict, going nowhere, achieving little. In my career, spanning almost four decades now, I have worked with leaders who have been exceptional thinkers but somehow unable to persuade people to see the brilliance of their plans. Their ability to analyse a situation, quickly seize on the key issues and decide on the actions needed was breathtaking. But they lacked that vital skill that enabled them to relate to people in a way that created buy-in and, in the end, after a great deal of pain for all concerned, they failed. On the other hand, it has been amazing to work with leaders who are more empathetic, and better communicators, who had a positive impact quickly in even the most disrupted of organizations.

'There's no point in having a vision or a strategy that you can't implement,' said one of the chairmen interviewed in this book. 'When selecting leaders, you have to decide whether they have good judgement, are clear thinkers, and will be able to take their people with them. That's all about communicating, communicating, communicating.'

Just about every leader in these pages identified communication as a top-three skill of leadership, if not the second most important. The ability to think clearly and strategically was inevitably placed at number one. (Clarity of thinking was also closely linked to effective communication.) Always, they pointed out, the best strategy was useless if people could not be inspired to help deliver it.

The Futures Company, which specializes in trends and future-facing research (and is part of the WPP Group), recently published the results of a poll that looked at the characteristics essential to being a good leader. 'Being a good communicator' ranked equal first with 'being willing to take responsibility for good and bad decisions'. In third place was 'identifying the most important actions needed by the business'.

Followers expect their leaders to be good communicators, and rate it a number-one skill of leadership.

Good communication, said the leaders in these pages, is about passion, empathy, simplicity, stories, conversations, great listening and compelling visions. It is about integrity and strong values, and a powerful sense of mission. It is about honesty. It is about building relationships, creating trust and enabling endeavour. Communication is what leaders do before, during and after decisions. It is what they do to achieve results. It is how they inspire us.

In the past few years the world has changed and the need for effective communication has never been greater. We live in a time of radical transparency and great uncertainty. Expectations of good corporate behaviour have been ramped up and empowered consumers and communities have changed the very nature of leadership.

The leaders in this book say the purpose of leadership communication is to influence and inspire in order to achieve great results. In that context, they talk about:

- why trust is essential to leadership, why that means you have to be authentic and why you have to learn to be more passionate in your communication;
- the need to articulate a mission that goes beyond profit as a motive;
- how they create leaders throughout their organizations by relentlessly communicating a framework of values that enable action and decision making;
- why they put into words a vision of the future which powers all their communication;
- how they bring external views of their organization into the organization in order to drive change;
- how they use conversations to engage and motivate people.

They say that if you want to be a more effective communicator, you have to:

- address the concerns of your audience *before* delivering your own messages;
- learn to listen better and master the most difficult communication skill of all;
- develop strong points of view on key issues;
- use more stories to capture hearts and imprint messages on memories;
- be aware of the power of unintended signals;
- prepare properly when appearing on public platforms;
- keep reviewing and honing your communication skills.

In the following chapters I will explore each of these themes, and share the dozens of stories these leaders told me. And yes, there is a framework in what they say, which you will be able to use to guide your own leadership communication.

This book is for all leaders. It is for leaders of large businesses, divisions of those businesses, and small teams in those businesses. It is for people who aspire to be leaders in any organization, big or small.

Dictionaries describe 'language' as 'a system of communication used by a particular country or community'. This book, then, is about the system of communication used by leaders. It describes... *The Language of Leaders*.

The leaders interviewed for this book

Dame Helen Alexander, Chair, Port of London Authority and Incisive Media

Ayman Asfari, Group Chief Executive, Petrofac International

Beverley Aspinall, Managing Director, Fortnum & Mason

Sir Anthony Bamford, Chairman and Managing Director, JCB

Kevin Beeston, Chairman, Taylor Wimpey plc

Phil Bentley, Managing Director, British Gas

Nick Buckles, Chief Executive, G4S

Damon Buffini, Founding Partner, Permira

Simon Calver, Chief Executive, LOVEFiLM

Barbara Cassani, Founder and former Chief Executive, Go Fly

John Connolly, Immediate past Senior Partner and CEO, Deloitte

General The Lord Dannatt, Constable, HM Tower of London

Jeremy Darroch, Chief Executive and Executive Director, BSkyB

Lord Mervyn Davies, Partner and Vice-Chairman, Corsair Capital

Mick Davis, Chief Executive, Xstrata Plc

Ron Dennis, Executive Chairman, McLaren Group and McLaren Automotive

Paul Drechsler, Chairman and Chief Executive, the Wates Group

Tom Enders, Chief Executive, Airbus

Dame Amelia Fawcett, Chairman, Guardian Media Group plc

Sir Maurice Flanagan, Executive Vice-Chairman, Emirates Airline and Group

Christopher Garnett, Member of the Board, Olympic Delivery Authority

Rupert Gavin, Chief Executive, Odeon and UCI Cinemas Group

Sir Christopher Gent, Chairman, GlaxoSmithKline plc

John Gildersleeve, Deputy Chairman, The Carphone Warehouse Group plc

Richard Gnodde, Co-Chief Executive, Goldman Sachs International

Philip Green, Immediate past Chief Executive, United Utilities plc

Moya Greene, Chief Executive, Royal Mail Group

General The Lord Guthrie, Director, N M Rothschild & Sons Ltd

John Heaps, Chairman and Partner, Eversheds LLP

James Hogan, Chief Executive, Etihad Airways

Baroness Sarah Hogg, Chairman, Financial Reporting Council

Tom Hughes-Hallett, Chief Executive, Marie Curie Cancer Care

General Sir Michael Jackson, Senior Adviser, PA Consulting Group

Antony Jenkins, Chief Executive, Barclays Global Retail Banking

Lady Barbara Judge, Immediate past Chair, UK Atomic Energy Authority

Lord Peter Levene, Chairman, Lloyd's

Graham Mackay, Chief Executive, SABMiller plc

Colin Matthews, Chief Executive, BAA Limited

David Morley, Senior Partner, Allen & Overy LLP

Heidi Mottram, Chief Executive, Northumbrian Water Group plc

David Nussbaum, Chief Executive, WWF-UK

Sir Nick Partridge, Chief Executive, Terrence Higgins Trust

Paul Polman, Global Chief Executive, Unilever

Dame Fiona Reynolds, Director General, National Trust

Sir Stuart Rose, Immediate past Chairman, Marks & Spencer Plc

Ron Sandler, Chairman, Northern Rock plc and The Phoenix Group

Chris Satterthwaite, Chief Executive, Chime Communications Plc

Lord Colin Sharman, Chairman, Aviva Plc

Lord John Stevens, Chairman, Monitor Quest

Dame Barbara Stocking, Chief Executive, Oxfam GB

Ian Thomas, Managing Director, Fluor Ltd

Professor Nigel Thrift, Vice-Chancellor, University of Warwick

Ben Verwaayen, Chief Executive, Alcatel-Lucent

Fields Wicker-Miurin, Co-Founder and Partner, Leaders' Quest

Sir Frank Williams, Founder, Williams F1

Sir Clive Woodward, Director of Sport, British Olympic Association

Sir Nicholas Young, Chief Executive, British Red Cross

With contributions from...

Peter Horrocks, Director, BBC World Service

Tony Manwaring, Chief Executive, Tomorrow's Company

Craig Tegel, President and Representative Director, Adobe, Japan

Peter Cheese, Chairman, Institute of Leadership and Management

PART ONE
Why you need to be a better communicator if you want to lead

Napoleon's leadership legacy

01

Jena is a university city in central Germany, on the river Saale. Population: 103,000. It is home to Zeiss, a manufacturer of optical systems. The world's first modern planetarium was built in Jena in 1926 by Zeiss, whose slogan is: 'We make it visible.' Being able to see clearly, and far, is a speciality of the city.

Even so, the city is most famous for being the site of the Battle of Jena-Auerstedt, fought on 14 October 1806, a day when lack of visibility was the key issue. Hardly anyone knows that Jena actually has a much more important claim to fame, one that has relevance for all leaders everywhere.

When the sun rose on the fields near the city that fateful October morning in 1806, a mist rolled in to obscure the vision of the 200,000 nervous soldiers lined up to do battle. However, the thick natural mist was nothing compared with the blinding fog of gun and cannon smoke that followed. On the one side, massed on the plateau west of the river Saale, were the forces of Napoleon Bonaparte of France. On the other side was the even mightier army of Frederick William III of Prussia. A little further north, near Auerstedt, thousands more soldiers of the two leaders were also preparing to attack.

The battle of Jena-Auerstedt began tentatively that morning, with the crack of musket fire and the roar of French artillery. The day ended with two spectacular and bloody victories for Napoleon, whose forces were significantly outnumbered in both battles. The Prussians were routed. The decisive victory left King Frederick William III shattered. His kingdom was cut to half of its former size. He was subjugated to the French empire.

The shots that echo through time

You might, at this point, be wondering why I'm telling you all this. It is because the sounds of those shots at Jena still echo through time – in the form of a military command philosophy – a legacy left for all leaders by Napoleon.

Lessons learned from that battle are still being used today by military leaders around the world – and an increasing number of business leaders.

In 1810, the Generals Scharnhorst and Gneisenau, who fought in the battle, and Prussian military philosopher Carl von Clausewitz sat down to examine what went wrong at Jena. The crushing defeat led them to conclude that their armies needed to be organized and commanded differently in order to cope with 'the fog of war'. Until then, soldiers were subject to a rigid command-and-control leadership philosophy. Nothing could be done without orders from the top.

They observed that the commanders behind the battlefield were unable to see or understand what was happening at the front, in the chaos of combat. The people who really knew what was happening were the subordinate officers fighting in the middle of the gun and cannon smoke. Key opportunities were missed by the Prussian commanders. Small opportunities were exploited by Napoleon's men, who were faster and more inventive on the battlefield. In the end, it was individual genius that had soundly beaten them. Why was that?

They concluded that the French leaders on the battlefield were reacting much faster to the situation at hand and took the initiative independently and without consulting high command. Thus they could quickly exploit any unexpected favourable situation or respond immediately to an unfavourable development.

'Create leaders everywhere!'

The Prussians knew they had to find a new system of command – one that would enable them to deliver the same degree of flexibility. It had to be a far cry from the rigid and hierarchical command philosophy of the time. What they birthed was *Auftragstaktik*: tactics focused on accomplishing the mission.

This new line of thinking was based on the premise that strict rules and rigid plans had no place on the field of battle. It was blindingly stupid to have to wait for orders at times when no orders could be given. It was better that commanders in the field should be able to act independently, but within the framework of a senior commander's intent. Auftragstaktik encouraged commanders to exhibit initiative, flexibility and improvisation, and actually enabled them to disobey orders so long as the overall intent of the commander was maintained. Competitive advantage could only be maintained if you did not have to run decisions up and down the chain of command. Once the commander's intent was understood, decisions had to be devolved to the lowest possible level to allow front-line soldiers to exploit situations as they developed.

Auftragstaktik was not only about more effective delegation; it also required a comprehensive reorganization and retraining of the Prussian army. It meant that military leaders would have to ensure that all ranks – from top to bottom – were always completely clear about the objective of any mission. The lowest ranks would have to be trained in how to lead. Senior commanders would have to make sure they gave no more orders than were absolutely essential. To do this they had to be extremely succinct in their articulation of commands. The objective was to create capable leaders everywhere; if they could do that, victories would follow.

They succeeded. The new command philosophy was perfected by Helmuth von Moltke the Elder, a German Field Marshall who, in the 19th century, embedded auftragstaktik deeply into the organization of the German Army.

After the Second World War, American and British military analysts began to ask the question: Why were the Germans able to move with such speed and flexibility in the early stages of the war? What they discovered was that 'initiative, flexibility and mobility' were the essential aspects of German tactics. They studied the German leadership philosophy, and both the American and British Armies adopted the concept of mission-oriented planning, which they still practise today.

The importance of understanding the commander's intent

In the course of my interviews for this book, I was lucky enough to be able to speak with three former British army generals. I also spoke to Tom Enders, chief executive of global aircraft manufacturer Airbus, himself a major in the German army reservists.

Each of them referred to the concept of commander's intent, and mission-oriented command, and related it to the needs of modern management. They made the point that in today's transparent world, where the business environment is more turbulent, fast and unpredictable, and more like the conditions faced in battle, long-term strategic plans are inadequate. Success depends on how quickly leaders throughout the organization are able to deal with difficult and unforeseen circumstances. They have to be able to take the initiative, while all the time mindful of the key strategic goal of the organization.

But what makes this possible? Using commander's intent, leaders focus on defining with crystal clarity the problem to be solved and the manner in which it needs to be solved. They then empower others to determine how. Empowering people throughout the organization to make decisions and trusting them to do the right thing require an extraordinary focus on communication.

'Mission command' is the name given to the leadership philosophy adopted by the army. 'Commander's intent' is the articulation of the mission's key goal. Everyone in the organization needs to understand the commander's intent and know exactly where they are going and why. Absolute attention has to be paid to articulating and communicating the why and what, while resisting the temptation to dictate the how. Teams must determine for themselves what they need to do to help the commander achieve his goal. Trust is a key ingredient in enabling this concept to work. The entire team needs to understand how those above them, below them and alongside them are going to behave and operate. And above all, they need to have a very good view of what is happening around them. All of this requires communication, communication, communication.

Communication is the glue that binds strategy and delivery together

General Richard Dannatt, the Baron Dannatt, is a former senior British army officer and former Chief of the General Staff, the professional head of the army. He has now been appointed to the ceremonial position of Constable of the Tower of London. He says: 'A leader doesn't just operate in a vacuum. A leader is leading something, some project, some enterprise, some mission. So the first thing the leader has to do is think through very carefully for himself or herself what it is that they're trying to do, what they're trying to achieve. The next thing they have to do is communicate that to those who are going to achieve it. In the military, we talk in terms of mission command.'

'Mission command has three elements. Thinking through what it is you need to achieve and setting out your Intent. That's Intent with a capital I. The second is then delegating tasks to subordinates. Third, it is supervising appropriately. The most important part is the communication of the Intent. A leader must discipline himself to set down his Intent and make it as clear and unambiguous as possible. People must know how they fit in the big picture. This is why, throughout their careers, officers are given so much training in communication. It is the glue that binds strategy and delivery together.'

Then, says Lord Dannatt, it comes down to the personality of the leader, and that is all about character and integrity. 'Success in the enterprise will be defined by the followers, the workers, the foot soldiers, who will look at the leader and decide whether this is the kind of person that they're attracted to, whether they're the kind of person that they want to follow. Their understanding of that person's integrity will actually determine the degree of enthusiasm with which they follow that person. Is that person to be trusted? Is that a person who's got their best interests at heart or is he or she only interested in short-term success or getting the right figures on the bottom line? So communication and character are both really important.'

Lord Dannatt is clear that, in addition to communication and character, courage is something a leader needs more today than ever. 'Courage is a word that everyone understands. Physical courage is tackling the guy who's about to score the try that's going to win the match, or charging into a machine gun nest. But that's physical courage. Moral courage – knowing what the right thing to do is and doing it even though it will be unpopular and lead to a great deal of criticism – is almost more important than physical courage.'

'The great thing is that people's stock of physical courage is a finite asset. But the more often you dig into your own reserves of moral courage, the greater the reserve in the bank is and the easier it is to do next time. Moral courage is born out of honesty and truthfulness, allied to self-belief, and means you will stand up for what you think is right even though that might be uncomfortable.'

'When you do that, followers will have a greater degree of trust in you as a leader and more confidence in the direction of travel. So the leader must put in front of his followers the things he thinks important and why. It's part of explaining what makes you as a leader tick – and you might as well understand that, folks, because the more you understand that, the more you're going to be able to predict how I'm going to react to a certain situation.'

Keep it simple

General Charles Guthrie, the Baron Guthrie of Craigiebank, was Chief of the Defence Staff between 1997 and 2001 and Chief of the General Staff between 1994 and 1997. For 10 years he was a non-executive director of N M Rothschild & Sons, a private investment bank with 50 offices around the world, and is now a director of Cold Defence and Petropavlovsk.

Speaking on the subject of a need for single-minded intent, he said: 'I remember when Michael Howard, then the Home Secretary, was trying to find a general to do a review of the Prison Service. The wretched prison service had 19 objectives! Well, how can you actually do that, how do you get that message across? The idea of having 19 objectives seems absolutely mad. You have to keep it very simple and have a mission, a clear statement of what you plan to do. To produce the best medium-sized helicopters in the world, that's a mission.'

'It must be very simple. I remember observing a young officer giving out his orders to attack something and he said: "We will capture hill so-and-so." And then he spoilt it all by saying: "We will then have a nine-phase operation." Well, in my experience, when you attack something it always goes wrong after the first phase and it's probably better not to have the debris of a plan that is not going to work cluttering your mind. You can overdo this sort of planning, I think.'

'A leader must have a mission. Then you must delegate as much as you possibly can by working out *with* people what their job is, then let them get on with it. How they do it, providing they operate within an agreed framework, is really their problem, as long as they deliver. Don't constantly interfere. I think a boss who is constantly trying to run everybody else's job is going to fail.'

Free people up with a tight framework

General Sir Michael Jackson is a retired British army officer and one of the most high-profile generals since the Second World War. He was appointed Chief of the General Staff in 2003, a month before the start of the Iraq War. He was succeeded as Chief of the General Staff by General The Lord Dannatt in 2006, and retired from the army after serving for almost 45 years.

'People respond to being given delegated responsibilities, there's no two ways about that. You've got to give real clarity about what you want to do to those whom you delegate to; you have to help them to be clear about their own objectives; you've got to give them the means and you've got to give them the operating envelope.'

General Jackson says that an 'operating envelope' (the manner in which things must be done) and a commander's intent give followers a handrail, which helps most when 'the great plan gets a bit wobbly, as they do'.

Tom Enders is CEO of Airbus, makers of the modern icon of the skies, the giant A380, as well as a range of other civil and military aircraft. Airbus employs 52,000 people around the world and recently sold its 10,000th aircraft. He says: 'Values are critical in business today, but I think it's not enough to be aligned only on values; you also need to be aligned on the mission of the company. Everyone needs to know what the mission is and it needs to be very clear and very simple. In our case, we defined it as: Make the greatest aircraft in the world.'

'You have to communicate the mission and values all the time and keep people focused on them. Does doing a particular project help achieve our mission? If not, why are we even considering it? This takes courage and persistence and character.'

Tom says: 'Character, competence and courage are the essential ingredients of leadership.' Then, in the middle of the interview, he leaps up to collect a framed set of words from a cupboard in his office. He shows me that the words 'character, competence and courage' are those of Major Dick Winters, Commander and leader of Second World War 506 Parachute Infantry Regiment, 101st Airborne Division, a man immortalized in the television series *Band of Brothers*.

Stand up for what you believe in

Tom says that leaders must stand up and speak out about things that really matter. This is what will give them credibility. It takes courage. 'You have to lead from the front. If you really want to motivate people, you have to give them your trust. In a book about the power of trust in organizations, I found a quote that pretty much captures the way I try to operate: I'd rather trust and be occasionally disappointed, than not trust and be occasionally right. It doesn't mean blind trust, obviously, but you have to give trust to unleash the enormous creativity in your company.

'When you delegate responsibility, when you truly trust people to do a job, they are wonderfully motivated. As Major Winters says, people can't do a good job if they don't have a chance to use their imagination and creativity. It takes courage to give your followers that freedom. Of course you have to be confident in the competence of people to whom you delegate that they behave responsibly. For that to work, you have to give them the bigger picture, they have to understand the mission of the company and the strategic objectives you try to achieve. There is also a strong correlation between lean organizations and trust. Lean cannot be deployed and flourish in a climate of micro-management.'

After hearing about Auftragstaktik, I started researching more about this command philosophy. I discovered many consultancies, particularly in the USA, offering their services to business leaders, promising to bring the discipline of this leadership philosophy into their enterprises.

The reason is clear. As nearly every leader I spoke to said: 'Above all, the modern world requires speed and agility.' At the same time, a single careless sentence or thoughtless act can lead to the destruction of your reputation. In these circumstances, ensuring that every person who represents your company has absolute clarity about your own sense of true north, your mission and your values, assumes ever greater importance.

Several important imperatives emerge from the military's leadership philosophy.

First, you have to be crystal clear about the mission, and you have to communicate it to everyone in the organization.

Second, people throughout the organization have to be able to lead; the more leaders you create, the greater your chances of success.

Third, those leaders must not only be clear about what the overall goal is, they must also be clear about their own goals, and how the achievement of their goal contributes to the overall goal. They must also be clear on the means at their disposal to get the job done, and the values they must apply to decision making. Leaders must articulate the values that matter, and live and breathe those values to help people understand the way things must be done. Those leaders, wherever they are, need to be encouraged to make their own plans.

Fourth, all leaders need to know what those above them, below them and alongside them are going to do. As the plan unfolds, they have to have a very good understanding of how things are developing, and what they must do to improve performance, or help others.

Fifth, leaders have to show courage and character to earn the right to lead, and must stand up for the things they truly believe. Equally, leaders must learn to show their character and their personal values, if they really want to inspire others.

Time after time, in the other interviews I conducted, I heard leaders talking about one or other of the concepts that are outlined in the military's leadership philosophy. But they also talked about other concepts as well. Running a business is very different from running an organization with employees who have little choice but to follow orders. Running a business or charity or any group of people in modern society requires more, and more nuanced, communications.

Let's examine why this is so in the next chapter...

KEY POINTS FROM CHAPTER 1

- Articulate your mission with crystal clarity.
- Take time and care to ensure it is easily understood, memorable, motivating and unambiguous.
- Values are crucial – they are the way you want things achieved. You need to articulate these, share these, live these.
- Your operating framework of values, combined with your goal, enables your followers to take action, and act with speed and creativity in pursuit of the goal. Ensure that everybody understands them.
- Converse with your followers to help them set their own goals. This will enable you to delegate with confidence, sure that they are clear about what you want achieved and how you want it achieved.
- This will free you to lead, rather than manage, and keep an eye on whether you are advancing to your goal.
- As a leader you must stand up for and speak out on what you believe in – it requires courage, but it shows your followers that you have a moral compass and are worthy of their trust. It gives them the confidence to follow you.
- You have to learn to show your character – people must know what you care about and what your beliefs are. This will make you more predictable, and inspire them to follow your beliefs.
- You must spend time helping teams to communicate with each other, so that everyone knows what their role is, and what other people will be doing in support of reaching the end goal.

Leadership transformed – life in the fishbowl

02

In some ways, the modern world of commerce is a little like a battlefield, but this is a misleading analogy. Yes, often employees (the troops) have to operate in difficult, fast-changing circumstances where they are cut off from their commanders. And yes, they absolutely have to know what the organization's mission is, and deliver their services and products in the right way, and within the operating envelope given to them by their leaders.

But their lives do not depend on them going that extra mile; employees retain a level of effort and commitment which they give at their own discretion, only if they are inspired to do so. That discretionary effort, however, can be the difference between an adequate performance and a great performance – and can be the difference between success and failure for a leader.

The task of a leader is to inspire others to achieve great results. It sounds simple, but leaders today are operating in an incredibly demanding environment. It is ironic, then, that so few leaders are taught the critical communication skills that enable them to be inspiring. How do you capture hearts and minds when life is moving at the speed of light? When there is no time for carefully crafting messages and scripts? When you can only rely on a personal sense of true north to help navigate a perfect storm of change?

The radical transparency of the modern world has, I believe, radically changed leadership. Let's have a look at a modern leader who is a prime example of someone having to lead while under the constant glare of scrutiny and public criticism...

Perpetual communication

Phil Bentley has been managing director of British Gas since 2007. British Gas is Britain's largest domestic energy supplier, with around 15 million gas and electricity customers, employing nearly 30,000 people in 30 different locations around the UK. Phil is proud of what he has achieved since joining the company, though you just know that it has not been without pain.

He says: 'When I took over, we were being voted worst for service, we were losing one million customers a year and the most profit that we'd ever made was £300 million. Today, we are regarded as best in service (despite what the media say), we're winning customers every day and we've quadrupled the profits of a mature, large business. We've won awards for best online website, best European call centre, great place to work and best brand turn-around, among others. These are all external recognition of a huge turnaround in British Gas.'

But, he admits, it hasn't been easy. Perpetual communication has been a feature of his job. 'It starts with the fact that we have 28,000 people in British Gas, so I do a huge amount of communicating internally. And, like it or not, British Gas requires a significant amount of external communication as well.'

At six o'clock every morning, Phil receives a text message informing him of the overnight media coverage of British Gas and the energy sector as a whole. This message could foreshadow a hectic day full of media interviews, including television and radio. It could also involve answering e-mails from dozens of irate customers, which he does personally. And it will involve communicating with staff to make sure that they're being kept abreast of developing news stories. Even if he has a day that doesn't involve dealing with the media, he will be out and about in the business, meeting staff and listening to what they have to say – always visibly taking notes, 'so that they know I am listening and I'm going to do something about what they're telling me'.

He adds: 'One of the most important things I can do is encourage people to bring me bad news and make them feel I will respect their views and take action where it is appropriate. That's what builds trust and commitment.'

When you look at that kind of day, it seems that communicating is the day job! Communicating, he says, is all about getting your message over and inspiring trust and belief. And, to do that, you have to be authentic.

'We used to read a story to the kids about an animal that was trying to be something different. The moral of the story was that you had to play the game you play. For me, there's no point in trying to be somebody I'm not, so I play the game I play, which is that I'm basically a hard-working northerner trying to do the best for my customers and my people in a difficult job. I try to talk plainly and avoid management speak. I hate sounding too formal and indifferent. And, at all times, I try to show my passion for customer care.'

Phil is acutely aware of the scrutiny he is under. Whether it is inside or outside the company, he knows his every move and statement is being watched and debated. 'We live in an age of 24/7 news, bloggers, social media and e-mail, and that makes it a pretty transparent environment. I think that's a great thing, which aids leadership rather than inhibits it.'

Aids it? How so? 'Well, for example, I put my e-mail out on national radio last week saying that if anyone had a problem paying their bill, they should e-mail me at Phil.Bentley@BritishGas.co.uk. I had a lot of people e-mailing to say that they were betting I would never reply. They got a message back straight away, along with a commitment to sort out the problem. I am of the view that people don't wake up in the morning and perversely decide they feel like complaining – they are compelled to complain because of something we've done to them. I love getting those e-mails, because it's how I find out what needs fixing in the business.

'Our business is built up brick by brick, conversation by conversation, winning over customers one by one. I want them all to feel that we will listen and we will follow up.'

The questions that really matter

Phil has driven a huge sense of urgency into the business and often personally oversees solutions for individual customer complaints. 'You have to lead by example and you have to send some powerful signals into the business.'

One such signal is a specialist team in his office dedicated to sorting out customer problems. He knows that he can call them at any time of the day or night and they will take the problem and find a solution. Any problem that comes into his office never leaves his office – it has to be sorted out by his team as quickly as possible.

'Sometimes customers will e-mail me and say that they have had a problem going on for 18 months, which has never been sorted out. They might even e-mail me on a Saturday night after a few drinks. They are staggered that by Monday the problem is sorted. They then write back and say why was that – how come it could in fact be done so quickly? That's a really good question. I then ask that question inside the organization – why were we able to sort out a problem in 24 hours that the organization as a whole has failed to deal with in 18 months?

'Those questions are really useful because they help us to understand how we can drive the same level of responsiveness across 30,000 people and not just the 10 skilled people outside my office.'

Phil recounts a recent interview on BBC when he was being grilled about price increases. The interviewer said that he had received an e-mail from a Mr Lowe, who was sitting under a duvet in his house because he couldn't afford to pay his bill. What advice would Mr Bentley give Mr Lowe?

'I said, well, Mr Lowe, we will contact you and will sort this out, and by the time I'd come out of the BBC, we had found out who the customer was and we had rung him to help and he was in tears (of gratitude). Quite often the elderly don't realize that they are entitled to far more than they claim. Everything I do is designed to demonstrate that every person has a voice and that we will listen.

'For example, we constantly monitor Twitter. If somebody tweets that their "bloody boiler has broken again and I'm once again waiting for British Gas", then we will ring them and say, can we help? It's the same for blogs. We monitor and respond.'

This focus on relentless customer care, constant improvement, perpetual communication and a willingness to receive and respond to criticism and bad news have been some of the primary drivers of change in the business, says Phil.

'Everything I say and everything I do communicates,' he says. 'My job is to make sure that I'm sending the right message and that everyone is receiving it and that those messages are inspiring trust in us as a business.'

I'm sure that Phil would not want me to represent him as the perfect example of a great leader. He is far too modest and decent for that. I start with the story of Phil Bentley because I think his story illustrates so many of the issues that have been raised by all the leaders I spoke to, and it is worth pausing for a moment to consider what insights his story gives us.

What can we learn from the way Phil communicates and leads in British Gas?

Leadership today is a product of our times, and the first observation is that Phil has embraced digital communications and the ability to interact directly with his customers with huge enthusiasm. Many other leaders I spoke to felt inhibited by the constant scrutiny and put off by the sheer volume of interactions required in a world that is so transparent and open. Somehow, they felt this put constraints on what they could do and say. Not Phil; he leaps at the chance to be directly in touch and to engage in conversation with his audiences. The business, he says, is built brick by brick, conversation by conversation.

He recognizes that he has to be visible and that he has to show up to defend British Gas even in the face of inevitable hostility and anger. It was crucial to ensure that he was delivering his company's point of view, no matter how uncomfortable. But he has to be visible inside the company too, constantly sending verbal and non-verbal signals into the organization.

He recognizes the need to be authentic and play the game he plays. He understands the power of listening and is passionate about getting feedback, both negative and positive. He uses the outside (customer problems) to drive change on the inside, and has created an environment where people can bring him bad news, secure in the knowledge that he will listen and respond.

He understands the need for speed, in a world where people's expectations are much higher – they expect better corporate behaviour, better service and faster and more responsive communication. He uses this relentlessly to drive people inside British Gas and wants and expects his staff to be as responsive as he is. His energy sends signals of urgency and his drive for change demands greater agility from everyone inside the organization.

He uses stories all the time to get people to focus on what needs to be done and he peppers his conversation with a string of anecdotes that all focus on customer problems and how they were solved. His passion for customer care is clear to everyone, not because he says it's important, but because he constantly shows that he thinks it is vital.

In one or other way, every leader I interviewed dealt with these subjects: they talked about a new world of transparency and scrutiny; that the job was about perpetual communication; they focused on the increasing need for a distinct point of view; they stressed the essential need for authenticity and passion; they all emphasized the crucial need to be a good listener; they spoke of the need to create an environment of trust, where negative feedback is an organizational asset; they underlined the need for speed and agility, and the need to create leaders throughout the organization as passionate as the leader of the organization, absolutely clear about what they were trying to achieve; they spoke about the need to be visible as a leader, showing up even when you are most uncomfortable; they highlighted that real leaders are accessible; but most of all, they worried about and unanimously recognized that reputation is today the single most important asset if you are to survive and thrive.

I believe that these communication demands on leadership are, in part, caused by a growing partnership between journalists and the public, which has forged a completely new dynamic in business. It is blindingly obvious that consumers and citizens everywhere have been empowered by the internet and digital communications. It is perhaps not quite so obvious that, just as Phil Bentley has embraced the accessibility he now has with consumers, so too have journalists.

The new partnership driving transparency

Few people understand how a modern newsroom really works, yet the changes in the way journalists operate have had a profound effect on modern leadership. Consumers, citizens and journalists now collaborate at lightning speed to provide news and commentary in a world which has become far more transparent. At the same time, it is also more complex, uncertain, volatile and ambiguous.

Under these conditions, being a leader is a demanding, intense and risky role. Everyone I spoke to is very conscious of constantly walking on the edge, just one step or one thoughtless word away from a crisis that could damage their reputation and possibly even the future of the business they lead.

Mostly, they recognize the need for speed and the increased risk of having to operate in a world moving at such a pace. Leaders who employ tens of thousands of people around the world know that every single one of those people could make a crucial mistake that could result in a catastrophe. More than half of the people I interviewed volunteered the saga of Tony Hayward and BP's Deepwater Horizon Gulf of Mexico oil spill crisis as an example of how even the biggest organization can be brought to its knees first by an accident and then by mishandled communications (see Chapter 14).

Perhaps none of them had stopped to think about what was behind a faster world, and what was really driving greater transparency and scrutiny. I have a view that it is this alliance between the public and the media, aided by the ubiquity of the internet, which has made speed the new currency of business. This, in turn, has forced on leaders the need to revolutionize their organizations in order to try to deliver far greater agility within them. And this has placed a huge emphasis on more, and more effective, communication.

Consider the following:

- the sheer speed of modern communication, on a global scale;
- the staggering increase in channels of communication, especially digital;
- shifting patterns of influence, and the rise of citizen and consumer power;
- the elevated expectations of all stakeholders, especially for speedy response;
- new and rapidly changing communities of interest, enabled by digital technologies and a new sense of empowerment;
- increased regulation and the consequent communications requirements;
- the aggressive pursuit of information by journalists, and the 'tabloidization' of business reporting;
- declining levels of trust in business, accelerated by the financial crisis and recession.

All of these issues weigh heavily on a modern leader's mind and have a striking impact on the way they think about communication.

First, let's look at how modern audiences forced a revolution on newsrooms. Peter Horrocks, now the director of the BBC's World Service, was the man who managed the revolution at the BBC – transforming 21 different news platforms into one of the biggest multimedia newsrooms in the world – all because audiences around the world have changed, radically, in the way they consume news. As he walked me around the BBC's newsroom, he told me that many people today use a combination of radio, TV, online news sites and social media platforms to find out what is going on. In response, the BBC has transformed its whole approach to news gathering and news delivery. Prior to the transformation, the BBC Newsroom operated through separate, discrete newsrooms across TV and radio, News 24, online and BBC World. Not only were they separate, but rarely did they collaborate on stories.

The competition was also very different then; ITN was the key competitor, whereas now there is a growing set of media – from broadcast to online newspaper sites, mobile news, news aggregators such as Google News and social media, including Facebook, Twitter and YouTube. This list will continue to grow and is driven by younger audiences who have a different approach to news consumption, where they prefer rapid browsing and have a far greater reliance on social networking and word of mouth for their news. These audience trends are reflected in the statistics: TV still has the lion's share of audience but is declining; BBC radio news is static; the two growth areas are online and mobile.

So how did BBC News transform itself across its 21 news platforms to become one of the biggest multimedia newsrooms in the world, delivering 24/7 news services, with 120 hours of output daily and 500 daily web pages? It involved radical and highly disruptive change requiring investment as well as staff reductions. Essentially, the corporation:

- changed the physical space, which was rebuilt to bring all channels together;
- restructured the editorial and newsroom teams to deliver much closer integration;
- used technology to be able to monitor audience behaviours and be in touch with audiences;
- put a new visual branding across all news services.

'The impact of all this change on BBC News and on our understanding of all our audiences is substantial,' says Peter Horrocks. 'Taking a multimedia approach means that news is highly networked, very much in real time, and stories move on at an amazing pace – what happened in a week in a newsroom now happens in a day.'

Within the BBC Newsroom there is hour-by-hour monitoring of top stories and analysis of the interaction and commentary from the audiences. Also, stories have to be adapted to the different channels:

- on mobile devices, stories need to be simpler and shorter;
- TV has to deliver visual impact;
- radio is more thoughtful and conceptual;
- online stories can go deeper but have to grab attention – average time on a site is two to three seconds.

Stories evolve at an incredible pace

Journalists have changed how they gather their news and develop their stories. The interaction and engagement journalists get from online forums and also from the power of blogging cannot be overestimated. By getting constant and voluminous feedback, their stories develop and change according to the needs of the audience, in real time. So, in the course of the day – because of this engagement with their audience – journalists can evolve a story or change direction at an incredibly rapid pace. All of this makes a modern newsroom a voraciously hungry news machine.

It also means that stories have a distinct life cycle and are often being adapted for the different channels in a particular rhythm. For example: radio peaks in the mornings and at drive time; mobile peaks during commuting times; online is strong at the start of the working day and then peaks at lunchtime; and TV peaks in the evening.

One of the most impressive things I saw on my tour of the newsroom was a team of people scouring the social websites for potential new stories. They were looking for angles that would be interesting and could be developed into good copy. No longer did they have to wait for someone to bring the idea to them.

The meaning for a CEO is clear. One disgruntled customer with a grudge and the motivation to go online with their views can reach directly potentially millions of other consumers on the web *and* attract the attention of one of the mightiest news-gathering machines in the world – within minutes of uploading their views. This is how small incidents or service breakdowns become major global stories.

Imagine the frustration of an airline which had not responded well to a complaint about a broken guitar by a journeyman country and western singer. The singer had spent a year trying in vain to get compensation but to no avail. He wrote a song chronicling his saga, which became a YouTube sensation and gave the singer the biggest hit of his career. The song was laced with humour and scathing criticism and packaged in a catchy tune and soon became a global media story. It cost the airline so much more than the price of a repair to a single guitar. United Airlines saw its share price tumble and could have avoided the whole issue if it had followed its own policy on customer service: 'In the air and on the ground, online and on the telephone, our customers have the right to expect – to demand – respect, courtesy, fairness and honesty from the airline they have selected for travel.'

A Virgin Atlantic passenger who was on a flight back to the UK from India did not enjoy his meal and took photographs of it. He then sent the photos plus a letter to Virgin, as well as sending it to newspapers and blogs. It had the merit of being a funny, but nevertheless accurate, complaint letter. The story soon took off, forcing Richard Branson himself to ring the passenger and thank him for his constructive if tongue-in-cheek e-mail, and thus defuse a story that could have stayed airborne for quite some time.

Internal e-mails can be very public

Even internal e-mails can become the subject of news – especially when disgruntled employees leak the e-mails to the media. Sir Andrew Cahn, who was then head of the government body UK Trade and Investment (UKTI), told colleagues just before the end of the year that the Foreign Office, which funds the organization, was 'heading for an underspend' and urged them to come up with ways of spending the cash.

His e-mail was leaked to the media and it triggered outrage that the department appeared to be fabricating ways to spend money unnecessarily while the rest of the country faced mass spending cuts. The Treasury reacted by saying it would dock the Foreign Office's budget by £20 million – a fine to set an example to the rest of Whitehall and warn all ministers and the civil service that any unspent funds should be returned to the Exchequer. That was a pretty expensive e-mail.

Most leadership communication is not fit for purpose

Dame Amelia Fawcett, chair of the Guardian Media Group, one of the UK's leading media organizations, says this new environment makes leadership much harder. 'Most communications are just not fit for purpose in the Facebook, Twitter, blog and 24/7 news world. News is now being produced by professionals and non-professionals working together – in what we call the mutualization of news. One correspondent on the *Guardian* has a following on her blog of 750,000 people. The *Guardian* has a circulation of 365,000. If you know how to engage with that sort of network it can be very powerful.'

This is why many leaders feel that they are operating much closer to the precipice. Reputation has always been important but today, they say, you can lose your reputation in seconds. Lord Mervyn Davies (Baron Davies of Abersoch), former chairman of Standard Chartered plc and a former government minister, argues that communication has assumed crucial importance in a world 'where news travels so fast; where bad and good news can move across continents in milliseconds. This has changed the nature of politics and changed the nature of business.

'It means that whatever you're doing, wherever you are, there is a chance that because of CCTV, YouTube, cameras on mobile phones, somebody is watching you. We live in a world where a small action can cause a big result.'

Kevin Beeston, who is chairman of Taylor Wimpey, one of the largest British housebuilding companies, and a former chairman of global support services group Serco, says: 'These days, everybody's got a camera with them. Everybody's got a mobile phone with a voice recording system or a video camera, so you cannot drop your guard. Make one mistake and you will not get away with it.

'But,' he adds, 'the opposite is also true – if you manage this environment well you have more ways of getting your message over and building your brand. And a strong brand is probably one of the most significant competitive advantages a company can have. So if you manage it effectively, it could be a big driver of shareholder value.'

Businesses are like open democracies

Graham Mackay, chief executive of SABMiller, one of the world's largest brewers, with brewing interests and distribution agreements across six continents, says that the modern world places much greater demands on leaders. 'Businesses are much more like open democracies. People expect to be communicated to much more and see themselves as part of a democracy where they consent to being led. As well as the need to communicate more with employees, there is increased regulatory scrutiny, the rise of global NGOs and 24/7 media. You have to represent yourself and explain your company and your actions all the time.'

Under such constant scrutiny, and criticism, leaders are only too well aware that business needs to be seen as a force for good and not just for profit. They have to have a much higher purpose than the simple profit motive.

Paul Drechsler, chairman and chief executive of the Wates Group, a family-owned enterprise which is one of the UK's largest construction services companies, says: 'A decade ago I would have talked about the business in terms of sales, profit, market share and competitors. When I stand up to talk about this business now, I talk about how many jobs we have created, what we are doing to reduce our carbon footprint and what positive effect we are having on society. We have had to broaden our storyline substantially. You've got to learn to tell your story in a way that will attract customers, attract employees and attract investment.

'It isn't that trust and reputation are more important today than they were before – it is that they are more vulnerable in today's world. I say to my colleagues in Wates that my number one concern is that, through their actions and behaviours, a brand and reputation that took 114 years to build up could be destroyed in an instant.'

Rupert Gavin is CEO of Odeon and UCI Cinemas, the largest chain of cinemas outside the Americas. Rupert believes that you cannot be a good business leader without also being a good leader in the community in which you live and operate. 'You cannot have a healthy business in a bankrupt society. In this regard the demands on the CEO are much more complicated than they were 10 years ago.'

Leaders must create leaders

Traditional command-and-control methods of management are simply not appropriate in this world. Leaders cannot leave themselves exposed to situations where employees are unable to make decisions because they cannot get hold of you. They have to be empowered to do the right thing when the critical moment arrives, and an angry customer needs to be placated or a mistake rectified. Leaders have to know what the minimum standards of behaviour are.

I regularly heard CEOs talking about the need to create leaders throughout their organizations, in order to be able to operate in this world. This thought resonated strongly with the military idea of creating leaders throughout the army. In fact, the idea that leaders must create leaders was among the strongest themes emerging from all of the interviews.

Key to creating leaders is creating a framework of well-understood values within which leaders can operate. The objective is to ensure that people throughout a company understand what the company expects of them, not only in terms of what they need to do, but how they should do it. Leaders need to spend a great deal of time trying to ensure that everyone understands what 'doing the right thing' really means.

Radical transparency needs radical thinking

Jeremy Darroch, CEO of BSkyB, the largest pay-TV broadcaster in the United Kingdom, with more than 10 million subscribers, believes you have to go further than simply embracing life in the fishbowl. You should invite people into the fishbowl with you.

'Everything is so transparent, you might as well invite people in to see what you do. Say: "We'd like you to come and have a look." This is because trust is going to be one of the great themes of business over the next decade and those companies that aspire to long-term success have to make building and maintaining trust an important part of their agenda. To trust you, people have to know you. They have to get a sense of who you are and what you stand for and what you believe in – inside and outside the company.'

Jeremy believes that this world of radical transparency has placed a burden on business to communicate more. Business has to get itself on the front foot and lay out the case for why business is good for society, in a much more compelling way. Winning trust isn't just a single-company issue, it is an issue for all businesses. And, he says, every leader must realize they are simply a steward of the organization they lead, destined to move on at some point. With that in mind, the job is to improve the long-term viability of the organization – to leave it in an even better state than it was when they inherited it.

Unanimous agreement, then, from the 60 leaders I interviewed: leadership has been transformed.

They said some of the same things that military leaders said, agreeing on the need for a clear mission and values, and about the need to ensure everyone knows what they are. They talk similarly about the importance of mission and values in creating leaders everywhere, and the need to drive speed and agility into the organizations they lead. But they also talk about a world in which there is an even more pressing need to inspire people, to lift employees to greater achievement through powers of persuasion. This is because people believe they work in an open democracy where their discretionary effort is their choice to give. In this environment, where trust and relationships are the engines of success, there is an increased demand for excellence in communication.

In addition, leaders today have little choice but to embrace transparency and work with the raised communication expectations of a digital age. It means they have to put reputation management at the top of their agenda, right up there with the need to build relationships of trust. To do that, leaders must communicate more clearly, more often and with the idea firmly embedded that communication, today, is about rapidly evolving stories and conversations.

Leadership is now more complex, demanding and stressful, but more rewarding and more meaningful if you can get it right. Leaders increasingly feel that they are only stewards of the businesses they lead, and have to make sure that those businesses are improved while they are in charge, and have an even better future ahead of them when they leave. This means thinking longer term about building a sustainable business, part of the communities in which they operate.

The communication demand on leaders is far greater today, requiring them to address a wider array of audiences and use an even wider array of channels. But, as Kevin Beeston says, if you manage this environment well, you have more ways of getting your message over and building a great business where everybody wins.

KEY POINTS FROM CHAPTER 2

- Radical transparency has radically changed leadership.

- Consumers, citizens and journalists are in a partnership where news and views travel the world in seconds.

- The sheer speed of modern communications, on a global scale, combined with the staggering increase in channels of communication and rapidly shifting patterns of influence, means that leaders have to build much more agile and speedy organizations in order to cope.

- Leaders must create leaders in order to build more agile organizations.

- Organizations are now much more like open democracies.

- People expect to be communicated to much more and see themselves as part of a democracy where they consent to being led.

- As well as the need to communicate more with employees, there is increased regulatory scrutiny, the rise of global NGOs and 24/7 media. You have to represent yourself and explain your company and your actions all the time.

- Every enterprise needs an articulation of a higher purpose than profit.

- Sustainability is the watchword. It applies to the organization's longevity as well as the social and physical environments within which a leader operates.

- Leaders must make trust a strategic goal.

- People want leaders that they can believe in.

- Life in the fishbowl requires leaders to speak to their beliefs and have a clear point of view.

- The scrutiny is intense. It won't go away. Learn to live with it.

- Leaders must embrace the digital age of transparency. The risks are higher, but the rewards are greater.

03

The 12 principles of leadership communication

The bosses I spoke with have a combined total of almost 2,000 years of leadership experience. Every interview was taped, and the tapes were transcribed. In the transcripts, there are more than 500,000 words.

These leaders are human: full of failings and faults, just like you and me. Most of them are quite happy to talk about their failings. All of them, however, have achieved success in their careers, and have risen to the top of organizations employing, sometimes, hundreds of thousands of people. They have had to appear in front of the media in a crisis, make speeches to influential gatherings and expose themselves to the full glare of public scrutiny. More importantly, they have had to lead change and improvement among teams, divisions and whole companies time and again. There is considerable wisdom in that experience.

After reviewing all those words, what have I heard? What can you use from their experience to power and inform the way you communicate as a leader?

My analysis tells me there are 12 principles of leadership communication that these leaders adhere to, to some degree or other. Rather like using a graphic equalizer on a stereo system, each leader dials up or down different principles, but all of them are always present, often changing in emphasis as circumstances change.

All the leaders are clear that leadership communication is about inspiring others to achieve great things. In this context, the 12 principles are:

1 Learn how to be yourself, better, if you aspire to being a better leader and communicator.

2 Give voice to a compelling mission and a powerful set of values.

3 Combine this with a vivid picture of the future, which you communicate relentlessly to drive behaviours in the present.

4 Keep your people focused on the key relationships that your organization depends on for success, and make building trust in those relationships a priority.

5 Make 'engagement' a strategic goal, and use conversations to engage.

6 Become a fanatic about understanding audiences, before trying to communicate with them.

7 Listen in new and powerful ways, and learn to ask the right questions.

8 Prepare a potent point of view to communicate your messages.

9 Use more stories and anecdotes to inspire the right behaviours.

10 Be aware of the signals you send beyond your words.

11 Prepare properly for public platforms – your reputation is at stake.

12 Learn, rehearse, review, improve – always strive to be a better communicator.

Why are these principles so important? Let's look at them one by one.

Be yourself, better

Authenticity in a leader is crucial. Followers will not commit if they do not trust you and believe that you have integrity. So, even if you are a highly introverted individual, you will have to learn to speak with more passion, talk to your values, and stand up more often to speak to your beliefs. Followers must feel your passion, and believe that you believe. When you are clear with yourself about the things you really care about, you cannot help but talk to them with passion. Most leaders have not spent the time articulating those beliefs, yet the ability to draw on and display that passion and commitment, consistently and predictably, counts for more than skills at oratory, and communicates more effectively than even the most perfectly crafted words. You have to be true to yourself, but you also have to learn to 'perform' yourself better.

Mission and values

Too often, leaders use financial or numerical goals to motivate people. They are more comfortable being rational and objective. Too often, followers say they don't get out of bed in the morning to achieve financial or other numerical objectives. They come to work and want to be inspired by a sense of doing something important, something that makes a difference. A strong sense of mission can help shape decisions to be made throughout the organization, and is even more empowering when coupled with a set of values which your people know to be true. In this world of radical transparency, values have assumed far greater importance, for many reasons. Values define how people in the organization behave in pursuit of their objectives, and their actions define a business to the outside world. Those intangible values – often dismissed as 'soft and fluffy' – translate into actions on the ground, which translate into hard numbers in the books.

Future focus

Every leader I spoke to used the future to drive the present. They knew precisely where they wanted to be in a given timescale, even if they did not know exactly how to get there. They were never satisfied with the status quo, and their restlessness was a tangible force. Every question they asked had to do with how people were progressing to the goals, and they kept those goals under constant review. They painted a vivid picture of success, often describing the future in both rational terms (the numbers) and emotive terms (how it would feel for all concerned). This bringing together of the rational and the emotional was key to inspiring people. Fusing the future vision (what success will look and feel like) to the purpose (what important thing we are here to do) and to the values (how we do it) was what stirred hearts and minds. This future, though, had to be expressed in benefit terms for all the people with a vested interest in the performance of the organization – customers, shareholders, local communities, suppliers and partners and, most importantly, employees.

Bring the outside in

Leaders have to live outside their organizations, constantly bringing stories of success and failure in external relationships into the organization to keep everyone fixed on what needs to improve. Successful leaders know that relationships are the engines of success; they keep a close eye on the state of all key relationships, and keep their enterprise focused on those relationships as well. You have to set up 'quivering antennae', as one leader described it – a radar system that keeps you in touch with the outside world. Too often I heard about the 'reputation gap' – the difference between the promise the business made and the experience customers or stakeholders actually received. Narrowing that gap, or even managing it away, is the goal if you want to be trusted. And you do want to be trusted. Trust is now the most valuable but most hidden asset on your balance sheet. Leaders are increasingly looking to make trust a strategic goal, measured and managed as preciously as any other key asset.

Engage through conversations

More and more leaders are now measuring levels of employee engagement, and using this measurement as a strategic tool to find the ways to keep people motivated and committed to the cause. Study after study has shown that companies with high levels of engagement among employees outperform their competitors, by some margin. Engagement is achieved through conversations – structured, potent conversations which allow employees to fully understand the big objective, and work out with their leaders what they have to do to help achieve the goals. It is in these conversations that the rubber hits the road, where the plan gets traction. Too often, these conversations are neglected, and middle managers are neither trained for nor measured on their ability to hold these critical conversations. Worse, top management doesn't check on the quality of those conversations, or seek to get the feedback from those conversations in a systematic way.

Audience centricity

Let us be clear: you have *not* communicated well if people have not heard you, have not understood you and do not feel motivated to think differently and act differently as a result of your words. You may have stood up and talked *at* them, but communication has only taken place when your words have had an impact. In any enterprise, leadership communication is all about achieving big goals. It is about changing behaviours. People listen from behind their own filters – filters which may be cultural or emotional, or they may be in place because of people's unique perceptions or even misunderstandings. You have to talk to them about their concerns, their issues, before you can be understood on your own. Every leader interviewed for this book, without exception, spoke of the need to be audience centric in communication, and to recognize that, when it comes to communication, it is all about the audience. You have to set out to achieve change in how they think, feel and act, but that requires you to know how they think, feel and act *now*.

Listening

Quite often, the people I interviewed treated the subject of listening as if it were somehow distinct from communicating. They rated it an essential skill of leadership, possibly the hardest to perfect. Sometimes the simple act of listening, they said, is an act of inspiration in itself. 'You have to give people a damn good listening to.' There is something more fundamental at work here, though, and I call it the listening contract – first you have to listen, if you want to be heard. When you listen *and* then respond with actions that remove barriers, or pick up on good ideas, you create enormous goodwill and demonstrate you are on their side, particularly when you encourage people to open up, and create an environment where people can bring you bad news, express their frustrations and voice their concerns without fear of repercussions. You have to listen beyond the words, into the motives and agendas, into the context, into the performance KPIs and the financial numbers and the mood, and you have to show you understand, even if you don't agree. You have to ask great questions, and learn to unleash your curiosity and interest in people. It really shows.

Point of view

The best leaders have a potent point of view, and it is always the person with the strong point of view who influences the group, who wins the day. As a leader, you are going to have to stand up and give your point of view, time and time again. You will have to take a position on issues, be courageous, and stand up for what you believe to be right. Too few leaders think about developing points of view – yet, when well articulated, these can help you win friends and influence people, and gain a stronger voice in shaping the future. In a world where people trust the motives, judgement and competence of business leaders less now than just five years ago, shouldn't we be talking to those issues more often, with more transparency, more conviction and, yes, passion? The ideal point of view should therefore bring together your purpose and your values, highlight your behaviours and draw attention to the benefits of doing things your way. And it should call people to action. Powerful stuff.

Stories and anecdotes

Getting people to listen to you is tough enough, but getting them to sit up and take notice, and then remember what you have to say is a supreme challenge. Every leader uses stories, knowing that we are wired to listen, imaginatively, when we are told stories. Good stories get under the cynical radar and touch hearts. Backed up by facts to cover off the mind, stories have the power to move people. The best stories tell us about customer experiences, good and bad, or make heroes out of employees delivering the values of the organization, or show up the frustrations of workers unable to do their best because of the system, or vividly portray the future, or reveal aspects of the leader to the audience. They deliberately avoid the tyranny of PowerPoint, and are the more memorable because of it. Some leaders I spoke with were uncomfortable with the word 'stories', and preferred 'anecdotes', saying this was factual rather than fictional, as some stories can be. But they all used them, loved hearing them and then retelling them, over and over.

Signals

Actions speak louder than words. A cliché, you might say, but nevertheless one of the hardest truths for a leader to grasp. Being a leader means looking, acting, walking and talking like a leader. Countless times, leaders forget that they are in a fishbowl and are being watched all the time. A look of frustration here, a preoccupied walk through an office without speaking to anyone, a frown of frustration when someone is talking – all of these send powerful signals that staff take away and dissect for meaning. Great leaders communicate positivity and optimism, and they often do it through a smile, or by walking with energy, or by standing straight and tall. Equally, there is nothing more corrosive than the conflict between saying one thing and doing another: for example, saying that bullying is offensive but then doing nothing about a high-earning bullying manager. That says one thing, and one thing only: money matters more than staff welfare. Leaders who clearly love what they are doing, who show it in everything they do, in every expression, are hugely infectious.

Prepare properly for public platforms

Many a leader has had their reputation dented, or even shattered, because they have not prepared properly for public speaking. Yet the more senior leaders get, the more likely it is they will have to appear on highly public platforms. Done well, such appearances can do enormous good, and drive up sales or the share price, calm nervous investors or unhappy customers, or persuade talented people to the cause. Proper training or coaching is highly recommended but is not enough by itself. Practice makes perfect, and rehearsal is the best practice. Never get complacent – it is just not worth the risk.

Learn, rehearse, review, improve

If you strive to be an excellent communicator, you will become a better, more effective leader. This is why all the leaders I spoke with focused on continuous improvement, fuelled by full and frank feedback on each and every performance. Brilliant leadership can be the difference between outstanding performance and disappointing failure. Great leaders steer organizations to success, inspire and motivate followers, and provide a moral compass for employees to set direction. They spearhead change, drive innovation and communicate a compelling vision for the future. The ability to motivate and inspire others is the characteristic most commonly cited as important when recruiting senior leaders. Communication is the tool that enables inspiring leadership. The simple truth is that you have to get better at it.

So that's it. The 12 principles. Simple.

Is that *all* the 60 leaders had to say? I hear you ask. No, they elaborated on these 12 points, and told stories to illustrate their points, and gave great case studies about these principles at work in their own organizations. There is huge learning in what they said. So the key question now is: If those are the key principles of leadership communication, how do you go about delivering each of them successfully in your own enterprise? How do experienced leaders think about these issues, and what lessons have they learned along the way – on each of these points – that might help you to be a more inspiring communicator?

For this is my goal: to help you become a more inspiring communicator, a better leader, not a technically perfect orator. You will be all the more effective if you can be both, but my observation is that you don't have to be. Passion, conviction, clarity, character, context – these things matter more. People set aside poor grammar, or even poor language skills, if the message itself is credible and really from the heart.

Which makes learning to be yourself, better, a good place to start...

PART TWO
The fundamentals

Learn to be yourself, better

04

BE YOURSELF,
BETTER

As a lifelong fan of Formula One motor racing, I was hugely privileged to interview Sir Frank Williams founder of the Williams F1 Grand Prix racing team, at his headquarters in Grove, Oxfordshire. He recounted how he had become addicted to motor racing at the age of 16, when he went to the British Grand Prix at Silverstone and watched Peter Collins drive a Ferrari to victory. 'Ever since that day, all I ever wanted to do was go motor racing,' he said.

In 1961, Sir Frank began racing his own Austin, funding his racing from his work as a travelling grocery salesman. He realized he was never going to be a great driver and instead turned his hand to running a Grand Prix team. The rest is history, and his partnership with Patrick Head resulted in the formation of a team that has, over the decades, seen both highs and lows in the intensely competitive environment that is the paddock of Formula One motor racing.

A car accident in March 1986 in France saw Sir Frank sustaining a spinal cord injury, which left him paralysed and wheelchair bound ever since. When I saw Sir Frank, he was seated behind his desk in his office, sipping with a straw from a cup of tea on a small block on his desk.

He was uncomfortable talking about the subject of communication and spoke quietly, but was considerate and considered. During the interview, he confessed: 'This is a somewhat unusual conversation for me.' He had not thought very hard about communication per se, and never really seemed at ease while talking about the subject.

Having exhausted all my questions, I then asked him about some of the things I really wanted to know. Who was his favourite driver? Who did he think was the best ever Grand Prix driver? (The answers were Alan Jones and Ayrton Senna.) As soon as we moved on to the subject of racing, his eyes lit up as his passion ignited.

'All I've ever wanted is to go racing, and it's racing that matters to all of the people in this company. We all share a common interest. We don't just want to participate. We want to win.'

In his own words: 'I'm a racer, pure and simple.'

After the interview, I stood chatting down in the foyer, and overheard a group of Williams F1 employees. They were talking about the new guy, Adam Parr, who, at the time, was about to take over as chairman of Williams F1. Sir Frank Williams says unequivocally he is the future of Williams F1, a man who is 'a great deal more competent at running the business than I have ever been'.

'Yes,' said the employees, 'but is he a racer?' To them, that was all that mattered... a clear legacy communicated to them and instilled in them by a man who exists to race Formula One cars.

Time and again I saw the same phenomenon: the passion of the leader replicated in the followers. As Sir Frank himself will admit, he is not a great orator. But one thing is for sure: he has managed to inspire and instil common values in his people.

Sir Frank can't move himself, but he moves people with his passion.

And therein lies the rub, as Shakespeare wrote. Too often leaders focus on trying to become technically perfect orators when they should be learning how to be more passionate orators. And that passion must be genuine, born of profound beliefs and dreams, or people will see through you in an instant.

What followers want from leaders

Leadership does not happen in a vacuum. Leaders operate in an ecosystem of interdependent people in an environment that they all inhabit together, and depend on. Leaders have followers. They have advisers. They have peers. They have competitors. They have customers. They have shareholders. They have regulators. And leaders have to communicate with all of these audiences.

Of course, many leaders are very often *also* followers. A CEO may take leadership from their board. A section leader may be guided by their director, before leading their own team. Equally, a director might be led by a subordinate when part of a team pitching to a client, for example. For any leader, though, the most important audience is followers. Nothing gets done without inspired and motivated followers. Customers won't be satisfied, regulators will be alarmed, competitors will be gleeful and advisers will have a field day, if followers don't perform.

If followers are the most important audience, then what do followers want from their leaders? That seems a good place to start. Above all, what they want in a leader is someone they can believe in. Followers respond best to leaders who have a strong strategic focus, with a clear vision of where the business should be going, who speak plainly and truthfully and, when necessary, courageously and with principles. They especially like leaders who stand up for them and defend them to the hilt. Leaders with a strong set of values built on honesty and openness and respect for other people are the most inspirational of all. They are predictable, and they are human.

Followers want leaders to be accessible, with genuine humility and even, occasionally, vulnerability. They want someone who listens to them and respects their views, someone who gives them energy and makes them feel involved and even electrified; they want someone whose passion and drive make it fun to work with them; they want to be trusted and in turn, to trust their leader; they want to be appreciated and to have their successes celebrated; and they want to feel valued, as much as they need to value their colleagues and the company for which they work. They want to have fun, and enjoy what they do, and they want to believe that what they do makes a difference.

Followers want leaders to make them feel inspired.

And that's the bottom line. Great leaders know that they must inject emotion into their communications or else they will be unable to make followers feel anything. The language of business is numbers, but for many that can be very boring. Action and commitment follow only when people feel uplifted and enabled and clear about what they are supposed to achieve. All too often I have seen leaders insist on staying in the world of rational argument, rooting their calls to action in the numbers. To be a great leader, you have to learn to communicate with passion, because passion begets action.

What do leaders want from the leaders they hire?

When I asked leaders about the most important skills of leadership, communication always featured as a top-three skill – often the second most important (behind strategic thinking) and sometimes the most important. I also always asked what else they were looking for in the leaders they hired in their own organizations. The answers were very consistent. Most often mentioned, in order of priority, were:

- raw intellect and the ability to think strategically, and with clarity;
- the ability to choose the right people and then align them to a cause;
- the ability to inspire people and take them with you; a good communicator, a good listener;
- a people person, able to be both challenging and encouraging, and able to create a strong culture and a shared set of values;

- a strong sense of mission;
- integrity, authenticity, strong values, honesty, openness and curiosity;
- domain excellence (knowledge and experience of the business they lead);
- energy, drive, resilience and persistence;
- numeracy, and a focus on performance and results;
- optimism, ambition and a willingness to take 'big bets'.

High on their list of desired skills and attributes are many of the same things wanted by followers: a future focus; strategic ability; a sense of mission; strong values; honesty; the ability to inspire; authenticity; integrity.

Authenticity came up a great deal. When I asked what it was and why it was necessary, here is what they said: 'It is about being true to yourself. And true to others.'

To do this, you have to do the following:

- Know your own strengths and weaknesses. You have to be clear about the beliefs that underpin your strengths. Figure out your sense of purpose. Articulate all of the above. Only then can you talk from the heart.
- Be trusted. You cannot lead if you are not trusted, and people cannot trust you if they don't know who you are, so you have to:
  - be visible: show up and be accessible;
  - have the confidence to be you;
  - treat people with respect, as one adult to another, and be interested in them;
  - be consistent;
  - always be honest, and admit to mistakes or that you don't know all the answers.
- Be a model of the behaviours you want. If you want to enjoy the benefits of being seen as a hero, you have to *be* a hero.
- Be authentic and true to yourself. When you are authentic, authenticity works its way through the whole organization.

Let's have a look at some of those points in depth. What did some of the leaders say about talking from the heart, being visible, being human, being yourself, knowing your strengths and allowing your emotions to show?

Talking from the heart

Fields Wicker-Miurin is co-founder and partner of Leaders' Quest, an international organization which works with leaders in the developing and developed worlds. She is a non-executive director of BNP Paribas, Ballarpur International Graphic Paper (India's leading writing-paper company) and CDC, the British government's development finance institution. Previously, Fields was chief financial officer of the London Stock Exchange and chief operating officer and partner of Vesta Group, an international venture capital firm.

She says: 'The most important part of being a good communicator is the secret ingredient of deep self-awareness, warts and all, and knowing and being comfortable with who you really are.'

'When we listen to a speaker, we know if that person is speaking from the heart and is authentic and honest. They somehow speak with complete confidence and vulnerability, all at the same time. Even if that person is not a very polished speaker, they will have impact. If you want to connect you have to learn how to speak from the heart.'

Yes, but how do you do that? 'It starts with knowing who you are. That's hard enough, because as we go through life we develop more and more mechanisms to protect and to shield ourselves and we learn how to conform in order to be successful. A leader has to reach a point of being comfortable and confident enough to say: "I know who I am and I can bring who I am to my leadership." This is not arrogance, because it needs to be done with a humility that enables you to be elastic, inclusive and porous enough to embrace and make space for lots of other types of people, perspectives and ways of seeing the world.'

'You cannot be consistent unless you are authentic. You have to understand what is core to your own belief system and figure out why you are here, what you believe in, and only then can you really be yourself and lead from your core.'

Often, if you are unafraid to show passion, your values will communicate without you having to put them into words. And you will communicate better, even if you are not skilled at giving speeches. Hollywood scriptwriters use a mantra: 'Show, don't tell.' What they mean is, don't tell your viewer that your main character is mean. Show him in a pub, sliding off to the washroom when it is his turn to buy a round. Let the viewer conclude, simply by watching the character in action, that he is tight-fisted. Equally, as a leader, don't say you are passionate about your subject, *show* that you are passionate.

Paul Polman, global chief executive of Unilever, a global consumer products business that owns many of the world's most famous consumer brands in foods, beverages, cleaning agents and personal care products, says authenticity is the most important factor behind inspiring communicators. 'I took my leadership team the other day to the Perkins School of the Blind, in Watertown, Massachusetts. I'm the chair of their international advisory board. A man called Andy, who was blind and deaf, gave a speech to my team. Technically, it wasn't a good speech, but at the end they were all sitting on their chairs, with tears in their eyes, and they were not clapping their hands (because Andy couldn't hear them) but they were stamping their feet so hard that he could feel it through the floor.'

Andy spoke haltingly from the mouth, but eloquently from the heart, and he moved his audience to tears.

Petrofac is a FTSE 100 business which provides facilities services to the oil and gas production and processing industries. Ayman Asfari is group chief executive of Petrofac, once a US company, which he joined in 1991 to internationalize the business and establish Petrofac International. Petrofac was listed in 2005 and it now employs around 14,000 people around the world.

Ayman is now a very rich man. 'But I am just as hungry as I was 30 years ago,' he says, 'still passionate about this business and our customers. That passion gives me an edge in communication. I am not a very good speech-maker, but if you know your stuff and you have passion, then you will have an impact on people. The one thing I do know is that if you don't sound like you're convinced yourself, it's very difficult to be convincing to others.'

Colin Matthews is CEO of British Airports Authority (BAA), the Spanish-owned operator of six British airports (including Heathrow Airport), making the company one of the largest transport companies in the world. Colin argues that people have an incredibly sensitive ear for sincerity or integrity.

'You can be a brilliant communicator but the most devastating under-mining of communication is lack of authenticity. And yet authenticity is simple – it is simply about presenting yourself truthfully.'

Why is authenticity so important? Because it enables people to trust you. You cannot lead, if people don't trust you. David Morley, senior partner at global law firm Allen & Overy, says authenticity underpins your ability to win trust. A&O operates in 26 countries, and David says it is the same in any country. 'If you are going to get your message across and influence the way people behave, which ultimately is what leadership is all about, then there has to be trust in you as an individual and in what you say. When trust goes, cynicism takes its place and it's very difficult to influence cynical people, or people who are cynical about you or your motives. Then it doesn't matter how brilliant a speaker you are – if people don't trust you, you may as well not be talking.'

What do you have to do to enable followers to trust you? The advice from all the leaders I spoke with was unanimous...

Be visible, be human and be straight

After qualifying as a barrister, Tom Hughes-Hallett spent more than 20 years working in the City before giving up his job as director of Fleming Asset Management to join Marie Curie Cancer Care in December 2000 as chief executive. Marie Curie is a charitable organization with more than 2,700 nurses, doctors and other healthcare professionals, and provides care for terminally ill patients in the community and in its own hospices, along with support for their families. This year, Marie Curie expects to provide care to more than 31,000 people with cancer and other terminal illnesses.

Tom feels the most important aspect of being authentic is that you have to be visible and you have to get around your organization. That is tough and a real commitment when you become a CEO. But you have to do it. 'If something needs to be communicated, then people should have a good idea of the bloke that is communicating, know what he looks like, and ideally have shaken his hand. Being authentic means being honest and straight – and definitely not pretending to know everything. You have to say "I don't know but I'll get back to you."

'Most important, you have to make it fun. I always promise people it will always be fun working here – always. People think I am potty saying that in an end-of-life care organization, but it attracts people. Fun actually means that you are being stretched, you are working hard, you know what you are doing and why you are doing it and it is just a nice way of codifying it.'

Richard Gnodde is the co-chief executive officer of Goldman Sachs International at Goldman Sachs Group Inc. He has been at this position since July 2006. The Goldman Sachs Group is a global investment banking and securities firm dealing primarily with institutional clients.

Richard says: 'Authenticity is being very straightforward, saying exactly what you think and being very candid, however difficult it might be. There is no good in sugar-coating something. Always strive to find a positive message to show people the way forward. That said, the message has to be an honest and credible one; don't try to pretend that your team is in a good place when it isn't.

'You really have to walk the walk. People are very perceptive and you are very visible all the time. Good leaders have to be very credible with respect to the message that they are communicating. You can see it in their eyes and you can see it in the way they carry themselves and you can see it in the way that they live their lives. A leader is just very visible.'

Lord Mervyn Davies, formerly a banker and then a UK government minister, now a partner and vice-chairman at Corsair Capital and non-executive chairman of PineBridge Investments, an asset management company, says: 'Authenticity is crucial. It means talking about your mistakes, talking about your weaknesses, and talking about things that are not going well. Never fall into the trap of thinking that you know everything. And you have to find ways of showing up and being visible, even in a global business. You have to recognize that there are so many different ways to have the dialogue and conversations, from face to face, to iPads and mobile phones and videoconferences.'

Heidi Mottram is CEO of Northumbrian Water, and the first woman to head up one of the big water and waste-treatment companies. She started her career in British Rail and went on to be commercial director for Arriva Trains Northern and then managing director of Northern Rail. Heidi was named Rail Business Manager of the Year in 2009 for being an 'inspirational leader'.

She points out that there are obvious parallels between the rail and water industries. Both are formerly nationalized, now heavily regulated, sectors, but there's also a tangible public service ethos. 'What really strikes you is just how committed and proud and passionate people are about what they do,' she says. Northumbrian Water employs 3,000 staff, scattered in small groups throughout a wide region. Heidi says her staff hate coming to big events, so Heidi goes to them – organizing regular visits to small groups of people at Northumbrian's waterworks and plants in a systematic way, even to the most difficult-to-reach places, on a regular basis.

'It is a big people business, blue collar, and I long ago stopped worrying about being a woman in a man's world. I turn up and have full and frank conversations with our staff, in their recreation rooms, and when I am there I give them my full attention. I learned years ago from two inspiring bosses how important it is to talk with people like I've just met them in a pub, adult to adult, where we both have important jobs to do, just different jobs to do. Talk about everyday things, have fun, and not only business issues. There is a real art in being real, one of the people, while still retaining respect,' she says.

'It is really important to me to understand how it "feels" to work in the business, so I ask a lot of questions about that, which brings out emotional issues – frustrations and concerns but also what's working well. I am at great pains to create the environment where they can talk openly and frankly with me about how they see things. Sometimes I have to be strong and push back, and be frank about why I am not going to do what they want, but at least they know then where I stand on issues. But I also take on board things they tell me, and take action, and that creates credibility as well.'

General Sir Mike Jackson says authenticity is sometimes as simple as being able to admit your mistakes.

'I always quote this example – and every young officer's been there: you're newly commissioned, you're on your first exercise, you've got 20 guys behind you, it's four o'clock on a January morning, it's pissing down, the wind's howling; people are wet, cold, fed up, tired... and you're lost. And they know that you're lost. Authenticity is how you handle that situation. The bullshitter will try and say, well, I knew where I was all the time; just taking a very clever tactical route. And the boys will just roll their eyes and say, what a load of cobblers. Instead, the officer should say: "Hey guys, that was a bit of a cock-up, sorry about that; I'll get it right next time." That's the authentic leader.'

To be seen as a hero, you have to be a hero

Ayman Asfari is clear that being a leader means you have to have integrity – and make sure that everything you say is important to you as a value is replicated in your work and your personal life. It *must* be. You have to be above reproach.

'A footballer can't be a role model for kids and then go out and be on drugs. The same applies to leaders. You can't have it both ways. Authenticity means being consistent. You cannot say one thing and do another. For example, one of our values is we want to be safe in the way we conduct our business. Being consistent to that means we've had to make some very difficult decisions. We've had to walk away from business that was very lucrative... we were making money out of it, but we walked away because we felt that the customers that we were working with did not share our values on safety, and we could not compromise. That sent very powerful signals to all our people about what safety really means to us.'

All-round authenticity

If you are authentic, you demand authenticity everywhere. And that is good for the brand, not just you. I came across two striking examples.

Sir Maurice Flanagan is the founding CEO of Emirates and is currently the executive vice-chairman of the Emirates Airline and Group. Emirates is the national airline of Dubai, in the United Arab Emirates. It is the largest airline in the Middle East, and flies to 105 cities in 62 countries across six continents. The Emirates Group, which has over 50,000 employees, is wholly-owned by the government of Dubai. In February 2011, *Air Transport World* gave Emirates Airlines the title of Airline of the Year for 2011.

On the subject of authenticity, Maurice says: 'Delivering excellence is a key value for us. For years I have lived and breathed the pursuit of excellence. If you really care about something, you will make sure that others care about it too. For example, if we care about being an excellent airline, that means giving our passengers excellent service. And that means making sure our cabin crew and ground staff are really nice to passengers. You cannot fake that. So, to make sure, we put prospective cabin crew through psycho-metric tests and we choose people who are inclined to want to be nice to other people. We select those who are nice by nature. That's authenticity.'

Beverley Aspinall is managing director of Fortnum & Mason, a world-famous department store and royal warrant holder (the Queen's grocer), situated in central London, with branches in Japan and a presence in many international markets. Fortnum's headquarters are located at 181 Piccadilly, where it was established in 1707 by William Fortnum and Hugh Mason. Beverley says: 'As a leader, you are on stage and being watched all the time, so you have to behave expecting that everything you do will be scrutinized. Above all, you have to be consistent. And you have to make sure your organization is consistent and authentic to your customers too.'

'Authenticity is actually one of our principal values, and that means every-thing we sell must be authentic – it has to be the authentic product, not something that looks like it or pretends to be it. We were having these debates just this week about the pottery industry and the demise of the whole industry in the UK, which is very, very sad. You are allowed to have China made in the Far East and then paint it in England and you're still allowed to pass it off as English pottery, but for me that's not the right thing to do. To be English, it has to be made here. There are still a couple of UK pottery companies struggling to actually make it work, so why wouldn't we go to them to buy? It's in those sorts of actions that I think your own, and the company's, authenticity is hugely important.'

Have the confidence to be you

Dame Helen Alexander was, at the time of the interview, president of the Confederation of British Industry (CBI), the premier lobbying organization for UK business on national and international issues. She is also chairman of Incisive Media and of the Port of London Authority (PLA). Until recently, her director-general of the CBI was Sir Richard Lambert, a former editor of the *Financial Times*. The role of the director-general is to be the key spokesman for the UK's business community in the media, on public platforms and with government. The D-G leads the CBI in the UK and represents it internationally. Sir Richard took over the reins from Digby Jones, Baron Jones of Birmingham, another high-profile British businessman. The post is currently occupied by John Cridland, who was previously deputy director-general since 2000.

Says Helen: 'Authenticity takes courage. Everybody was asking John in his first days whether he was going to be a Digby Jones or a Richard Lambert. His answer was simple – "I'm going to be me." I was so delighted when he said that, because that has to be the right answer. You just need enough confidence to be able to say it.'

Nick Buckles is chief executive of G4S plc, (formerly Group 4 Securicor) a global security services company headquartered in Crawley, in the United Kingdom. G4S is the world's largest security company. It has operations in more than 125 countries, and employs more than 625,000 people. (It is the world's second-largest private sector employer, after Walmart.)

He recalls: 'My most seminal learning as a communicating leader was realizing that just being yourself and being natural and being confident is the best way of communicating. You have to be authentic. Yes, you have to have some structure, and you have to think about what you're saying, and you have to think about your audience, but then you have to make sure you say something that is of interest to them, that is genuine and from the heart. As a leader you want to change behaviours, and leave people feeling inspired to do something different, without having to give them instructions.'

'Before that realization, I would often just go through the motions of giving a presentation because I was asked to give one. Without passion, without real feeling, it was just giving information. Half of the people might think, yes, that was all right, but the others could just as easily say it was a complete waste of time.'

Nick is very clear: 'The task of a leader is to inspire, to make people think differently, act differently, to want to improve even if they're doing well.

You've got to stop complacency. You've got to be very generous with your praise but at the same time (and you can do it in a humorous way) you've got to make people believe they can do more and better. I believe absolutely in self-improvement and continuous improvement. We should always try to be the best we can be. By talking to this passion, I can convey how deeply I care about it, and I don't have to use lots of facts to convey how important it is to me. People soon get the message, and start behaving accordingly.'

Know your strengths to be yourself better

Sometimes, leaders have not stopped to think about and articulate what they really care about, and are reserved about projecting their personal beliefs on to others. That is a problem! No passion means no inspiration. And you can't fake it. People can spot insincerity in an instant and you cannot live a lie for very long. This places a great onus on leaders to dig deep and articulate their own passions and beliefs, consistently and with confidence. Leaders must accept that they have a personal brand and that their reputation is key to their leadership. They are the brand that leads the brand and often, their reputation is also important to the reputation of their company.

How you position yourself, how you choose to be seen, the themes on which you communicate: these things define you – and you define your organization.

Sir Christopher Gent is chairman of GlaxoSmithKline, a global pharmaceutical, vaccines and consumer healthcare company headquartered in London. GSK is the world's third largest pharmaceutical company, measured by revenues. Sir Christopher was previously CEO of Vodafone, a global British-based mobile phone company.

He says leaders have to think carefully about how they want to position themselves. 'Confine yourself to talking about your company's issues, and define what you want the world to know about you and what you will talk about. Unless you do that, you expose yourself to more and more people writing about you, and sometimes saying untruthful things about you. In today's Google world, a lie once told can take on an eternal life.'

So stop thinking you don't have a reputation; you do. If you aren't managing your reputation, then someone else will, so it had better be you. And that means you'd better talk up about what matters to you. Managing your reputation means identifying your strengths and ensuring that they are seen better in the glare of the spotlight you will be under. Managing your reputation successfully can never equal cynical manipulation. The CEOs that I interviewed said a good reputation itself is the wrong pursuit. It should be the consequence of everything you do and everything you say.

Lord Tim Bell, my chairman at Chime Communications for the past 12 years and an adviser to me in two different corporate communications positions for eight years before that, says reputation is not only the consequence of what you do and what you say, but also what others say about you – increasingly important in today's digital and viral world. People will talk about you, so it's best you make sure they talk about the things you care about.

How do you go about identifying your values and mission?

By way of example, I will tell you the story of George, the CEO of a global management consultancy. I have changed his name to spare his blushes, but 'George' had worked in this professional services business since leaving college. He asked for my help when he was in the running to become chairman. The chairmanship, however, was an elected position. George needed to show the company around the world that he had the vision to secure the prize. He wanted help with his key messages. After just two working sessions, I could see he had a much more worrying problem.

George worked daily with the chairmen of multinationals. The ones he admired – like the chairman of his own company – had gravitas, grey hair and exuded 'captain of industry' status. George was not like that and he knew it. His 'gravitas' messages rang hollow because, at heart, he doubted that he was a chairman.

'Rather than wordsmith ideas, let's look at your strengths,' I suggested. Together, we drilled down to what George truly valued, what he was passionate about. 'It was uncomfortable at first,' he told me afterwards. 'I had never done this before, gone down deep to what I really believed in terms of my business, and boiled it down to the essence.'

As we worked, George's true strengths began to emerge. He was a great collaborator who valued warm relationships but also had a fierce belief in high standards. This combination gave him the desire to draw the best from people and move them forward. We mapped this onto the needs of his company, wrote it down, refined it. As George distilled his core beliefs on the page he became excited. 'I could see how to make this resonate with people. It was rigorous, I could measure it by the new insights I gained.'

George's vision was to achieve the great client relationships that would drive his business to be a global leader. He tested this vision, cautiously at first. A colleague and close confidant told him it was not only logical, and necessary for the business, but also very authentic. George now knew he had something he could take to the world. 'It was a pledge, a promise I could make to our people because it was fundamentally what I believed in.'

George's message was clear, as was his leadership platform. Much more important, by finding his real strengths, he had banished the nagging anxiety that he might not actually be 'chairman material'. He now saw he could make the role his own by being himself. 'I became so much more confident to lead the firm with a real belief in my underlying values, and using those in my messaging. I could go and talk to anyone in any country with real conviction, knowing this wasn't just something I was saying because I thought people wanted to hear it. The response was so strong because underneath I had a solid foundation of authenticity. That was the key.'

George phoned me one April morning. I knew at once what his news must be. 'Congratulations, Mr Chairman,' I said.

A springboard to action, a leadership platform

So, what do we draw from George's story? When I work with CEOs, as I did with George, we look at every aspect of the leader's situation – their challenges, aims and concerns, their business environment, past and defining moments. I am deep diving for their strengths. Amazingly, most leaders find their own strengths an extraordinary revelation – they have often thought of them as run of the mill until we put them into perspective. They have the view that everyone must have those strengths, because the strengths come too naturally and easily for them to appreciate their skills. When leaders do realize their true strengths, it's cathartic, enlightening and, crucially, the springboard for action. That is because their strengths are hard-wired in to them, from childhood, probably, and those strengths are accompanied by strong beliefs and an even stronger attitude to issues. Unearthing those beliefs and then giving them expression are what is so liberating.

For George the revelation was that there are many valid leadership styles. By being himself he could lead with his personal style – collaborative, warm, with a drive to offer the best to every client – that drew people to him like a magnet and truly inspired.

Finally, understanding your strengths allows you to locate the channels you can employ with authenticity and confidence to communicate emotionally. It might be through video streaming, a speech from the podium or the old-fashioned practice of 'walking the floor'. Or it might just be about listening to small groups, responding to what they say and being seen to be out there doing it.

Whichever way you choose, it is 'your way', the one that sits most comfortably with you. A great example of this is John Connolly, the immediate past senior partner and CEO of Deloitte Touche Tohmatsu Ltd, and also the immediate past senior partner of the firm in the UK. Deloitte is the largest private professional services organization in the world, with about 170,000 staff at work in more than 150 countries, delivering audit, tax, consulting, enterprise risk and financial advisory services.

His 'way' is to send his staff a voice message, which he does regularly. They can hear him talking about things that matter, and he scrupulously commits to doing regular messages. He knows his successor will more likely be more modern in his communication style, using blogs and Twitter, but whatever the medium, the passion has to be the same. 'A leader has to be prepared to show passion and not be embarrassed to show it. They have to have character and show courage, they have to be positive and enthusiastic and energetic and ambitious and want to talk with people about the things they care about. Emotion is crucial.'

The need for emotion in business

So, authenticity means playing to your strengths, and gaining insight on how to use them as a power source to achieve your objectives. It entails discovering your own appropriate style to be a great communicator. Because it is only when you understand your true strengths and operate from your own value system that you can know and passionately communicate what is right for your business. This has long-term benefits: it makes you consistently convincing because you are consistently yourself.

However, knowing what those passions are is often only half the story of my coaching. I often find I have to help leaders understand why there is a real need for emotion in business communication, which can be a challenge. Many of the leaders I have worked with are highly rational, fast- and clear-thinking people who have got to where they are by being challenging, numerate and results focused. Emotion seems fluffy and soft to them. But, as I keep saying, how people 'feel' determines how they act. Are they committed to the necessary action? Will they go the extra mile that will make the difference between success and failure?

Business plans have stretching targets in them – cold, hard numbers that have to be achieved. Those numbers won't be achieved if people don't change their behaviours – if they don't work smarter, or differently, or innovate, or sell more, or build key relationships. Behaviours deliver the numbers, and are the link between tangible results and fluffy feelings.

The success or failure of any business strategy depends significantly on the 'emotional engagement' of employees and front-line managers. Leaders have to articulate strategies that are not only smart and intellectually rigorous, but also have real emotional appeal. Emotional, engaging communication is the link between the business plan and people's behaviours.

Having worked in dozens of companies, I seldom meet employees who agree that their company's strategy is either exciting or inspiring. Yet emotional communication is not vague or abstract: any leader can achieve it and benefit. Because the power of emotional communication is centred in leaders themselves, it is leaders who are able to change behaviours in a positive way. And that, let us remind ourselves, is the fundamental purpose: to change behaviours and achieve results.

We have to examine not only what success for the leader and their business would be like, and feel like, but we also have to look at what prevents success and what communications will get over the hurdles. These will be communications that carry integrity, and be effective because they stem from the leader's own passionately held beliefs – mapped against established organizational values. Leaders can indeed 'be themselves, better' because authenticity in business means leaders match their beliefs and values to the values of the organization, understand where they overlap and use the overlaps to gain powerful results.

We do not exclude reason and logic. The best narratives have logic, as well as emotion, and a whole lot of the communicator's character in them. Aristotle described three main forms of rhetoric: ethos, logos and pathos. An ethos-driven message relies on the reputation of the speaker. Logos is appeal based on logic or reason. Pathos is appeal based on emotion. To me, what is critical is the use of emotion to support logic.

David Morley, senior partner at global law firm Allen & Overy, agrees this is true even in the legal profession: 'As lawyers we tend to be very logical, reasoning people. Emotion is almost squeezed out of you because you're trained to be objective and critical. But we live in a world where people are bombarded with messages and information and we respond on an emotional level as well. So if you want to motivate people, win them over and persuade them of the case you are trying to make, you've got to appeal to people's emotions. Not in a blatant or manipulative way. But if you can get your passion across, you can persuade people to go the way you want to go.'

As we will see in a later chapter on listening, showing your passions and being emotional yourself are one thing. Encouraging people to talk about their emotions is equally important. More than half the leaders I spoke with said they actively encouraged people to talk about their emotions when they walked the floor, by asking the question: 'How do you feel about this?' As they said, it surfaces issues they really need to know about, and demonstrates they understand what motivates and demotivates people.

Being yourself better is a skill leaders have to work on, and seldom comes naturally. They have to think about it, choose to show parts of themselves that help engender trust, and bring out their own emotions and the emotions of followers more. This means taking the time to articulate what is important to you. There is an old saying: 'How do I know what I am thinking if I cannot see what I am saying?' Writing out your beliefs and purpose is a very powerful action, which equips you with a powerful point of view you can use any time, anywhere.

That's what you have to map onto the organization you lead, if you want to create a framework for empowering and enabling everyone to do the right things the right way...

KEY POINTS FROM CHAPTER 4

- Authenticity in a leader is crucial.
- Followers will not commit if they do not trust you and believe that you have integrity.
- To know you is to trust you: you have to communicate who you are.
- You have to learn to show your character – people must know what you care about and what your beliefs are. This will make you more predictable, and inspire them to follow your beliefs.
- People want to feel inspired. Feelings are emotions, so leadership communication needs to be more emotional.
- Even if you are a highly introverted individual, you will have to learn to speak with more passion, talk to your values and stand up more often to speak to your beliefs.
- Followers must feel your passion, and believe that you believe.
- Passion and authenticity will inspire people more than a technically perfect presentation or speech.
- When you are clear with yourself about the things you really care about, you cannot help but talk to them with passion.
- Most leaders have not spent the time articulating those beliefs.
- Writing out your beliefs and purpose is a very powerful action, which equips you with a powerful point of view you can use any time, anywhere.
- To communicate who you are, you have to articulate your own purpose and values, and talk to them with passion.
- Show that you are human – admit mistakes or that you don't know.
- You have to be visible, and people must see you are willing to engage on the things that really matter, no matter how difficult.

Provide a framework for leadership and action, through mission and values

05

The advertising industry has a saying: 'Give me the freedom of a tight brief.'

It means that the more closely the client defines success and the manner in which it is to be achieved, the more freedom and creativity the agency can apply to the advertising, and the more likely it is to get the right result.

A tight brief is the opposite of constraining; it is liberating, it focuses people on an outcome and generates more ideas, not less. Ironically, a loose brief is a problem. It leaves too many questions open, and paralyses creativity by creating uncertainty and confusion. There is too much need for clarification, consultation, consensus building – and everything bogs down in the syrup of confusion.

As we have seen in previous chapters, leaders today know they need to create more leaders, throughout their organizations, if they in turn are going to create more agile, responsive and faster companies. They need to give those leaders a framework for leading, a tight brief that enables decision making where it is needed, when it is needed, confident in the knowledge that those leaders will be able to use it to make the 'right' decisions.

To be able to make those decisions, people need to know what they are trying to achieve (commander's intent: What is our mission?). They also need to know, exactly, what values and beliefs should be applied to those decisions (operating envelope). And, finally, they need to know what the commercial goals are, what the picture of success is, in order to be able to make the right decisions.

It is for this reason that leaders must articulate a clear, compelling and simple mission, allied to a statement about what the enterprise stands for, and how it expects employees and suppliers to behave. They must also articulate clear and concise commercial goals, a vision of what success in the mission looks like. Of course, their own sense of mission and their personal values (as outlined in the previous chapter) must resonate and reflect the corporate ones.

Sir Anthony Bamford of JCB, the world's third largest construction equipment brand, which sells more than 150 products in more than 150 countries, says it is important to distinguish between the mission and the vision. 'There is a difference,' he says. 'Mission is what you do all the time. It is your purpose in life. A vision is about how successful you will be at what you do, and this will be expressed as a five-year business plan. The plan will be translated into annual goals, and even monthly and weekly goals. The plan has to work in tandem with your mission.'

Business in the Community (BITC) is a business-led charity with a membership of more than 850 companies, from large multinational household names to small local businesses and public sector organizations. BITC advises, supports and challenges its members to create a sustainable future for people and the planet and to improve business performance. Two leaders interviewed for this book had been heavily involved with BITC: Sir Stuart Rose is a past chairman and Philip Green is still chairman of the BITC environment leadership team.

In guidelines to members, BITC says: 'A company's statement of values is a high-level statement that describes how the company behaves. It is not a mission statement that describes what task the company aims to fulfil. Neither is it a set of commercial objectives. The "rule of thumb" is that if it describes time-limited objectives, task-oriented goals or aspirations of achievement, then it is a mission statement, or goals. Corporate values are about what the company stands for and how its employees behave. They are about framing a role for the business that gives it a purpose beyond profit.'

'It is not easy to do. For every one genuinely values-driven company there are many more where the corporate values statement simply exists as a poster on the chairman's wall. The result of such circumstances is that employees in the call centres, and possibly even those working on the other floors of head office, do not recognize the value statement as describing the actual values and behaviours in the workplace. To change corporate culture requires full and consistent commitment from the top, excellent communication throughout the organization, and empowerment of staff to begin to use the values as their guide to making decisions.'

BITC says that research has shown that a key factor common to companies that have been enduringly great performers – at the top of the market for 100 years or more – was precisely a base of values that were strong enough to provide employees of the company with a common bond – a purpose beyond profit.

Getting it right, says BITC, can win all sorts of benefits:

- employees who are loyal to and supportive of the company, and more likely to stay if offered an equivalent position elsewhere;
- customers who are more likely to trust the company, because they see employees doing the right thing;
- enhanced relationships with investors, who may see that the company runs less risk of corporate scandals or controversies;
- good relationships with government and local communities, who begin to see the company as a good neighbour.

'Values statements can be very simple indeed,' stresses the BITC guidance. 'One company simply has the maxim that you should always "do the right thing by the customer and by the employees". This can be the worst kind of fatuous platitude, or a profound guiding star for the behaviour of all employees – it all depends on the implementation. Most statements of values, however, have more detail that leaves little room for ambiguity in what they might mean.'

From all my discussions with leaders, I believe that the vision of the future needs to describe the commercial goals of the business, and also describe what that success will 'feel' like to all the stakeholders who will benefit from that success – shareholders, customers, employees and suppliers, and local communities.

Feelings and emotions are the driving force of our lives. It is why I put so much emphasis on the word 'feel'. Leaders have to embrace the idea that good communication has to be about feelings as much as it is about facts. Head and heart. For this reason, I believe firmly that the vision can only work well in conjunction with the mission and values. For the purpose of this book, however, I am going to tackle these two subjects in separate chapters, which interlink.

I heard so much about both these areas from the leaders I interviewed, and each is different, but with huge overlap. The leaders also tended to use a variety of words to mean the same thing or, sometimes, the same words to mean different things. For example, the words 'vision', 'mission', 'purpose', 'goals', 'objectives' all became quite blurred. For the sake of clarity in this book, I will define them as follows:

- Mission is why we exist; what we are here to do.
- Values are our principles, or the qualities we consider worthwhile or desirable, and which drive all our behaviours.
- Standards are the minimum standards of behaviour acceptable, when values are applied.

These are all on the emotional side of the story, and are what employees find most inspiring.

By contrast:

- To me, a vision is the leader's concept of the future, described both in numbers and in terms of the quality of key relationships, if all the organization's goals are to be achieved.
- The goals are the four or five things to which the endeavour of the organization is directed, critical to the achievement of the vision.
- Objectives are the clearly defined, decisive and attainable supporting goals which must be delivered if the main goals and the vision are to be achieved.

These last three are the highly rational, intellectual, measurable aspects of the story.

All six are needed for the full story – and it is only when all six are articulated that the story is complete in an employee's mind. I include standards, because these are measurable, and another way that leaders can ensure that values are brought to life in the daily actions of people in the business. Without minimum standards of behaviour, which are appraised and rewarded, the danger is that your values will become important words on a poster on the wall.

Let us look first at mission and values, and how (if they are tightly framed) they can create a framework for freedom inside companies, liberate the creativity and imagination of employees, and enable leaders everywhere on the hierarchy to make the right decisions when the pressure is on.

Values build trust

Paul Polman, global chief executive of Unilever, says values build trust. 'I can visit my colleagues in any country of the world and I find that they may speak different languages and be working to different issues in their different countries, but within Unilever, they all have the same values. That creates trust, and trust enables us to work together – it helps us to fill the cracks that are in any system you design. And that's the basis of prosperity. So, there can be no prosperity without trust, and trust comes from having the right values framework.'

'You have to enable people to make decisions at the lowest possible level inside the company. I believe the best way to galvanize success in a company like Unilever is to be sure that decisions are being taken at the level where the knowledge is. That's a very important statement – that decisions need to be taken at the level of where the knowledge is. So as a CEO, as a leader, you always have to drive the decision making as far down in the organization as possible. You have to show people the operating framework and make sure they understand it. It isn't about rules and regulations – which stifle innovation – it is about having the right values and trust, which stimulate innovation.'

Rupert Gavin, of Odeon and UCI Cinemas, feels you have to know who you are and what you stand for and be clear about your values if you are to be able to communicate those well. It is only when you communicate those really well that you can truly empower and enable your staff to make the right decisions. The acid test is that any person in your organization, when hit with the challenge on Saturday at five o'clock in the afternoon, unable to get you, is going to come up with the right answer by themselves 99 per cent of the time – the answer that is right for the organization.

'Instilling those values in the organization is what will help you sleep at night,' Rupert says. 'You can only do so if you are secure in the knowledge that John or Mary, when challenged by a customer, will respond in the way that you would, in the way the organization would wish them to. And they need to know that if they make an honest mistake while trying to do the right thing, they will not be blamed, but be supported.'

Why people love a motivating mission

Within a few weeks of arriving at British Airways, as the proud new director of communications, I was given a preview of the company's new mission statement. I was asked to think about how best to communicate it to staff and to the world. British Airways was still very much regarded as 'the world's favourite airline' at the time, and operated 290 aircraft, including the awe-inspiring Concorde. Managers in the company had, apparently, spent the previous two years debating the new mission, and had finally settled on: 'To be the number one in world travel.'

A new corporate branding was also unveiled to me, a radical idea about how to use art on our fleet of aircraft to show the 'new' British Airways. This was what became known as 'the infamous tail fins' – where art from different countries was painted on the tails of aircraft in the fleet. It led to a barrage of criticism, mainly in the UK. The year was 1996.

Just a few days old in the job, I wondered whether it was wise to tell the then chief executive, Bob Ayling, that I didn't think the new mission statement would be very inspirational to staff. After all, his managers had been debating this for two years, and the new statement, along with the new livery, had been decided. They were part of unveiling a strategy for the future that required a radical overhaul of the airline's costs, partnerships and positioning.

Being the newcomer, I wondered what being 'number one in world travel' really meant. Were we going to buy hotel chains and car hire companies, for example? The answer was no. The definition of 'number one' would be explained in the text of the full mission statement.

At the time, the airline was in heated discussions with all staff about ways to reduce the company's wage bill – Bob Ayling had already announced his 'billion pound cost-cutting' programme, which he felt was needed to keep the airline competitive, so the tensions between staff and management were running hot. I recommended we should run focus groups throughout the company to get the feedback that would enable us to communicate the new vision with the greatest chance of success, and the management team agreed. We arranged to speak to mixed groups of people, comprising pilots, cabin crew, baggage handlers, check-in staff and admin staff, in various locations and countries, so as to get as wide a range of feedback as possible. In a carefully constructed session, these groups were introduced to the concept of mission statements, then they were shown a variety of mission statements from other companies, and finally they were shown the new British Airways mission statement.

I anticipated a great deal of hostility from the groups – after all, they were angry about the cost-cutting programme and would be, I thought, cynical and unhelpful. What I learned during those focus groups changed my view of mission statements forever.

Talking with these colourful and outspoken groups, we learned:

- Employees *do* like a good mission statement, and felt the right one was inspiring and necessary.
- They were *very* clear about the difference between good ones and bad ones.
- 'Good' ones spoke to an enduring and meaningful purpose, something that made them want 'to get out of bed in the morning, for a reason other than to earn a living'.
- 'Bad' ones were about achieving numerical goals that made no difference to employees, or were so bland and generic that they could be used for any company.
- The best ones were a constant reminder to employees of why the company existed, and enabled every individual to see how what they did contributed to the mission.
- Examples they shot down were 'Thinking about tomorrow, today' or about 'Being number one in the market' or earning '£1 billion by the end of the decade'.
- They most admired the mission statement that NASA (National Aeronautics and Space Administration) used for the Apollo project, the moon landings (more about this in just a few paragraphs).
- They believed the British Airways mission should be on the lines of 'Enabling people to experience the joy and benefits of travel'.

Eventually, the new British Airways mission statement was launched, but with only a few concessions to the staff feedback. Management agreed to employee suggestions to put people at the heart of everything they did, and portray a people focus as the centrepiece of the mission statement. But it still went out as BA wanting to be 'the number one in world travel'. The management had a tailwind of two years of debate behind them, and understandably did not want to pause to reconsider and revise. They were happy with what they had.

Employees *want* a good mission statement

The most powerful lesson for me though, was to do with how highly employees rated good mission statements. Until that point, I had never fully appreciated how much they mattered to people. What all the British Airways staff pointed at as desirable ('Enabling people to experience the joy and benefits of travel') was something that explained, in uplifting terms, why we existed. It explained what we were there to do, and why it mattered to people. They could see how what they did, no matter what their role was in the airline, helped to deliver the mission. They wanted to feel that what they did was important, and that they could be proud of it with friends, family and drinking chums in the local pub.

I came away with a strong view that employees take huge inspiration from the right mission statement, and are hugely cynical about what they judge to be the wrong one. Crafting one that resonates with all staff is important. Ever since my BA experience, I have had this view reaffirmed, in dozens of enterprises.

Especially important is the 'clear line of sight' between what employees do in their daily working lives, and the company's purpose. Really good managers take the time and effort to make sure that each employee can see how their actions contribute to the mission. In the case of the BA employees, they most loved the NASA statement. Let's have a look at why.

In May 1961, the president of the United States of America, John F Kennedy, said: 'I believe this nation should commit itself to achieving the goal, before this decade is out, of landing a man on the moon and returning him safely to the Earth.'

This came very shortly after Mercury astronaut Alan Shepard became the first American in space. President Kennedy's exciting and daring challenge set the nation on an incredible and epic journey. Eight years of focused and aligned effort by thousands of Americans came to fruition on 20 July 1969, when Apollo 11 commander Neil Armstrong stepped out of the lunar module and took 'one small step' in the Sea of Tranquility, calling it 'a giant leap for mankind'.

On the successful completion of the mission, the then president, Richard Nixon, told Apollo 11 crew members Neil Armstrong and Edwin 'Buzz'

Aldrin, that 'For one priceless moment, in the whole history of man, all the people on this Earth are truly one.'

In and of itself, the mission was inspiring and incredible. So you might discount it on the grounds that not every organization can have such an inspiring purpose. But what the BA staff most enjoyed was the story of the janitor who spoke to President Kennedy before that fantastic mission was completed. Many leaders I speak to remember this legendary JFK anecdote.

The president was apparently visiting NASA headquarters and stopped to talk to a man who was holding a mop. 'And what do you do?' he asked. The man, a janitor, replied, 'I'm helping to put a man on the moon, sir.'

Employees need to feel part of the story

The lesson I took away from the BA employees was this: Leaders need to tell a compelling story about why their enterprise exists. And they need to make every employee feel like an essential part of that story. Knowing their part in your organization's story engages people and gives each of them a sharp sense of purpose.

But there's more. We know that emotional engagement is key to the success of leaders. Being number one in a market or achieving a revenue or profit target is not emotionally engaging and inspiring to most employees. Knowing what their financial or other performance goals are is crucial, but only part of the story. They are measures of success, not the reason itself. All too often, though, it is on the numbers that leaders choose to focus.

I believe that is because these are the goals that are key to each leader's strategy, and are therefore key to the leader. Most leaders are highly rational, logical people. So it is best to stay in the world of rational and logical argument, they think.

But if they do use rational argument only, they are losing sight of the need to communicate with people on the things that matter most to them, if they are to communicate successfully. As I have already argued, you need logic and emotion and character all wrapped up in your story if you want to inspire people. This view has led to me advocating that employees are most motivated by the sense of mission they glean from their organization only when it is allied powerfully to the values of that organization. Do they feel inspired and empowered by the culture? And is that culture rigorously upheld? Are there minimum standards of behaviour that are required, where crossing over those boundaries will actually have consequences?

The need to raise people's sights

Helen Alexander, of the Confederation of British Industry, said: 'You know the NASA story, don't you, with the janitor? Not everybody knows that.

I was talking in a school the other day where the teachers are the heroes and the admin staff are not. I told them about the NASA mission statement and the admin staff said: "That's amazing. Can we use that story?" I said of course they could – because they were also helping to educate the talent of the future, and that sense of a higher purpose is really important. You need to raise people's sights about why what they do is important. It is incredibly important.'

Ben Verwaayen is chief executive of Alcatel-Lucent, a global telecommunications corporation, headquartered in Paris, France. It provides voice, data and video hardware and software to service providers, enterprises and governments around the world. It holds Bell Labs, one of the largest R&D houses in the communications industry, and operates in more than 130 countries. In 2010, Alcatel reported revenues of almost €16 billion.

Ben says: 'As a leader, it is extraordinarily important to be a good communicator, in order to do your job. Leadership is all about good communications and leaders must recognize they have three essential communication jobs to do. The first is to put a dot on the horizon for your people to see. In my case it is 80,000 people around the globe. I cannot say for those 80,000 people that the dot on the horizon is to grow our earnings per share or something else that is irrelevant to the vast majority of them, right? So you need to give them something that is inspiring and is relevant throughout the organization.'

'Allied to this relevant vision is the need to set the tone from the top with all the right values. Together this will give people enough freedom to add their own intelligence and creativity to what they need to do. Then you need to reinforce the values by making sure you model them yourself and are very tough on people who do not deliver the values. I cannot say that I am against bullying if I leave in place a person that everyone can see is a bully. My actions speak louder than words and are most vivid in the people I choose to lead. It is through these three things that you change the DNA of a business.'

Externally, a purpose wider than profit is needed

People expect more of business today. As we saw in Chapter 2, transparency has changed everything. In a world where people are so much more empowered, leaders in business have now to do a far better job of explaining what business is for. To customers, they must explain the benefits of their endeavours. To the wider public, they must explain how and why they are a force for good.

It is not enough simply to explain themselves to their shareholders or, if they are not publicly listed companies, to their financiers. Leaders, when thinking about crafting their mission statement, must now think about a broad range of stakeholders and make sure that all of them are included as beneficiaries.

Tony Manwaring is chief executive of Tomorrow's Company, a business-led think tank based in the United Kingdom. It believes that business can and must be a force for good, and that this is in the self-interest of business because this will be how companies can best deliver long-term and sustainable value. Tomorrow's Company works with leading businesses and business leaders around the world, and is respected for the quality of its thought leadership, as well as the practical value and policy impact that this achieves.

Tony says: 'The world is undergoing a period of unprecedented change and it is becoming clear that the current frameworks within which the market operates are leading to unsustainable outcomes. The survival and success of companies are bound up with the health of the natural environment, the social and political system and the global economy. Companies must play a role in all three and they need all three to flourish. Companies can be a force for good and are uniquely placed to deliver the practical solutions that are urgently required to address these issues.'

Tony says that Tomorrow's Company has identified ways in which leaders can ensure that they expand the space in which they operate. These are contained in a special report available from the think tank, entitled 'Tomorrow's global company: challenges and choices'.

First, says Tony, leaders should expand their view of success and redefine it in terms of lasting positive impacts for business, society and the environment. Having done that, they should then stand firmly behind their convictions and use them as a basis for the business strategy and decision making. 'Second, shared values are essential to provide cohesion in companies, especially those that are global and diverse. Once values have been established and communicated, they must be rigorously followed in practice and people should be held accountable for observing them. Those values should provide the bedrock upon which a company's behaviour should be based.'

John Connolly, immediate past senior partner and CEO of Deloitte, says: 'I believe that we have come to a stage where we have now to imagine a new definition of the purpose of business. What is it for? How does it make a positive contribution? There has to be more of a focus on long-term sustainable success rather than just short-term gain. It is only if you think long term that you build more value in your business. You cannot sustain your business in an environment, either social or physical, that does not have a future. Leaders must recognize that they not only must articulate this better, but must be prepared to stand up more often and talk about it, both inside and outside the enterprises they lead.'

Be an engine of progress for humankind

Sir Christopher Gent, chairman of GlaxoSmithKline, says: 'Having a strong set of values throughout the company – that are part of the DNA of the organization – is the best way of reducing bureaucracy. That way you don't need endless manuals about how to behave. You must create a culture which is ethical, and will stand up to both internal and external scrutiny. It is crucial for a leader constantly to give voice to a purpose and values that are authentic and relevant in today's world.'

'Having a higher purpose and a sound set of values is more important than ever. Companies are rooted in the society they serve. Socially engaged capitalism is critically important and to me is an engine of progress for humankind. All constituencies are interested now in business endeavour, but not always necessarily interested in ways that are sympathetic to business. Therefore, as a leader, you have to communicate what you're doing and express it in terms that convey the benefit you're trying to achieve for society as a whole and not just shareholders.'

'You provide employment, you provide benefits to pension holders, as well as shareholder returns. And there should be an agenda of public benefit broader than just profitability. There aren't many firms that aren't in the position to do that. I'm not trying to make this sound overly grand but I do actually think it makes the world go round.'

Paul Drechsler, chairman and CEO of the Wates Group, says: 'Trust in business, in my mind, has taken a major walloping over the past two or three years, particularly trust in business leaders. Yet business is a tremendous force for good. Now we are going to have to expend as much energy proving it and explaining why and how, as well as actually being a force for good.'

Jeremy Darroch, chief executive of BSkyB, argues that being open and forthright about what you do is crucial if you want to be trusted. 'Organizations that aspire to long-term success have got to have trust as an important part of their agenda.'

'You never trust somebody you don't know, whose motives you don't understand. So, as a leader, you have to give people inside and outside the company a sense of who you are and what you stand for. That's what will help people decide whether they are willing to trust you.'

'You've got to make sure that your mission and values are relevant to a broad range of audiences, and that they understand your endeavours are making a contribution beyond the narrow profit motive of your business. What is good for you as a business is generally good for others too, whether you are a partner, an employee or a customer. So you have to be prepared to stand up and explain why your success is good for all of those people.'

'There is no good in doing a lot of good and then not communicating it. Business has got to get itself on the front foot. Leaders have got to start laying out the positive case for business and private enterprise in a much more compelling way.'

Chris Satterthwaite is chief executive of Chime Communications plc, the holding company for a portfolio of 52 companies which include public relations, advertising, digital, marketing, sports marketing, market research, corporate responsibility and design businesses. (Chime is also my employer.)

Chris says: 'A lot of people think that the scrutiny of this fishbowl world is a monstrous intrusion, but it has brought a greater sense of responsibility to actions and means that leaders are much more accountable.'

'Reputation is a reflection of what you believe, what you do and how well you explain what you do. It is that last part – how well you explain what you do – that is part of the new accountability of business. Leaders must now think in terms of being trustworthy, which means you have to have values and standards that you apply to everybody, which enable people to know what to expect from you and what you expect from them.'

Involve everyone in your mission

Paul Polman, global chief executive of Unilever, puts it like this: 'All I have to do is ignite the flame that links the passions of our people to a great sense of mission, then we are up and running. That's what makes a high-performance organization.

'However, your mission cannot just be about the optimization of profits, because that leads to the wrong behaviours. The recent financial crisis we had was really a crisis of ethics that has highlighted how business should be done.'

'We at Unilever see the fishbowl as a great opportunity. There are things in life that you cannot do anything about, but as a leader there are things that you can influence and do something about. In my business brands build trust. When consumers are more uncertain and look for brands to trust, it is a huge opportunity for brands. It is not surprising to me that last year we had the highest volume growth for 30 years in this company.'

'Unilever recently launched a sustainable living plan which actually capitalizes on the fact of being in the fishbowl. We think it's a unique opportunity to leverage consumer power through transparency to really say, look we're trying to be a company that is responsible. If you see us doing bad things, let us together correct those.'

'We're trying to say to people that they, as individual consumers, might not think they can make a difference but, if they buy a Lipton teabag and it is sustainable tea, they might think it's a drop in the ocean, but think about two billion consumers of our products and harness that power. How can you harness that positively? Leaders who don't understand that, who run away from the need to be more vocal about their mission, or that try to protect themselves, over time will become dinosaurs.'

'It all goes to building trust, which is a very transparent asset on your books. Look at the market cap of a company like ours, take off the tangible assets, and then what you see is a difference of £60 billion. People call that reputation. It's trust in your brands and it is trust in your organization. So the biggest asset I need to protect is the reputation of the overall company. That can be wiped out in one day nowadays. But don't fear that. Turn that into a positive. We are, and by doing so we set much higher standards for our individual brands. I believe that is a catalyst for growth. So the only way I can run this company globally is because the values are so strong and the values drive trust.'

Reputations at risk

Sir Stuart Rose was, until early in 2011, the executive chairman of British retailer Marks & Spencer, which has more than 700 stores in the United Kingdom and another 300 stores spread across more than 40 countries. M&S specializes in clothing and luxury food products.

He is worried about the demonization of business: 'I was chairman of Business in the Community and I think it is beholden on business leaders to spend time in educational establishments, especially schools, and explain to children that work is not a bad place and that unless they are unusual they are going to spend 30 years or more in work. One of the downsides of the financial crisis is that there is now a feeling in schools that the creation of wealth is a bad thing. We've got an obligation to explain to the community at large that business growth is good, otherwise we wouldn't have roads, universities, trains, planes, and all the other infrastructure we need. People need to understand that the government is spending the money that business makes. This is hugely important and I've been quite vociferous about it.'

Another reason that leaders have to define their mission and values and then drive them into the business is because their own reputations stand or fall by whether or not employees in the organization behave according to those values.

Ron Dennis is the executive chairman of McLaren Automotive and McLaren Group, and is also a significant shareholder in both companies. He was the team principal of McLaren, the group's Formula One team, until 2009.

'One thing I'm absolutely sure of is that, if you're going to lead, you're going to have to push hard for the benefit of the people in your company, for your shareholders, so you are going to make mistakes, and you'd better come to terms with the fact. Taking responsibility for your own mistakes is hard enough. The most painful part for me, of leading a company that attracts a lot of publicity, is you actually have to take responsibility for other people's mistakes, and that is really painful.'

'In all big companies, a leader can do no more than instil values into the DNA so that they ensure people deliver the right behaviours, but you're a fool if you think that you're not going to have the odd bad apple. When that happens, the world cuts you no slack. You have to take the responsibility, because even if it's an individual that's caused that problem, you're responsible for the system, and you're responsible for the monitoring, you're responsible for everything.'

'If you work in a slow-moving organization, that's tough enough. Running a Formula One team, when you have to work in margins of half a second, you'll succeed or fail very publicly if you call it wrong, and you have to operate at incredible speed. You are on a roundabout where you're stuck to the walls, being centrifuged out, and you're trying to hang on. In this situation, I think it's a harder challenge. And you cannot do it if you don't ensure everybody subscribes to the values.'

The need for speed and the need to create leaders

The main reason for clarity on your mission and values and standards is to create a liberating framework that enables employees throughout the enterprise to be leaders themselves – leaders who are able to take decisions without constantly having to go up the chain of command for decisions.

Philip Green is the immediate past chief executive of United Utilities, which owns and operates the water network in northwest England. He says: 'Leadership isn't one person; leadership in a decent-sized company is hundreds of people.'

Leaders that I spoke to constantly talked about how leaders need to create leaders if their organizations are to thrive. The modern business arena shares many of the same attributes as a battlefield. The troops on the ground are the ones who are in the thick of the action and know most about what is going on around them. Everything happens at fantastic speed. There is little time to go up and down the chain of command, and employees need to be able to take action in the heat of battle. Leaders have to invest in them the ability to make decisions that are appropriate and in the spirit that they would themselves make decisions. If the sense of mission and the values of the enterprise are truly ingrained, then employees need only go to their hearts at times of crisis to make the right decisions – the decisions that are good for customers, good for the community and good for shareholders.

John Gildersleeve is the immediate past chairman of New Look, a British global fashion retailer with a chain of high street shops in Britain, Belgium, France, the Netherlands, Ireland, Malta, Singapore and the United Arab Emirates. He was on the board of global grocer and retailer Tesco for 20 years and, until recently, chaired Carphone Warehouse, Europe's largest independent mobile phone retailer, with over 1,700 stores.

He believes that a strong sense of mission and a defining set of values are an essential part of a leader's armoury. 'Lots of companies have a set of values but they make the mistake of putting those in the annual report and going about their business as if they don't exist. Successful companies use values successfully. These sets of values are communicated relentlessly. Leaders go around the business asking questions of employees, and vice versa, about whether what they are doing adheres to the values. It gives people a framework, not a rigid set of rules, and acts as a true north that keeps them pointing in the right direction.'

Lord Sharman is chairman of Aviva, the sixth largest insurance company in the world, created by the merger of Norwich Union and Commercial Union and employing 46,000 people. He says the big issue for leaders today is speed. 'You simply don't have as much time to think as you did before. You have to empower people – it is a business imperative. You can only do this through a very clear set of ethical and behavioural guidelines. Those values and standards are the most important thing. If you've got that strong framework in place then people understand how to behave and they can make their own decisions about what feels right.'

Standard Chartered is a multinational financial services company headquartered in London, with operations in more than 70 countries. Lord Mervyn Davies says the only way he could run Standard Chartered when he was chief executive was by instilling a strong set of values that influenced the culture.

'How do you get engagement and communicate across 75 countries with tens of thousands of people that you don't see regularly? Well, how do you do that? First, you decide on the values of the company, what sort of culture you're going to have; and then you decide how you are going to consistently communicate those values to people. You've got to break through that permafrost that you see in lots of different companies, where messages come from the top and get stuck in the middle. So the key is: know your audience, get your culture right, get your values right, get your messaging right, and then communicate, communicate.'

Three examples of mission and values at work

Xstrata plc – where information knows no hierarchy

Xstrata is a global mining company headquartered in Switzerland, with its registered office in London. It is a major producer of coal (and the world's largest exporter of thermal coal). It has operations in 19 countries across Africa, Asia, Australasia, Europe, North America and South America. Mick Davis is the chief executive. A South African, he was previously finance director for mining giant Billiton plc.

He feels that Xstrata operates differently from most other mining companies, with just 40 people in the two head office sites. 'We have a devolved management structure. We have high levels of accountability at business unit level, high levels of responsibility and high levels of authority. Authority is key; we vest a lot of authority in our people to take decisions and to act. To enable this to happen, it was essential for us to establish a set of principles about how we want to behave. So our values go round the importance of people in our organization, the safety of the people who work in our organization, the health of the communities and environments that we operate in.

'One of our values is that we are a value-conscious organization. We're here to extract as much value for our shareholders as we can. Every day I expect people to come and say, how can I run the business differently today than I ran it yesterday, for more value? Another example is the value of momentum, continuously moving forward; don't sit back. Organizations with momentum are able to act and capture opportunities. They're very simple but powerful propositions everybody buys into.'

'We don't tell leaders how to implement the values, we simply tell them these are the standards you have to meet, and they know that it is for them to determine the actions they need to take. There isn't anybody at head office who's second-guessing them. The system works because we have built an emphasis on open communication – we have strong informal networks of communication in the company, where hierarchy matters only when instructions have to be given.'

'If you work for me I can give you an instruction. You can give the people who work for you an instruction. I cannot give the people who work for you an instruction. That hierarchy is followed absolutely. But information flow and discussion in this company know no hierarchy. I can phone the fellow running a mine in Queensland and ask how things are going. I'm asking for information and Bob's boss knows that I'm not going to give Bob an instruction. I might encourage Bob to talk to his counterpart in South America, in order to help the spread of best practice.'

'We strongly pursue this informal network and that does two things: it empowers people throughout the organization to share experiences and it embeds an open and honest and sharing culture. That level of transparency, allied to our strong values, is what enables us to deliver.'

The National Trust – freedom within a framework

The National Trust is a conservation organization which works to preserve and protect the coastline, countryside and buildings of England, Wales and Northern Ireland. It owns many heritage properties, including historic houses and gardens, industrial monuments and social history sites. It is one of the largest landowners in the United Kingdom, owning many beauty spots, most of which are open to the public free of charge. It is the largest membership organization in the United Kingdom, and one of the largest UK charities by both income and assets.

Dame Fiona Reynolds has been director-general of the National Trust since January 2001. Before taking up the post she was director of the Women's Unit in the Cabinet Office and was previously director of the Council for the Protection of Rural England.

She explains: 'The scale of our conservation responsibilities is huge: more than 600,000 acres of countryside, 700 miles of coastline and over 300 historic houses and gardens. Each property is different, and needs the care of expert staff and dedicated volunteers. Both the places themselves and we, as a charity, need to be sustainable for the long term: financially, environmentally and in our strong relationships with those who love our sites, from the original donor families, to our tenants, members, visitors, staff and volunteers.'

'At each location we must celebrate a distinctive spirit of place. Each too must nurture a web of human links – with those who loved it in the past or will do in the future, with neighbours and local communities, and with visitors for whom this special spot of earth can become like home, a vital part of their lives. So, though the heritage we all share is immense, it is also personal and local. The heart of our strategy is to cherish these intimate qualities, so that millions of people each year can grow close relationships with the unique places in our care.'

'In order to deliver this, we are implementing a new strategy of localism, trying to move away from being too corporate and too samey. To do that, we have had to create what we call "a framework for freedom" – a reinforcement of our purpose and our values that enables leadership and empowers people throughout the organization.'

'We are re-engineering and redesigning the Trust to enable this local empowerment. Freedom within a framework is the mantra for localism. It means talking constantly to values and ensuring that everyone understands what our purpose is and what our values are, and how those should be delivered in their own unique environment. It is only through that level of local empowerment that we will truly be able to deliver our promise and ensure that people keep trusting us.'

'Trust is fundamental to our brand: staff have to trust me, they have to trust our brand, and people outside have to trust that we will do what we promise. People who leave us huge legacies need to trust us to fulfil their wishes. Trust runs in our blood and we work very hard to protect that trust. Trust is won through people engaging with you, seeing where you want to go, debating it with you, and that is what leaders throughout the organization need to be doing, not only with employees but with visitors and donors as well. To do that, they have to understand the framework.'

'This is what will enable the organization to be very much more innovative and imaginative in things like interpretation and presentation. With this framework in place, already our language has utterly changed. It's about how do operations feel? Do they feel free and confident to really fly with the ambitious ideas they've got for their properties? That's totally different from sending them an instruction from some senior person to make their properties more interesting.'

Serco – be clear about the reputation you want

Serco is an international service company that works for national and local governments in important areas of public service, including health, education, transport, science and defence. More than 70,000 employees deliver these services in over 30 countries. The scale and scope of Serco services are extensive, including operating traffic management systems covering more than 17,500 kilometres of roads worldwide, providing secure computer and software support services to all 66 UK law enforcement agencies, managing 192,000 square miles of airspace in five countries, and transporting more than 275,000 passengers every day on driverless trains on London's Docklands Light Railway.

Former chairman Kevin Beeston, now chairman of Taylor Wimpey, one of the largest British housebuilding companies, says that in large companies, where tens of thousands of employees are representing the company, they need help in understanding how to behave. A good reputation is the foundation stone of success and how employees behave determines the reputation.

'You have to live the reputation you want,' says Kevin. 'But that means being clear about what reputation you want. Do your mission and your values enable you to deliver that reputation? Focus on helping your employees to understand the expectations of customers and the outside world so that they understand what doing the right thing means.

'As a leader you have to spend time articulating in a very clear way what your mission is and how you expect people to behave. We did two powerful things at Serco. One was to articulate a set of what we called governing principles. These were very short and simple and defined what we expected of all of our employees, how we wanted to live our values in the organization. The other was giving our sense of mission a very public presence in the form of a strapline: "Bringing service to life". We used this strapline everywhere, in our corporate literature, on our website, in all our marketing collateral.'

'This was a promise we made to the world which guided the behaviours of 70,000 people in the company. It was one of the most empowering things that we did. No matter what you did in the organization, whether you were sweeping streets for local councils or whether you were engaged in high-level engineering and IT, you knew that you'd got a customer and that the service we provided to them needed to be of a very high quality. That made people feel very proud and it was driven by knowing that customers had had a good experience.'

Make sure the values resonate

Frequently, the leaders I interviewed spoke of how it would be impossible to run a business if their own values did not reconcile with those of the people they led.

Jeremy Darroch, CEO of BSkyB, says he would not be leading Sky if his personal values were not aligned with those of the company. 'We spend a lot of time talking about and making sure that anybody who joins the business understands the culture and our values. I've had several conversations with senior people where I had to say that if our culture doesn't motivate them, then they might not fit, in spite of their strengths and experience. But if they do get it and believe in the values then they are likely to do very well in the company.

'My job is about upholding the values and standards that we set ourselves. When everyone gets the values, that is when the organization starts to become really efficient. Even though communication is critical, when values are understood, a lot of the day-to-day stuff can be unspoken, because everyone is pushing in the same direction.'

'You can't write a set of rules for 17,000 people doing all sorts of different things, all over the world. You have to base communication on shared values and standards, and conversations need to be about that. Leaders need to spend time bringing those values to life, encouraging people to explore what those values mean in the margins, then you can have confidence that everybody will be approaching this in broadly the right way. Values are more powerful than rules, because you can't provide for every likely scenario and when people get into difficult situations, a rulebook doesn't help to orientate them. Values and a sense of common purpose will get people on the right path.'

The value of values

In every interview, I asked the leaders to tell me what the values of their business were. Many admitted that their values could be common to almost any other organization, because often values represented the moral norms of the societies within which they operated.

Some companies had worked hard to use the values to differentiate themselves and say something about them that was unique. Nearly all of the leaders made sure that their purpose and values became part of the company's brand and were used as a source of competitive differentiation. The purpose and values were also used with suppliers and partners to ensure consistency everywhere on the value chain and ensure high standards.

Leaders were unanimous in their view that articulating values and purpose was one of the most important jobs of leadership. It was a conversation without end, on board and management agendas, discussed on roadshows and workshops.

A shared sense of mission and values was inspiring, empowering and liberating and created enormous value in those companies that really brought them to life.

However, having a compelling mission and a strong set of values is irrelevant if you don't have a destination in mind. What does successfully carrying out your mission look like? Who will benefit? What is the reason why all your stakeholders should take an interest and help you get to your destination?

When you paint a picture of success in the future, and ally it with your mission and values, you have a much stronger story to tell.

KEY POINTS FROM CHAPTER 5

- Too often, leaders use the achievement of financial goals as their purpose. They are more comfortable being rational and objective.

- Too often, followers say they don't get out of bed in the morning to achieve financial or other numerical objectives.

- They come to work and want to be inspired by a sense of doing something important, something that makes a difference.

- Leaders with a strong set of values built on honesty and openness and respect for other people are the most inspirational.

- The right mission statement is inspiring; take care to craft it in a way that is compelling, easily understood, memorable and unambiguous.

- In today's world, businesses need to articulate their mission in a way that shows how they are a force for good in society.

- Every employee needs to feel part of the story, with a clear line of sight between what they do and the organization's overall purpose.

- A strong sense of mission can help shape decisions to be made throughout the organization, and is even more empowering when coupled with a strong set of values.

- The values you articulate must be the values that you live.

- In this world of radical transparency, values have assumed far greater importance, for many reasons.

- Shared values enable trust, and liberate employees to be leaders; they can then take action within a framework that enables speed, creativity and agility.

- They create competitive differentiation.

- The way your people act with their 'customers', whoever they are, says more about you than all the words you ever utter. So take care to define, and live, the values that you want delivered in daily behaviours.

- Those intangible values – often dismissed as 'soft and fluffy' – translate into actions on the ground, which translate into hard numbers in the books.

- Values must be measured for impact; people who don't live up to them should shape up or ship out.

Communicate the future to drive the present

06

MISSION & VALUES — BE YOURSELF, BETTER — FUTURE FOCUS

Leaders have to spend a great deal of time talking about the future, if they want to shape the future.

John Connolly, immediate past senior partner and CEO of Deloitte, says: 'You have to talk about what the future looks like, how you are going to achieve it, and you have to explain the case for change. You have to talk with people about their role in achieving the vision, and make sure they see how they fit in. You have to make sure they understand what you stand for, why what you are doing is important, and how everyone will benefit from success. Human beings work best when they believe in who they are, what they are doing and in the way in which they are doing it together.'

I conclude from speaking to so many leaders that they actually do 'see' the future. They are able to visualize some unique idea, a destination, and imagine the future.

This is not a book about how to build a business vision; it is about how important it is to articulate that vision. However, it seems to me the whole point of leadership is working out where you want to go from where you are now. That process itself involves a great deal of communication, both in and outside the company. Having decided on a future, you have to make sure others see it as clearly as you do by talking about it, often, and everywhere.

Followers love leaders who are forward looking. It strikes me that leaders who aren't are probably spending too much time firefighting in the present to be able to envision tomorrow.

To talk about the future, you have to be very clear about the future

Damon Buffini is one of the best-known figures in the world of private equity. He was chairman of Permira, one of Europe's largest and best-known buyout firms, until 2010, when he stepped down to focus on deals. Permira owns brands such as Birds Eye, AA, Saga and New Look. (Birds Eye Iglo Group (BEIG) is a branded European frozen food company that produces fish, vegetables, poultry and ready meals. The AA is the UK's market leader in roadside assistance, attending over 3.5 million breakdowns every year. Saga provides financial services to people aged over 50 in the UK. New Look is a global fashion retailer.)

Damon has years of experience in appointing leadership teams to build Permira's investments into better businesses. He says great communication depends on having a clear vision.

'I often think that poor communication is the result of not being clear about the direction you want to go or the goals you are setting. People will forgive poor communication technique if they have a very clear understanding of what you're trying to achieve and how they fit into it. You have to explain to your team with crystal clarity where you are going, what they need to do and why it's a good thing for them and the people they serve.

'That means you have to be incredibly clear in your own mind as to what it is you want to achieve, over what period of time and what actions are needed to get there. You have to be explicit about what you expect from the people who are going to deliver those actions. You must take the time to articulate your vision, and share it widely. Thereafter, leadership is all about being able to inspire people in the different ways they need to be inspired.'

Once a leader has that clarity, as described by Damon, it becomes easier to paint this picture for others, bringing it vividly to life with details that help others to see what is possible. The picture must describe not only what things will look like, but also how people will be feeling in the future, how people will be relating to each other and how the different stakeholders will be benefiting from the achievements in the future – all stakeholders, not just shareholders.

Using this picture, leaders can then help their colleagues face up to the reality of the situation they are in, and inject optimism and energy into realizing a better future.

Back to the future, over and over

Often, leaders do not know exactly how they are going to achieve that future; and they aren't afraid to say so – they just know it has to be achieved. They engage their people in that future by talking about how to achieve it, not whether to achieve it.

That is a really important point. Having set the direction, they engage people with the future by talking about how to achieve it, not whether it is the right future.

Followers know it is the job of the leader to decide the direction, but they hate having the route mapped out for them, step by step. That stifles creativity and limits commitment and effort. Often, leaders talk of setting seemingly impossible goals, stretching the powers and potential of everyone in the organization, of placing 'big bets' on the capability of their people to achieve more than they thought was possible. And, somehow, with that uplifting, ennobling future vivid in everyone's mind, they achieve it.

Barbara Cassani is the founding chief executive of Go Fly, the low-cost airline spun out of British Airways in the late 1990s and subsequently sold to another low-cost airline, easyJet, in 2002. Later, Barbara became chairman of London's bid for the 2012 Summer Olympics, before handing over that role to Lord Sebastian Coe.

Talking about the days when she was building Go Fly, she says: 'I have been in a number of situations in my career where being a good communicator was the difference between success and failure. The airline that we set up was a pipe dream, it was not really supposed to be achievable. I look back now on that time and I think "Oh my goodness, how did we do that?!" I believe a lot of that was to do with setting up an environment where really good people understood really clearly what they needed to do in order to make this crazy idea a success.

'There was just so much power in that clarity of vision. We could see and feel and taste success. We were clear about the future, and we had that in our minds constantly. Using that, we were able continuously to check and get feedback on our progress to our goals, and what changes we needed to make to stay on track. We experienced highs and lows together, we felt every crisis together, through open and honest communication.

'I found it was so important to involve and talk with every single person in the company on the journey. I believed that everyone, whether it was the receptionist or my most senior colleague who ran operations, every single one of us was important to the success of the airline. And you know, people stay in touch with me now, 10 years later, needing to stay in touch because it was such a special experience. That's what you can create when everybody has that clarity, feels the passion, and is striving to achieve the impossible, then does.'

James Hogan is CEO of Etihad Airways, which operates close to 1,100 weekly flights to 67 destinations in 45 countries from its main base in Abu Dhabi, capital of the United Arab Emirates. He has overseen rapid growth of this UAE airline over the past four years, adding more than 33 new destinations and 35 new aircraft, and increasing the number of passengers carried each year from 2.7 million to 7.2 million.

'Four years ago we said the vision of the airline was to be the best airline wherever we operate in the world. It seemed crazy at the time, but it's already happening. It means where we decide to compete, we're best in class. It doesn't mean we're going to get bigger. It doesn't mean we're going to be all things to all people. It means people will recognize we are the best.

'We are already rising up the rankings: we were 52nd best airline in 2006. We were sixth last year. Being the best to us means best in safety, best in service. So our vision is to be the best, and our values include being safe, being service oriented and being respectful.

'Mutual respect matters a lot in an airline which employs so many different nationalities and operates in so many different countries, so I make sure that people have a voice. Our employees come from different backgrounds and different cultures, and I spend a great deal of time ensuring they all understand our mission, and that I understand their issues.

'Everybody has to feel that passion to be the best if we are to achieve the vision, and it is that passion that empowers your people. I can't be in all 67 cities, so I have to make sure – from top to bottom – that we all believe we can achieve those objectives.'

Keep people engaged in the future

Often, as situations evolve, leaders have to adapt and change their view of the future.

Simon Calver is CEO of LOVEFiLM, initially a venture capital-backed UK start-up but now a British subsidiary of Amazon.com. LOVEFiLM provides online video rental (rental by mail) and resale of DVD video, Blu-ray and video game console discs, as well as on-demand video streaming over the internet of movies in the UK, Germany and Scandinavia.

He says: 'When we started out, with just a few of us in one office, communication of the vision was easy. But growing to nearly 500 staff operating over six different locations, the ability to align and engage staff behind a common vision became much harder. Yet being clear about your vision and your expectations of people is the most important thing a leader must do. Once you've been clear about your expectations, monitoring and managing performance against that becomes a lot easier.

'I describe the task of a leader as threefold. First, am I doing the right thing, have I made the right analysis and decided on the right strategy? Second, am I doing it the right way, with integrity, building trust, acting in a way which is mindful of our customers, neighbours and the environment? And then the final point which, I think, determines the success or failure as leader in most situations is: Am I bringing others with me?

'So it is about clarity of vision, creating a framework and a culture within which people can be creative and unleash their potential, and persuading them and inspiring them to the vision.

'But your vision can change, and with it your tactics and strategy. So you have to evolve it depending on your circumstances, and you have to keep talking with your people to ensure they are still engaged. With us, when we first started, we were competing against the likes of Blockbuster (a chain of video rental stores). Now we are competing against television broadcasters, other online video and games rental businesses, and even cable and satellite companies.

'Our purpose has always been about providing people with more choice in the way they watch films and what they watch – we *love* movies. But now we have become an important part of people's entertainment experience. Now our purpose is to give better entertainment to people at home. Our people are excited by the fact that we have been redefining an industry, and that's powerfully motivating.'

Your future must embrace all stakeholders

Paul Polman, Unilever's global chief executive, says: 'Companies have a greater and wider responsibility than just to their shareholders. It is very clear that if you want to have a long-term success, you need first to do what's right for your consumers and for your employees and for society at large. If you do all of that well, the shareholders will be rewarded.

'For a long time we have been too myopic. For a speech I was giving recently I looked at how long shareholders keep their shares in UK FTSE 100 companies. In 1960 it was 20 years. In 1980 it was 10 years. Then in the 90s, it dropped to five years. Now, it's less than six months. In less than six months the whole company market cap of the top listed companies gets turned over. That tells me the interest of the shareholder is not necessarily aligned with the long-term interest of the companies they invest in.

'Our Unilever Sustainable Living Plan is a 10-year plan. That is because I firmly believe that any vision of the future has to be really long term, and it must be focused on delivering benefits first to your stakeholders, and then to your shareholders. The ability to do the latter utterly depends on first being successful with your customers and staff and the communities in which you operate.'

Four examples of how leaders bring mission, values, vision and goals together

When leaders talk about the future, they are very specific. They are clear what their mission is. They know how they want people to behave, and what culture they want. They work hard to release the creativity and commitment of their people, by making them part of the story, in every way. They set very specific goals for their mission, as far out as five or 10 years, and ensure that they have goals for every year to the target date. They ensure that everybody knows the goals, and what they have to do to achieve them. They also set goals for all their key relationships, from employees to customers to shareholders, and they measure progress, tuning in to what is happening in a variety of ways, in order to continuously correct and improve.

Often, I heard leaders talking about getting people to imagine what relationships would be like in the future. They would tell a story of how people would be behaving and interacting, because they recognize that relationships are the engines of success. Relationships are all about feelings, and great communicating leaders lock onto this to get emotional buy-in.

Most importantly, they recognize that what people do is the link between the numbers in their plans and the successful delivery of their plans. Unless people change their behaviours, there can be no change. So people have to be provided with a reason to change, and be given a vision of compelling benefits that enlists their support. The benefit messages have to be strong enough to persuade customers to buy more, employees to work smarter, government to create an environment that enables success, shareholders and financiers to invest more, and local communities to support their activities. Communication in this context is not 'for information', or a 'nice to have'. It is an essential part of achieving the behaviours that deliver the plan.

Here are some examples of leaders delivering a seamless story of the future, where their stories embrace all of the above.

McLaren – the power of precision

Ron Dennis, executive chairman of McLaren Automotive and McLaren Group, explained his vision to build 'the world's finest sports car'. I was struck by his commitment, passion and precision.

'I saw an opportunity to build what I wanted to be the world's finest sports car. People would say to me I was brave, taking on Ferrari in this recession, building a factory, building a sports car in a declining market. First of all, I had to tell them, I'm building this factory at least 30 per cent cheaper than I could have built it three years ago, and 40 per cent cheaper than I could build it in the next three years. So I think that's pretty smart, right?

'Point two: I think it's pretty smart that we saw not just the downturn of the sector of the market that we're going to bring our sports car into, which is a price sector, I saw that five companies were at the end of their product lines, and they didn't have the money to push on with their new products. So I'm coming to the market with a new product when others have old ones. My main competition was going to be the 458 Ferrari; we knew when it was coming. We had to think, how do we second-guess what the 458 performance is? Because one thing's for sure, we've started later than them. They were going to come to the market early. We don't know how good it's going to be.

And we had to make something that's better, and yet we didn't even know what the targets were.

'So we set our own targets – for performance of the car, for first orders, for financing, for the date of the first car off the production line. We had a vision, really clear, pointing true north. And then came the recession. All around me were doom and gloom. I got all the guys together. I said: "This is an opportunity. We're going to power into it." I didn't have any problem motivating my management. It was harder motivating the investors. But we got there.

'The power of the vision has enabled so much. We raised the money. I am on target for first deliveries. The car is getting great reviews. We have sold over a year's production already.

'So these were the milestones we set for ourselves, and so far we have achieved all our milestones. We said we were going to do that four years ago. People ask me now, how do you do it? Really, how do you do it?

'The answer is that we had a compelling vision, we had very clear milestones, everyone knew what they had to do and they were highly motivated to do it. And we have a culture of hitting deadlines – we couldn't be in Formula One if we didn't. Simple as that.'

Barclays Global Retail Banking – including all stakeholders in the future

Barclays is an international financial services company, with retail banking core to the business. Global Retail Banking, led by chief executive Antony Jenkins, comprises four business units: Barclaycard (international credit card and loan provision), Barclays Africa, UK Retail Banking and Western Europe Retail Banking. In the UK, Barclays has over 1,600 high street branches (including former Woolwich branches) and it has also joined up with Post Office Ltd to provide personal banking services to customers who live near a post office in the UK. Worldwide, Barclays plc operates in over 50 countries, employing around 150,000 people.

Antony says: 'It is incredibly important for leaders to have a sense of purpose and a moral compass. Barclays was founded by 20 Quaker families over 300 years ago and they were, as I understand it, quite hard-nosed business people but they also had a broader sense of purpose.

'That is really important to me as a leader. I am very much of the camp that you have to manage a business for all of your stakeholders and you have to be able to optimize across them, through the short and the long term.

'We have two big ideas that inform Global Retail Banking. One is our mission, which is "Lives made much easier", which is customer centric. It's been highly catalytic in the organization because it provokes us to think and talk about the role of a bank in people's lives. We think the role of a bank is to help customers do things, and if we can do that in a way that's easier for them, then their lives will be better, and they will reward us with more business.

'The second idea is this notion of balance, which we call the four Cs: company, customer, citizenship and colleagues. We manage a balanced scorecard and we have goals in each of those categories. This year, as a result of the strategy work we've done, we've defined those goals out to 2015. We asked what success would look like in 2015. And then we've worked back to this year to say what we need to achieve now to progress towards it.

'We have to succeed in each of the C categories. So you can have a great financial performance but if your customer satisfaction or employee opinion survey scores are declining, that's not a good performance.

'Making a contribution in the communities we serve is also important to our long-term success and is how we will be seen to be a force for good. So when I assess the performance of the business, I measure it on each of those four areas.

'There's no doubt that in our industry we have an enormous mountain to climb to restore trust and we're doing that in an environment which is very challenging, both economic and regulatory. There's never been a time when leading, when communicating, when this moral compass notion, have been more important.'

G4S – building values into the business plan

G4S is the world's largest security company. It has operations in more than 110 countries, and employs more than 625,000 people. The CEO is Nick Buckles.

'We state that our purpose is to secure your world,' he says. 'We believe that no growth is possible unless people feel safe and secure. What we do is fundamental to the success of governments and companies around the world. To have a mission that really matters, and makes a difference in the world, is invigorating for the organization.

'To be reminded what they're there to do on a day-to-day basis and be able to describe it in a way that isn't exaggerated, but makes people feel they've got an important role to play in their job, makes people proud. Having pride in what you do makes a difference to performance. Otherwise, for some of our people, you could just say: "I come to work to sit at a reception desk and wear a uniform and smile at people when they come in." That's very different from thinking that I'm there to help provide a safe and secure environment for everyone who works there – it makes you think that you are adding something to society and the world. I think that can be very inspiring.

'I firmly believe there is a link between people feeling proud about what they're doing and our profitability. How people feel at work and why they come to work may be soft issues in business but they have a definite impact.

'Our values are crucial as well. For example, we include integrity and teamwork and collaboration among our values. Integrity is crucial in many of the places that we work and we simply wouldn't be able to provide a good service to clients if we did not collaborate as colleagues and as suppliers.

'It's important for leaders to concentrate on these areas and commit time and effort to communicating mission and values. These are intangibles that deliver very tangible results. When you draw up the values of the business you do that through a team effort and everybody chips in.

'We actually did our strategic plan by putting all the actions and objectives under the values so that it gave real momentum to delivering the values. We actually built the business plan around the values to make sure people delivered growth, but in line with the values. To stop people saying "What do the values mean?" we put some tangible objectives around them.'

Northumbrian Water Group – talking to everyone about the values

Heidi Mottram is chief executive of Northumbrian Water Group, which operates in the northeast of England and also in the counties of Essex and Suffolk, serving 4.5 million customers. It employs 3,000 people. She took up the post in April 2010, after a career in the rail industry.

'Ever since I've been in a position of influence, I have pursued mission and values with some passion. I have worked in some businesses, not at a senior level, where the values were at odds with mine and it was very uncomfortable. Within a month of taking up my new role here, I was in dialogue with all the employees, asking them what it was they thought we stood for around here, what sort of business we were. What were the things people would say about us and what would we like them to be saying about us?

'People spoke of the need to be ethical, customer focused, results driven and collaborative. It was very important to preserve those values because they resonated within the organization. Then we had to think about introducing some values that would be important in moving us in the right direction. Once we had done that it became very important to use measures so that people could see we were serious about values. What would they mean for middle managers? What would they mean for the board? What would they mean for me? What would we be doing or not doing if we were living by those values?

'Then we made those standards completely transparent so that everybody could see what we expected of people at their different levels. Anybody can see the sorts of things they should and shouldn't be doing. Those values work in conjunction with our mission statement, which is to be the national leader in sustainable water and waste-water services.

'To bring that to life, we've got the five pillars of our plan, the first of which is to do with our customers. What does being the best company look like for the customer? What is it for the environment? What is it in terms of competitiveness and efficiency? What is it in terms of our people and working for the company? And what is it in terms of the communities that we do business in? How would you have to score a leader in each of those different pillars?'

'Once we had shaped that with the leadership team, we then did it in collaboration with 3,000 people. We embarked on a roadshow and I literally met every single employee at 51 events in total. In those roadshows we said: "Look, guys, this is what we're thinking." Then we broke out into sessions and asked them to tell us whether or not they could buy into that; whether they thought we were wrong; where we needed to do better. We received a massive amount of feedback from that. What we got in the main was a vote of confidence in the direction of the business. The exercise was hugely empowering.'

Bring to life the customer's experience

Leaders use their customers to help engineer a better future. We all have customers, whether we are in commercial organizations or charities. We also have customers within our own organizations, particularly if we are in a service department. Our customers are the people we serve, and whose trust we have to earn and keep if we are to keep them.

Inspiring leaders keep talking about the views and experiences of their customers, in order to ensure a real understanding exists inside the company. It is only when employees get to 'feel' what it is like to *be* a customer of their own organization that true understanding and commitment to change can be engineered. That is why leaders are increasingly bringing those outside experiences into their own companies – as we will see, in the next chapter...

KEY POINTS FROM CHAPTER 6

- Paint a vivid picture of success.
- Describe the future both in rational terms (the numbers) and emotional terms (how it will feel for all concerned).
- This bringing together of the rational and the emotional is key to inspiring people.
- This future, though, has to be expressed in benefit terms for all the people with a vested interest in the performance of the organization – customers, shareholders, local communities, suppliers and partners and, most importantly, employees.
- Leaders make sure their vision presents sustainable success for all.
- Leaders must not only explain the future, they must also explain why it is necessary to change, and give a sense of hope and optimism to the businesses they lead, through what they say.
- Leaders ensure their people understand what quality of relationship will be needed with their key stakeholders.
- Fusing the future vision (what success will look and feel like) to the mission (what important thing we are here to do) and to the values (how we do it) completes the picture.

07

Bring the outside in and focus on building relationships and trust

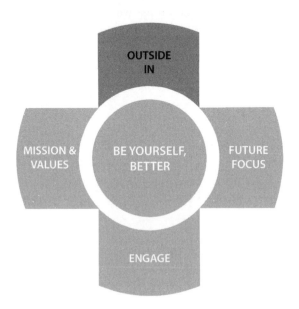

In the *Oxford Dictionary*, risk is defined as: 'a situation involving exposure to danger or loss'. A little earlier in its pages, the dictionary defines reputation as: 'the beliefs or opinions that are generally held about someone or something.'

We all know that what is generally believed about any enterprise is the result of thousands upon thousands of actions – all the positive things an organization does over years and years, all the things it says about itself, and all the things that others say about it. Every day, as any organization goes about its business, interacting with perhaps millions of people, there is a risk of being exposed to situations that could lead to danger or loss.

A good reputation is an intangible asset of immense financial worth – so much so that loss of reputation is now considered by the leaders I interviewed as their single greatest risk. As we have seen already, this risk is constantly on their minds. It is why they recognize the need to build cultures with strong values frameworks, which enable their employees to do the right thing in the heat of the moment. It is why they stress the importance of relentlessly communicating those values, probably one of the most important things they have to do.

They worry about the reputational damage that can be done when employees 'do the wrong thing' and a crisis erupts. As Fields Wicker-Miurin, co-founder of Leaders' Quest, says: 'What comes out in a crisis is how well a leader has done their job before the crisis – how well they instilled the right culture and behaviours in their organization.'

Most leaders now regard trust as the hidden asset on their balance sheets, worth – in some cases – billions. Richard Lambert, former director-general of the CBI, said he had spoken to business people the length and breadth of Britain after the financial crisis. He found they were deeply mindful that reputation and trust are now more important than ever. 'We live in an age of transparency, and leaders must ask themselves before every business decision: will this pass the *Sunday Times* test? We have to be more willing to look in the mirror and apply conscience, not just be compliant, if we are to win back trust.'

Sir Stuart Rose, former chairman of M&S, stresses: 'For a business leader, building reputation and trust *is* the day job, which makes communication the day job too.'

John Connolly, immediate past senior partner and CEO of Deloitte, says: 'Leaders have always placed emphasis on their own and their organizations' reputations. Unfortunately, we are now in an environment where leaders are concerned that reputations can too easily, and perhaps sometimes unfairly, be damaged – and that damage can be permanent. When you live in a world where one mistake will be allowed to eliminate everything good you've ever done, and destroy the trust you need to operate, even if it is a relatively minor mistake, the consequence is that leaders not only become more risk aware, they become risk averse as well. And that can lead to little or no progress, for part of leadership is about pushing hard in order to progress.'

Baroness Hogg has been chair of the Financial Reporting Council, the regulator and standard setter responsible for corporate governance and financial reporting as well as the audit, accounting and actuarial professions in the UK, since May 2010. She is also senior independent director of BG Group plc, lead independent director of HM Treasury, a director of the John

Lewis Partnership, a member of the Takeover Panel, senior adviser to the Financial Services Authority and a member of the prime minister's Business Ambassador Network.

'The problem is that there are lots of people who think that their brands exist if within their control when actually their brands exist in the minds of their customers. There is a divergence between the internal brand and the external brand and that's always troublesome. You lack authenticity if your internal brand and how other people see you from outside are not the same. Closing that gap is critical.'

Loss of your 'licence to operate'

So, leaders know that trust matters, and they especially know that trust matters most in a crisis. More than half of the CEOs I spoke to volunteered the example of Tony Hayward, the CEO who had to resign as the head of oil company BP because of the Gulf of Mexico oil leak crisis. They cited this as the ultimate example of how quickly trust can be lost and your licence to operate revoked (see Chapter 14).

At the heart of what they are all saying, though, is the idea that their very future is pegged to the strength of the relationships they have with all the people upon whom their success depends. Those relationships are not only precious but also increasingly fragile. The reason is because relationships change, and in a world transforming at the speed of thought, power has spilled out of the corridors of government and big business and onto the street. Here, people have become less deferential and much more demanding.

Why? It is because they have greater access to information and to each other. That means they have much more choice – and they're getting smarter. Not only are they smarter, but they are also faster than most companies are to respond. To them, trust is as critical as delivery, and they sit in judgement of every act and every utterance of leaders.

These people represent what I call 'the court of public opinion', and in this court, judgements are handed out rapidly – and ruthlessly. If they don't like what they see or hear, if they lose trust in a company or brand, they can walk out of this relationship and into another, just like that.

Managing the intangible asset of relationships

The worst risk is therefore not in the loss of reputation, but rather in the consequences of a bad reputation – the destruction of relationships. So you could argue that managing reputation is actually about managing the risks around the intangible asset of relationships – for it is upon these relationships that the future of the company depends.

For this reason, I kept hearing from the leaders I interviewed that they regularly ensure they bring the views of external stakeholders into their organization to help focus on what needs to be done, and then use those views to drive the right conversations, with their people, about how to improve. They focus on closing the gap between the external perception of the brand and the internal one.

Phil Bentley, managing director of British Gas, demonstrated how he was doing this in Chapter 2 – where we looked at how he had set up a system that allowed him to be alert to what people outside the organization were saying, so that he could respond in an instant. He was willing to enter into dialogue with his consumers, in order to earn their trust and turn them into advocates of his business.

A report published by United Kingdom Department of Trade and Industry in 2001, but still hugely valuable today, is entitled 'Creating value from your intangible assets'. The conclusions outlined were drawn from the general question: 'What have you got that is valuable that is not included in the balance sheet?'

The report identified seven areas of intangible value for leaders:

- relationships;
- leadership and communication;
- culture and values;
- reputation and trust;
- knowledge;
- skills and competencies;
- processes and systems.

In this book, we have been paying attention to the first four intangible assets.

On relationships, the report has this to say: 'Only by developing an effective strategy for managing and maintaining excellent relationships with all its key stakeholders can a company hope to achieve its full potential. A successful company is one that looks constantly to build on its existing relationships, be they external (customers, suppliers or anyone else whose ideas and coopera-tion may assist in meeting goals and solving problems) or internal (different functions and their teams working together to seize opportunities and create value).

'Understanding how to identify, develop, organize and sustain an appro-priate network of relationships that bring new ways of working, ideas and opportunities plays a key role in the quest for competitive advantage.'

In particular, the report highlighted the need for organizations to improve the quality of dialogue with stakeholders: 'For your company to reach its full potential in this area, it is essential that you not only consider how you can develop and improve your current relationships, but that you also care-fully consider how you can develop and improve the relationships necessary for your future success.'

The virtuous circle in relationships

I believe there is a powerful virtuous circle in bringing the outside in. If you are in dialogue with your stakeholders, and bringing their perspectives and ideas into your teams, it means you will be much better informed – and only in high-quality relationships can you get great feedback. Not just feedback on how you are perceived or what might be going wrong, but also ideas about what you can do to make a difference.

That, in turn, leads to better debates inside the company and, ultimately, to better decisions. Those better decisions enable better performance. In turn, a better performance has a positive impact on relationships and reputation.

Whether we work in the commercial sector, the public sector or the third sector, we are all subject to the same governing law, which is that good relationships are the engines of success. Leaders must ensure they are monitoring those relationships, understanding how people feel, feeding that insight back into the organization, influencing the decision making, and ensuring there are strong, two-way communication processes in place that sustain healthy and supportive relationships.

For relationships to thrive there has to be trust. Yet trust is bust, we keep hearing. Or, at the very least, it is in intensive care. And in a world that has been reset by the widespread impact of the recession and the financial crisis, it cannot be business as usual. The cost of a loss of trust to business, to governments and to charities will be huge, for one crucially important reason: Trust can earn us real money. And a lack of trust can cost us even more.

The real value of trust

If you are trusted, you can bring products to market faster, more cheaply than your competitors. You can win that pound from a member of the public for your charity more easily. You can bring about change and deliver public services more effectively and with greater cooperation and even collaboration. It is like being paid a massive dividend.

If you are not trusted, you will face an uphill battle – more regulatory hurdles, more time, more effort – and a heavy tax is imposed on the organization. (The British Chambers of Commerce recently estimated that the cost of regulations introduced by the Labour government after 1998 amounted to £77 billion – a staggering amount.)

So, in every sense, trust means money. I am convinced that leaders who put the winning of trust at the heart of their corporate strategies will gain competitive advantage. *Are* leaders more aware of the value of trust? Absolutely. Every leader I have spoken to talks to the value of trust.

Marcus Agius, group chairman of Barclays, says: 'Reputation and trust are essential to the recovery. Trust is the hidden asset on company balance sheets.'

Philip Green, former CEO of water company United Utilities, says: 'You can't run a big business without having trust and reputation high on the agenda. For a big corporate, your reputation is one of your most important assets – more so in companies like retailers, utilities and financial institutions, where trust is at the heart of the proposition.'

Just a decade ago, business leaders were still, overall, trusted. But corporate disasters like Enron and the banking crisis, allied to media more likely to scrutinize and popularize business stories, and a savvier, better connected, more empowered public, have changed everything. Members of the public have raised their expectations of organizations – and are far more demanding, more suspicious and less inclined to trust.

Watch out for the reputation gap

A brand *is* a promise – of quality or service – and in today's world, consumers are going to express themselves widely when they are disappointed. The risk of instant recrimination and widespread viral criticism is ever present when businesses fall into the reputation gap – the gap between what they promise and what they deliver.

Some brand experts say that a brand can represent up to one-third of a company's value, because the brand is equally a promise to shareholders of growth and profits to come. But when consumers doubt these promises, they throw doubt and risk into future profits. And that can have a major impact on your share price if you are a publicly listed company, or on the willingness of your financier to keep providing you with cash.

Faced with such compelling reasons to act, one would think that leaders would be doing far more about making trust an explicit objective, constantly measured and improved. I heard many leaders talk about the importance of trust, but few could say they had made it an explicit objective. Only a few measured it. Why?

Most don't know how to think about measuring a 'soft' intangible factor like trust. The problem is, if it remains that way, then leaders won't know how to get their arms around it and work to improve levels of trust. Trust, to many leaders, is a word hard to define and therefore difficult to measure.

I first became intrigued by this when I worked with a well-known fast food business in the UK. They were in the midst of a publicity storm about how unhealthy their product was, and tried to respond by bringing healthier foods into their high street restaurants.

They commissioned research into how they were seen by the public and, in particular, how they were trusted. The research showed that levels of trust in their brand were plummeting. Yet strangely, sales were going *up*! How did that work? The answer lay in the fact that they had failed to distinguish what the public meant when they talked about trust. Did the public trust the leaders of the business to 'do the right thing' about obesity and unhealthy eating? No. Did that matter? No. Why? Because the public trusted them to deliver a high-quality product in their restaurants, and that mattered more.

The three dimensions of trust

I have come to believe there are at least three dimensions to trust. David Kenning, psychoanalyst and strategic adviser to the public relations and communications group Bell Pottinger, says: 'The three dimensions of trust are: trust of judgement; trust of will or motive; and trust of delivery or competence.'

Trust of judgement represents recognition of another's experience, wisdom or insight, explains David. 'Without trust of judgement, we would be in a perpetual state of confusion, suspicion and paranoia. The two most important questions in this regard are: Is this person or organization giving me their honest opinion? And what's their track record of getting things right?'

The second kind of trust, says David, is trust of will or motive, and is quite different. 'This is where we trust someone to look out for us without taking advantage or seeking personal gain. When applied to a corporation it entails integrity and transparency and a genuine, demonstrable consideration for the customer's interest and point of view. We should never underestimate our unconscious desire to project this kind of trust onto government, employers or our favourite brands. In doing so, we make ourselves vulnerable. A failure of trust of judgement may elicit feelings of frustration, disappointment or anger. But a failure of trust of will or motive will elicit much deeper feelings of betrayal, disgust and even paranoia, since its loss can be crushing.'

The third kind of trust, says David, has to do with trust of delivery or competence – namely the trust we acquire through experience that certain people, brands or organizations can be relied upon to do what they have said they will do. 'This is more robust than trust of judgement in that – up to a point – we can be more forgiving if things go wrong. A good track record counts against occasional mistakes becoming permanent trust breakers.'

Why leaders need to inject more character into their communication

My view is that trust instils confidence in people – and that confidence is born of a positive view of a leader's character and competence. Character is about their integrity and motives. Competence is about their skills and track record of delivering on their promises. After nearly 40 years in communications, I feel safe saying that most organizations are usually pretty good about talking to their skills, results and track record. Whether through advertising, public relations or sponsorship, leaders are well versed in talking about the value of their products or services, and the benefits they bring to their stakeholders.

But in this reset world, where it is now so much more about character and trust, I feel equally safe saying leaders are far less practised when it comes to making explicit what they stand for, how they see the world and what values they will draw on when making their decisions. In other words, leaders are not very good when it comes to communicating 'character', which has come to matter so much more.

In this new world, authenticity is now the Holy Grail. However, it is only when you make your values and beliefs more clear that people will be able to judge whether you are being authentic. Not everyone will agree with your values or your view of the world, but at least they will know where you are coming from, and that will stand you in good stead, for people will be able to trust that you will consistently behave in a certain way, and know what to expect. (For more on this subject, see Chapter 11.)

This places an imperative on leaders to frame trust in economic terms, and focus on making the building of trust an explicit organizational objective. Trust must become like any other goal – it must be focused on, measured and improved. When the dividends of trust can be quantified, this enables a compelling case for building trust.

The health warning on building trust

There is, however, a health warning on building trust, says David Kenning. 'As companies strive to create an emotional connection between themselves and their stakeholders (and as a result, enjoy commercial benefits of greater loyalty and advocacy), this leads to a more personal and private relationship between the company and its customer, staff and partners.

'Stakeholders trust the company – and its brands – to embody and uphold their own values and ethics, and also to make decisions in an emotional rather than commercial way. When this doesn't happen, people feel badly let down. The sense of betrayal can be very intense – and the bad publicity much more damaging.'

Leaders need to be sure that they can keep the promises they make and need to have plans in place to manage situations that arise from an actual – or perceived – breach of that trust. Trust impacts on us all day, every day, and underpins every relationship, for which, after all, leaders are supposed to be responsible.

This means leaders should spend far more time on values-based communications – and focus on what the organization they represent stands for and believes in. They should encourage more conversations and show their willingness to be more transparent. They should ensure more direct communications with their publics through the marvels of digital communications and the internet, and have less reliance on reaching them through the media.

Sir Nicholas Young has been chief executive of the British Red Cross since July 2001. The charity delivers emergency response in the UK and around the world, community care services which meet the needs of vulnerable people in UK neighbourhoods, refugees and asylum seekers, and provides education in life-saving skills. He feels that trust has become more important and has required organizations to raise their game when it comes to communicating.

'Communicating with all our stakeholders just gets ever more important. It's a very competitive world. There are something like 200,000 charities in the UK. The top 500 of those are all much better at communicating now than they used to be. It's ever more important for us to communicate about what we believe, what we do, about the difference we make, the impact we have, and what it is that your giving pound will achieve. That's not only specific communication about particular projects or challenges, but also about our brand. That has to include an element of trust, of credibility, of authority or integrity.

'People have to trust us. Our beneficiaries have to trust us to get them the relief and the rescue that they need. Our donors obviously have to trust us, because we're using their generously given donations, to meet needs around the world. Governments and health authorities need to trust us, because we help them with our task of caring for the population. In the UK it's absolutely vital people have that sense of trust and confidence in us. They have to believe in our ethic, trust our judgement and know we can do what we say we can do.'

How to unlock the value in relationships

How much value is locked away in our key relationships – these most precious, but intangible, of assets? Could more value be released if we managed this asset more systematically? As we have seen, the increasing volatility in relationships has serious implications, what with so much of a company's value lying in the state of those relationships.

Stripped right down, the role of any leader is to ensure they achieve the mission – and that usually means ensuring their enterprise makes profits, returns value to shareholders or investors, and can do so on a sustainable basis. In a charity, one of the roles of leadership is to secure the funding that enables the organization to continue to service the needs of its end users, whoever they might be. If relationships are bad, leaders will struggle to deliver either of those goals, and certainly compromise their chances of sustainable success. If those relationships become really bad, leaders can end their own careers and even put an end to the organizations they lead.

On the other hand, great relationships represent a real competitive edge, and help to deliver a better performance... which delivers better results... which delivers a better reputation... which delivers greater value. Yet how many companies today actively audit the state of their relationships, as well as their reputation, and then institute plans to address the issues raised by their stakeholders?

Most of the organizations I spoke with did actively engage with stakeholders this way, but, more widely, experience tells me that all too few organizations really spend time on and absolutely know how their stakeholders feel and think. When leaders don't listen to their stakeholders, they can't respond to their concerns, and failure to change becomes the reason for loss of reputation.

If listed companies did conduct relationship audits, they could get more recognition of their intangible assets and uncover pearls of insight, which could help in driving up their share price and releasing even greater shareholder value. Such audits might also be of far greater value than conventional audits. These audits need to include one super-critical question of each key relationship: 'What would it take to improve our relationship?'

The answers will enable management to know what action to take, and to cost those actions against likely returns on their investment. Once the right actions are identified, management can communicate what they are doing, why it is important, and what benefits the company and its stakeholders will derive. It is this that builds trust and credibility. The opposite is achieved by promises made but not met.

Financial audits are all about past performance. Relationship audits are the predictors of future performance.

Thinking about which relationships are key is a good starting place. Which people are most important in your court of public opinion, and why? Mapping out these relationships becomes a strategic process, which enables better insight, action and better performance.

When leaders manage reputation in this way, they significantly improve their chances of successful change, because they are more aware of the real issues. They are far more likely to deliver a transformed organization – listening better, acting faster, improving performance and building better relationships, by the day. When they bring the outside in, and help employees to understand – to really understand – how their stakeholders feel, employees 'feel' the need to change. They are inspired.

The leaders I spoke with all brought the outside in, in a variety of ways, always with a mind to taking action as a result of what they heard. They loved customers' stories – good and bad – because they gave them a chance to do something.

Tuning in to the court of public opinion

Sir Stuart Rose argues that because we live in a world which is so fast-moving, 'you have to have your antennae permanently switched on 24 hours a day and they have got to be literally quivering.

'Let's just say David Beckham came out of a party in LA last night with a white tie on, customers of Marks & Spencer would expect stores to have white ties in pretty quickly. Equally, leaders inside have to know what is going on in the food arena. Is healthy the agenda? Is sustainability the agenda? Is carbon footprint the agenda?

'So, it is keeping an eye on that and making sure that we are absolutely in tune with what the consumer expects of us. There is a constant rumbling and we measured that very carefully, and brought it into the company. In addition, we listened to what NGOs were saying, whether it was pressure groups on Burma or Madagascan vanilla or whatever. Be sure there are hundreds of pressure groups, so you have to keep listening.'

When you listen and bring the outside in, it presents you with opportunities too. Sir Stuart explains: 'Not too long ago there were a couple of smart girls who happened to be quite well endowed, who complained that Marks & Spencer were charging a premium of a couple of quid extra to a girl with a double D cup bra. We were! It costs more to make a double D cup bra because of the required engineering.

'These girls talked about this on their Facebook page and within minutes had something like 10,000 followers. M&S had a 27 per cent share of women's lingerie in the UK and I could smell that this was going to go the wrong way. I got our marketing director, Steve Sharp, in and said that we were going to take the tax off the bras and give the girls a discount for a couple of weeks. He came up with this wonderful advert.'

At this point Sir Stuart breaks off to find the advert and hold it up for me. The full-page ad, placed in national newspapers, showed a photo of a large-breasted woman, with the words 'We boobed' strategically placed. The ad read: 'It's true our fantastic-quality larger bras cost more money to make, and we felt it was right to reflect this in the prices we charged. Well, we were wrong, so as of Saturday 9 May, the storm in a D cup is over! Every woman can now experience the difference a well-made quality bra will make.'

Sir Stuart continued: 'The newspapers all said this is a listening company and our market share went up within about five minutes. In addition, we had 30,000 people on Facebook within two days. So, it pays to be in tune!'

Get your hands dirty

Tom Hughes-Hallett, CEO of Marie Curie Cancer Care, believes leaders have to go out and experience the external world, if they really want to bring that world back into the organization.

'After a period here I became extremely frustrated with the way our care and services were being managed. But I knew I was not a nurse, a doctor or a physiotherapist, so who was I to criticize? Perhaps I really did not understand. So I actually became the head of our caring services for a year and came to fundamentally understand that business.

'It was a good thing to do, because I learned very quickly that it was about clients and customers and we had become too detached from their needs, too professional. It was what the nurse thinks the patient needs rather than what the patient wants, so I turned it on its head. Since that day, we have trebled the amount of care we provide, with fewer staff, and it is the care that the patient wants. It is the thing that I am most proud of in my whole career. I think getting your hands dirty in the business is not something every leader can do but one or other way you had better take a bit of time to find out about it. Go listen.'

If need be, actually bring the client in

Lord Sharman, chairman of Aviva, tells the story of when he became senior partner of global accounting firm KPMG. 'I kept telling people they had to actually put themselves in the shoes of the customer. I didn't want our people to keep telling our clients what they should think. I spent hours talking about client relationships but nothing worked as effectively as the day I brought a client to our senior partners' meeting to talk about how he felt as a client of ours.

'He got up and he said: "Look, I've been asked to talk about managing client relationships. You guys all sit there and you think managing client relationships is about taking me to the opera, being nice to me, getting me on side, but you couldn't be more wrong. I don't want a nice cuddly bloke looking after my audit. I want a real bastard. I want somebody who's going to hold my management's feet to the bloody fire and tell me what's wrong. So forget the opera." That stopped my partners dead in their tracks. It's those sorts of things that you need to do.'

The customer experience brings the vision alive

Paul Polman of Unilever says bringing customers into the organization helps everyone understand the purpose of the company.

'I was in Egypt just before the crisis of early 2011 and I went into a consumer's home about an hour outside Cairo. The lady doesn't have anything. She has sand on the floor. There are a few mattresses, two or three rooms that look dark. She was explaining to us how she works and she said in the morning she does her laundry in one of those petrol barrels that she had made her washing machine. She fetches wood and puts it under the barrel to heat up the water. She goes to the well about three times to bring the water. Then she turns the laundry with a stick, which is all that she has, and puts some powder on top of it and prays that it gets the clothes clean. Then she has to rinse.

'She has to go back to the well three or four times to rinse. It takes the whole morning. In the afternoon she does the same with the cooking. She has to get the water boiling. More wood. She has to get whatever she's making for dinner prepared for when her husband comes home at night. He gets angry because the laundry isn't done properly or the food isn't done to his liking. Tough life.

'What people forget is that's how 90 per cent of the people still live in these areas. So if we can make a little detergent that doesn't need so much rinsing or that gets her clothes slightly cleaner, or a little cube of Knorr that gives her food more flavour, then we give her more time. We give her more time for her children, or to start a little business. We give her time to invest in education for her children. We give her time to give her husband. That's what we do and there's no better way to make that come alive than to bring our purpose alive through customer experiences.'

How to develop quivering antennae

As Sir Stuart Rose says, you have to find a way to develop 'quivering antennae'. Yet too few companies understand how to use the internet to develop fast ways of getting fresh, free and authentic insights into the way their organizations are perceived, says Nicholine Hayward, Bell Pottinger's planning director.

'From search engines to social media, the internet offers an easily accessible repository of authentic insight and intelligence. The insights come not from people sitting in a focus group filling out a questionnaire or standing on a street corner talking to a researcher with a clipboard, but from unguarded conversations and forums, social networks, blogs and searches on Google. I call it the world's largest, most honest and unselfconscious focus group.

'By looking at what millions of people are asking for and talking about online, we can see what the public is asking for, in their own time, in their own words, and sitting at their own PC, and we can put this intelligence to work at every stage of a business or marketing strategy. There are so many ways that leaders can learn more effectively to bring the outside in, and using the internet more imaginatively is one of the easiest.'

But what do I do with the insights?

Gaining the right insights is all very well, but the big question becomes: what to do with them. I have frequently been surprised at how little market research really is shared with all employees. When it is, when employees gather to consider the views of customers and work out how to improve those views, exciting innovation can take place at a stunning pace.

To do this, leaders need to engage employees in the right conversations...

KEY POINTS FROM CHAPTER 7

- Successful leaders know that relationships are the engines of success, and they keep a close eye on the state of all key relationships.

- They keep their enterprise focused on those relationships as well.

- Define and map your key relationships; and find ways to listen to those people continuously. Develop 'quivering antennae' to ensure you stay in tune with how they think and feel.

- Use your own valued external critics, tap into Twitter and the blogosphere, employ newsreaders, market researchers, trend spotters, undertake personal visits to customers' homes and offices – anything that keeps you grounded in the experience your organization is delivering to the world outside your office walls.

- Bring customers 'into' your organization through stories, anecdotes and research – or bring in actual customers, so they have a real voice in your enterprise.

- Help your employees to 'feel' how your stakeholders feel; this emotional engagement drives pride and action and improvement.

- You have to live the reputation you want.

- Define the reputation you want – as expressed by every external audience relevant to your organization.

- Use that definition to manage quality inside the organization.

- Mind the reputation gap – the difference between the promise you make to customers and the experience customers or stakeholders actually receive.

- Narrowing that gap, or even managing it away, is the goal, if you want to be trusted.

- Communicate your values and beliefs to external audiences more: if people don't know you, they won't trust you.

- You do want to be trusted.

- Make trust a strategic goal, measured and managed as preciously as any other key asset.

- Make the building of trust in all relationships a strategic objective; and understand what you need to be most trusted for.

08

Engage and align through conversations

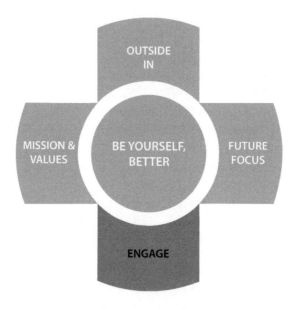

OUTSIDE IN

MISSION & VALUES

BE YOURSELF, BETTER

FUTURE FOCUS

ENGAGE

Sir Nicholas Young, CEO of the Red Cross, tells an amusing story about advice he received when he first joined the organization. He says that the chairman of his board of trustees at the time was Lady Sylvia Limerick.

'She called me into her office and said: "Oh, Mr Young, you're new aren't you?" I said: "Yes, Lady Limerick, I'm in charge of our UK operations."'

'She said: "Yes, very good. Well, let me tell you something. You must remember this. If you want to get things done in the Red Cross, it can take five years. If you want to get them done quickly, it will take you 10 years."'

Sir Nicholas says that point has always stuck with him and is a story he has often told. 'It's such an important point – you have to spend time talking with people to get them on board to changes you need to implement. You just have to take the time.'

If there is one character trait common to the leaders in this book, it is that they all seem to have a restless urge to do better. They are typically challenging and demanding, and that translates into a constant urge to change things, to enhance performance, to do more.

This primal drive in leaders to strive for difficult goals, if thwarted by employees unwilling or unable to change, can boil over into some very poor leadership behaviours. Frustrated leaders resort simply to ordering people to do what is needed; sometimes, it even becomes rage. In that case, employees will do what they are told, but not willingly, not with real commitment, and so change takes longer, and results are mediocre at best.

Ordering people to do something is often the right thing to do in a crisis, when there is no time for consultation, and somebody has to take absolute charge. In the event of a fire, nobody in their right mind would suggest a meeting to debate potential courses of action in order to reach a consensus. In those circumstances, one appreciates being told exactly what to do and where to go in order to escape danger. However, most challenges facing organizations do not have that same life-or-death urgency attached to them. There is more time to align people to the cause, more time to get their ideas.

Sir Christopher Gent, chairman of GSK, agrees fully. 'To get people engaged and fully supportive of decisions, you have to go through a process of vigorous debate. This conversation may take longer than you would like, but in the end, you will implement faster and more successfully if you do take the time.'

What is an engaged employee?

Both Sir Nicholas and Sir Christopher are talking about the need to engage people in change. It seems so obvious that, as a leader, you have to truly engage hearts as well as minds if you want to unlock the potential in every employee, and achieve a step change in workplace performance. But, sadly, many leaders I have encountered over the years have failed to truly grasp the power of engaging staff. They still make decisions and then say: 'What shall we tell the troops?' They have honest and good intentions to make sure that they communicate well, but they lose sight of the fact that broadcasting messages at people is not the same as engaging with them.

What is 'an engaged employee'? Tom Hughes-Hallett of Marie Curie Cancer Care says: 'I believe it means someone who is emotionally committed to their organization, to their colleagues and to the job they have to perform. People who are engaged are fully involved in, and enthusiastic about, their work. Everything they do is aimed at improving performance and delivering a better service or product to the people who are their customers. Usually, engaged employees are having fun. The difference in attitude is palpable.'

Myth: 'People are our only asset'

I have often heard leaders talk about people being 'our only real asset'. This is a fantastically misleading concept. People who are not committed and turn up to do the minimum amount of work are a drag on performance. Even worse, people who resent change and resist it can be toxic to the organization that employs them.

The truth is that only committed and inspired employees are an asset. People who are inspired give of their very best, tend also to have fun – and they make a difference. They are the ones who are truly 'engaged'.

In the autumn of 2008, the British government's Department for Business, Innovation and Skills commissioned a special report into employee engagement. Ministers wanted to understand more about the potential benefits of greater employee engagement for the UK, for companies, organizations and for individual employees.

In particular, they wanted to know whether a wider take-up of engagement approaches could impact positively on UK competitiveness and performance, as part of the country's efforts to come through the economic difficulties of the recession, as well as meet the challenges of increased global competition.

Entitled 'Engaging for success: enhancing performance through employee engagement', the report concluded, unequivocally: Yes!

The report's authors said: 'Of course a sustainable business strategy and access to cash are vital, just as good policy and planning are for successful public services. But, in a world where most factors of production are increasingly standardized, where a production line or the goods on a supermarket shelf are much the same the world over, employee engagement is the difference that makes the difference – and could make all the difference as we face the realities of globalized competition and the millions of graduates and even more skilled and committed workers that China, India and other economies are producing each year.'

Engagement at the heart of strategy

The report said: 'If it is how the workforce performs that determines to a large extent whether companies or organizations succeed, then whether or not the workforce is positively encouraged to perform at its best should be a prime consideration for every leader and manager and be placed at the heart of business strategy.'

It went on: 'Many company leaders described to us the "light bulb moment" when an understanding of the full potential significance of employee engagement dawned. Tesco chief executive Terry Leahy recorded his reaction when he realized that his company knew more about its customers than it did about its employees. Tesco then set about understanding what the workforce wanted, what motivated them at work and what workplace approaches would best build on those understandings.'

Increasingly, I am finding that leaders are making 'engagement' itself a strategic goal of their business, and they measure it, monitor it and manage it. They see it as a key enabler of success. Why? Because, when employees are motivated to go beyond that which they have to do to that which they very much want to do, the results can be transformational. This 'discretionary effort' can be the difference between success and failure – the difference that makes the difference. Anyone doing a moment's research online can find evidence that higher levels of employee engagement bring better financial performance.

What we really mean when we say we want better engaged employees is that we want employees with more positive behaviours. We want them working smarter, we want them to innovate more, we want them to provide a better service to customers. But employees will not go that extra mile unless they feel valued, empowered and motivated, so that often means we – as leaders – have to change our behaviours first.

The key question is what do we, as leaders, have to do to inspire people to feel committed and positive and willing to change their behaviours? When we answer that question, we stand a better chance of engaging employees better.

Choice, not change

I think part of the secret lies in a simple choice of words. People prefer choice to change. They prefer dreaming up choices and then selecting from those choices to the idea of having change imposed on them.

We all know that the leader's job is to make strategic choices. Leaders have to decide on the destination. Ideally, we would like to know that our views had been taken into account before any decision was made. But, when we are in the role of follower, while we accept the right of the leader to make the choice of destination, we hate being told exactly how to get there. We like to be given the chance to generate options for the route, and make choices, together, about the best way of getting there. We'd like to be in a role where we are empowered to make the choice of route by ourselves. This is when we are truly committed – when we have made the choice. If leaders want to achieve this commitment, they must facilitate these conversations, and deploy great skills in communication to enable them, guide them and keep them happening.

Many of the leaders I interviewed said that it was not enough to be a good communicator yourself. You have to make sure that the whole organization is communicating. This means ensuring that managers everywhere are encouraged to get out and talk with employees, to draw them into discussing issues and coming up with ideas about how to solve them.

Colin Matthews, chief executive of BAA, says: 'The communication between employees and their direct managers is critical. If you think of communication as a cake, then corporate communications from the top is the icing, and the real substance is in the discussion between front-line supervisors and employees. Too much icing, without the cake, can make you ill.'

'Leaders should ensure that those front-line managers have the tools and skills to have quality conversations with their staff. Leadership isn't something you do by yourself at the top; you have to have leaders everywhere in the organization.'

The ingredients of engagement

The government's report on engagement points out that there are differences between attitude, behaviour and outcomes. Leaders have to discern between these to make sure they're addressing the right issues. An employee might feel pride and loyalty (attitude); but they might not be a great advocate of the company to clients, or go the extra mile to finish a piece of work (behaviour). Outcomes may include lower accident rates, higher productivity, fewer conflicts, more innovation, or reduced sickness rates and employee churn. All three – attitudes, behaviours and outcomes – are part of the engagement circle. Engagement is not the same as culture, motivation or satisfaction.

The report says: 'Leaders must be careful of manipulating employees through mechanistic approaches. Employees see through such attempts, very quickly, and they can lead to cynicism and disillusionment. Engaged employees freely and willingly give discretionary effort, not as an add-on, but as an integral part of their daily activity at work.'

The report concludes that there are four key enablers of engagement:

- leadership which ensures a strong, transparent and explicit organizational culture which gives employees a line of sight between their job and the vision and aims of the organization;
- engaging managers who offer clarity, appreciation of employees' effort and contribution, who treat their people as individuals and who ensure that workers are organized efficiently and effectively so that employees feel they are valued and equipped and supported to do the job;
- employees feeling they are able to voice their ideas and be listened to, both about how they do their job and in decision making in their own department, with joint sharing of problems and challenges, and a commitment to arrive at joint solutions;
- a belief among employees that the organization delivers its values, and that espoused behavioural norms are adhered to, resulting in trust and a sense of integrity.

We have already heard about all these points from the leaders in this book.

The first and most important task of a leader when communicating with employees is to show up! All too often, one hears stories about leaders issuing instructions by e-mail and not bothering to have face-to-face discussions with their staff. Leaders need to find ways to ensure that managers and supervisors are engaging with their employees.

Measure and monitor engagement

Tom Enders, chief executive of Airbus, has made engagement one of the four pillars of success for his company. 'When I first started here I thought hard about what we needed to do to propel us into the future. Competent people are, of course, a big asset. But competent people who are not motivated don't get you very far. I realized that we had to put engagement at the heart of our strategy.'

'As a leader at the top of the organization, you must hold your own conversations with people throughout the company. I love to get out and meet people, and talk with them about what is happening, because this is how I pick up indications of problems, or information about things that are going wrong. This is part of my job that I really love – doing site visits, talking to young people, spending more time with people on the shop floor. If you stay on the executive floor or in the boardroom, you will never fully understand what is going on in your business. But my doing that is not enough.'

'We have roughly 2,500 management units, and we require the managers of these units to sit down with their people and ask about what really motivates them. We survey staff to find out how they feel, which enables us to talk with managers about why their engagement scores are low. Many of our managers, who had bad scores in the first round of our employee survey, told me that it gave them a real wake-up call. They hadn't realized that they simply weren't spending enough time with their people, and now that they were, performance was improving.'

As discussed in the previous chapter, I believe that relationship audits, in this case employee engagement audits, are a more reliable predictor of future success than past financial performance.

Leaders today face an environment of constant change. But constant change leads to uncertainty, and uncertainty leads to a loss of confidence, which in turn leads to low morale. Positive, forward-looking companies become negative, backward-looking, failing companies. The challenge of change is that leaders must keep people motivated in spite of uncertainty.

Line managers and front-line supervisors must be the most important communication priority. Leaders must spend time, money and effort on communicating with those leaders and enabling them to have better-quality face-to-face conversations with front-line employees.

As Phil Bentley, managing director of British Gas, says: his business is built up brick by brick, conversation by conversation.

Input equals buy-in

Damon Buffini of Permira says his style is to set aggressive goals and then sit down to discuss with people how to achieve them. 'When you do that, people are going to want to talk with you about what their concerns are, and they are going to want to feel that you are engaged.'

'You set the direction but then you consult on the how, that's how you create buy-in. Getting people engaged in your vision is fundamental to any business. The only way to get people engaged is if they have had some input into the process. The only way they can have input into the process is if you sit down to talk with them about it.'

Simon Calver of LOVEFiLM says leaders cannot create alignment unless they have given their people time to understand and talk about what is going on. 'My way is to have what I call brown-bag lunches with different groups of people. We simply get sandwiches in a brown bag and then get together and talk about issues. We talk about what's working well, what's not working well, or what I can do to help them. What are the issues in the business that they're worried about?'

'As the leader, you have to have these open sessions with open dialogue. But you also have to make sure that managers are getting out there and talking with their people. Our way is to set employees quarterly goals upon which they are measured and rewarded. Managers have to appraise their staff every three months. That way, I'm forcing communication between the manager and an employee.'

Philip Green, former CEO of United Utilities, feels that conversations are crucial 'because your people want to be heard. They care about the organization that they work for, they want to contribute to thinking and want to give their opinions to their leaders. It is really important for them to have that opportunity. When leaders do sit down with employees to talk, you get a lot of really good ideas. People on the shop floor are often more in tune than most boardrooms, so you find out what is actually going on.'

Sir Nicholas Young says he and his Red Cross managers have a deliberate process of consulting staff and volunteers on big decisions. 'In a commercial organization, I can see leaders feeling our way is ridiculous, that it takes too long and is too consensual. But actually, it's really important to get our volunteers and staff along with changes, so we take the time to go out and ask them, and discuss ideas with them.'

'It really makes it much easier to inspire people if you know where they are coming from, if you know and understand what their issues are. It is only through these conversations that you can encourage and support and inspire others to achieve.'

Don't dominate the conversation

But, says Professor Nigel Thrift, vice-chancellor of the University of Warwick (a public research university located in Coventry, United Kingdom), you have to be extremely careful about showing up and then dominating the conversation.

'Leaders tend to be forceful and the danger is that you interrupt too much. My wife tells me that I tend to obtrude into conversations too much of the time, so I have to be really careful when I sit down with groups of people, to let them have their say. People need to tell you things, they want to tell you. And it's their right to tell you and you have a duty to really understand what they're saying. But as a leader, there are times when you do have to guide a conversation, and you do have to put forward your point of view. You should never be afraid of doing that, but you do have to get the balance right.'

Barbara Cassani, formerly of Go Fly, says conversations with staff have to be about their agenda, first and foremost. 'I deliberately scheduled plenty of time in my diary to talk with groups of 15 people, usually from different departments, and I would go and listen – that was what I was there for. My agenda was them. I had to learn, though, and I used to make a note to myself that said: "Ask everyone first!" instead of "Here is my agenda."'

'Ultimately, when you do this, you realise your objectives more readily. You may even end up modifying your objectives. Leaders who don't take this time can hit invisible barriers. I mean, we all feel that if someone has not taken our thinking on board, we will resist change. And, frankly, it is just disrespectful not to ask employees their views.'

Beverley Aspinall says she has regular interactions with groups at Fortnum & Mason. 'I very much see my role is to ask the question and then listen to the answers or draw out people's viewpoints. I find if you ask the question and then let people discuss issues, nine times out of 10 if you ask the right questions in the right way, the answer will emerge without you having to give it. Just occasionally, two competing answers may arise and then your role is to say: "Well, you know, bearing in mind what I've heard, this is the path I think we should take." But it's very rare that that happens, very rare; people nearly always come to the right solution themselves, as long as you keep asking the right questions.'

'Absolutely the wrong thing for me to do is to go into meetings and express my view before anybody else has, because that just renders them impotent. It completely negates the point of them being there. The problem is, as people become more senior, it becomes more and more tempting just to jump in and say what you think. You must avoid that.'

Dame Barbara Stocking is chief executive of Oxfam GB, a leading UK charity set up to fight global poverty. Oxfam was founded in Oxford in 1942 as the Oxford Committee for Famine Relief. Oxfam is now an international confederation of 15 organizations working in 98 countries to find solutions to poverty and injustice. Oxfam GB is also the largest second-hand bookseller in Europe and has 20,000 volunteers in the UK.

Barbara says that, when meeting with groups of employees, leaders must remember that there are three parts to communication. 'There is what you say, there is what you hear and there is the interpretation of what you hear. Good leaders will sit in on these conversations and try to understand where people are coming from, what it is they're really trying to tell you.'

'We do regular staff surveys to understand how motivated employees feel, and one of our challenges at the moment is that employees don't feel our managers are listening well enough. We're looking at ways to enable our managers to go out and meet their teams and communicate better. That means listening as well as talking. It is almost more important to be a good listener than a good orator. In a volunteer organization, motivation is fantastically important, and that depends on how engaged people feel and whether they feel their views are being taken into account.'

If communication is so important, where is the training?

This brings us to 'the big gap'. All too often I heard leaders talking about the importance of communication, but then later worrying about the lack of communication skills among managers and supervisors. Many complained that managers either did not bother to communicate key messages or were inclined to put a 'spin' on the messages when they did deliver them. Often the spin was unhelpful, if not damaging. In spite of putting enormous effort into cascade briefings, leaders found time and time again that people on the front line had not heard about key initiatives and were not clear about what they were now required to do.

Frequently, leaders talked about using employee feedback to determine where line managers were falling short. Where they picked up signs of poor morale and a frustration at the lack of communication, they used this in their appraisal of line managers, which in turn would lead to individual coaching to help the managers improve their people skills.

When I asked whether leaders gave their managers communication training, all too often the answer was no. As Colin Matthews of BAA says, communications from the top is crucial, but it is in the conversations between line managers and front-line employees that the rubber hits the road. So the critical question for leaders is: How best to encourage your managers to engage with their staff? And how will you know if they are doing so? Just showing up for a conversation can make all the difference, even without training.

But imagine how much more potent those conversations could be if leaders throughout the organization were given more training in communication, especially listening skills. (More in Chapter 10.)

It is in these meetings that leaders can most usefully 'bring the outside in'. By helping people understand what effect their actions will have and how people outside the organization will feel when they are successful, leaders can engage the emotions of their employees. As Unilever's Paul Polman says, it is when people have this sense of external emotional purpose that their passions are ignited.

'The single great problem about communication is the illusion that it has taken place,' said George Bernard Shaw. One of the greatest barriers to communication is a lack of understanding of the audience. Delivering carefully crafted messages to an audience that is more interested in something else is a definite recipe for creating the illusion of communication. Thinking about the audience is the first and most important stage of being able to communicate successfully...

KEY POINTS FROM CHAPTER 8

- The saying that 'people are your only asset' is trite and dangerously simplistic.

- Employees who turn up to work to do the bare minimum are a drain on resources, slowing everything down, and people who actively resist change are toxic.

- Your real 'people asset' is that group of people motivated to give the organization their discretionary effort, wholeheartedly. It is that effort that drives super performance.

- Measure levels of employee engagement, and use this measurement as a strategic tool to find ways to keep people motivated and committed to the cause.

- Study after study has shown that companies with high levels of engagement among employees outperform their competitors, by some margin.

- Take time to engage; ultimately you will achieve your aims faster and more effectively.

- Engagement is achieved through conversations.

- Conversations must be structured in a way which allows employees to fully understand the big objective, and work out with their leaders what they have to do to help achieve the goals.

- These conversations create a 'clear line of sight' between the organization's purpose and goals and the actions of the individual.

- Because of these conversations, employees can make choices, and they don't feel victims of change.

- Their choices make the difference between success and failure.

- Too often, these conversations are neglected, and middle managers are neither trained or equipped for, nor measured on, their ability to hold these critical conversations.

- Top management doesn't check on the quality of those conversations, or seek to get the feedback from those conversations in a systematic way.

- If you require leaders throughout your organization to have regular conversations with employees, you must model this behaviour with a programme of your own conversations.

- During those conversations, encourage people to voice their opinions, and guarantee them a no-blame culture.

- Be prepared to guide the conversations, but only after listening.

- You must spend time helping teams to communicate with each other, so that everyone not only knows what their role is, but also what other people will be doing in support of reaching the goal.

PART THREE
Communicate, communicate, communicate

It's all about them – the need for audience centricity

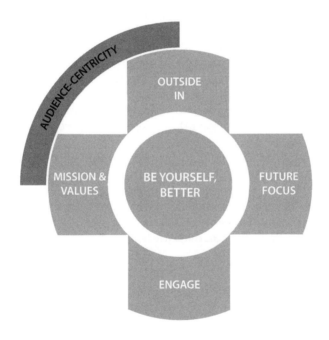

09

Imagine, for a moment, that you are a soldier on the eve of a major battle. Tomorrow, you're going to have to launch yourself into the jaws of hell. Your mission is to overrun a heavily armed enemy who have dug themselves into positions that seem impenetrable. The terrain is open, barricaded and landmined. It provides little cover from the enemy's deadly fire. Somehow, you are going to have to dislodge them. The picture is terrifying.

What's on your mind? What is your overriding concern? Most probably, it is the thought that tomorrow, you are going to die.

'This is what General George S Patton knew when he addressed his Third Army troops on the eve of the Allied invasion of France in June 1944, the day before the D-Day landings at Normandy,' says Lord Sharman, chairman of Aviva. 'So the first thing he said to them was that not all of them were going to die – only 2 per cent would die in a major battle.'

'Immediately, the guys on the receiving end are thinking: "Great, I have a 98 per cent chance of survival!" That gave them hope and did wonders for morale. Not only that, but General Patton also used a great deal of profanity whenever he talked to his troops, knowing that this was the way to relate to them, to make a connection. The way to inspire them was to allay their fears about dying.'

'If you really want to communicate, and make a connection with your audience, you have to understand what it is that they need to hear, where they're coming from, and you'll need to address those issues upfront. You will also have to talk with them with the right tone. Unless you do both of those things, they are unlikely to hear anything you have to say. You might give a brilliant speech, but you won't have communicated.'

(Patton's speech is available on the internet and is a marvel of inspiring communication. He was speaking to his troops on 5 June 1944, the eve of the Allied invasion of France, codenamed 'Operation Overlord'. His prediction of 2 per cent was nearly right. On D-Day, the Allies landed around 156,000 troops in Normandy. A total of 4,414 people are estimated to have died that day – about 2.8 per cent of the soldiers who crossed the Channel on 6 June 1944.)

Lord Sharman was just one of many leaders who talked about the need to understand your audience before attempting to communicate. Nearly all of them said that they had come to this understanding by failing to connect with audiences in speeches and talks they had given early in their careers. Those had been painful experiences. But as a result, all of them knew the importance of thinking about the audience before attempting to communicate with them.

It's not what you say; it's what they hear

At the beginning of every interview, I asked each leader to rate themselves as a communicator. On a scale of 0–10, where 10 was the maximum mark, they averaged between seven and eight in their self-assessment. Most felt that they had now become good communicators, but all said they still had to keep on learning and developing. They had not yet mastered the art.

Many commented that they would rate themselves differently on different days, depending on their performance that day. On some occasions they could be as low as 4/10. When they rated themselves highly, there was a single common factor.

It was all about 'connection'.

They all gave themselves poor marks when they felt they had not made a connection with the audience. They may have given a brilliant speech, with perfect technique, but because they could not engage the audience, they recognized that they had not achieved the task – which was to create an emotional link with the people they were speaking to.

On those occasions when they felt they had made a connection, when they enjoyed the 'buzz' of an engaged audience, they would sometimes give themselves 10/10.

In business, communication is all about changing behaviours. Communication is what turns strategy into action. If you have not made that emotional connection, then you are unlikely to change the way people feel and think. And if you can't do that, then you will never change what they do.

Says Dame Fiona Reynolds, of the National Trust: 'When people say that you have given a brilliant speech, it might not have been objectively brilliant. It was that they felt inspired and moved by it. 'To do that you have to think about the audience beforehand, you have to think about how you are coming across and you have to really think about how to empathize with people.'

Paul Drechsler, chairman and CEO of the Wates Group, points out that successful communication is not what you say, it is what is heard. 'The acid test is whether people have really understood you, and what they take out from what you are saying. If you want to turn ideas into action then you have to engage people. You have to engage with employees, you have to engage with customers and you have to engage with everybody who is important to business.'

This connection only comes when leaders have spent time thinking hard about the audience. Few people possess the skill of being able automatically to connect with an audience without having done some considerable research beforehand. Damon Buffini of Permira says: 'Great communication always reminds me of an iceberg. Hearing someone talk is just the tip of the iceberg. When someone succeeds in moving you, you realize that so much has gone on before you have heard the message, because there's been so much thinking about the audience beforehand.'

What do you want them to think, feel and do?

David Nussbaum is the chief executive of the World Wide Fund for Nature (WWF) in the UK. The WWF is the world's largest independent conservation organization, with five million supporters. Its mission is to build a future in which humans live in harmony with nature. Moving people to action is the staple diet for the WWF.

'Being persuasive is not about being a great orator. It is about taking people with you and creating alignment. Before you can do this with any audience, you have to ask yourself these key questions: What do I want them to know? What do I want them to feel? What do I want them to do?'

'It isn't just about what they want to hear – you have also to ask yourself what they should be prepared to hear. What will interest them and make that connection? What will engage them and make a difference? What are the crucial things that they must hear? You have to remember that communication hasn't taken place unless it changes the opinion and the behaviour of the people that you are talking to.'

Ron Sandler is executive chairman of Northern Rock plc, and non-executive chairman of the Phoenix Group and Ironshore Inc. Northern Rock plc is the British bank now owned by the UK government. It is best known for being, in 2007, the first bank in 150 years to suffer the humiliation of seeing thousands of customers waiting in line outside its branches to withdraw their funds in case the bank became insolvent. Ron Sandler was brought in by the government to run the business when the bank was nationalized in early 2008. The Phoenix Group is a closed life assurance fund consolidator that specializes in the management and acquisition of closed life and pension funds, and operates primarily in the United Kingdom. Ironshore is a speciality property and casualty insurer, headquartered in Bermuda and with global operations.

Ron is therefore no stranger to having to deal with controversial issues, and says that being able to relate to people is 'all about being able to adapt message, tone, style and delivery to the needs of the audience'.

He continues: 'You cannot make a connection unless you have translated your thoughts into accessible ideas for people through an idiom or a vernacular that they recognize and with which they feel comfortable. Clarity of thought leads to clarity of content, and is essential for clear communication. But your ability to engage successfully with people depends on whether you talk with them in a way they are comfortable with, so that you can draw them out, and so that you can have a meaningful dialogue.'

Fields Wicker-Miurin of Leaders' Quest says that a good leader has to be able to communicate effectively to a heterogeneous population. 'Whether it is institutional investors in New York or China, NGOs or local business communities in Kenya, whether it is ministers in Downing Street, the media or your own staff, leaders need to understand, first and foremost, the audience.'

'You have to be able to understand how people from around the world with different belief systems and cultural roots receive and process information, what filters they use to edit out as well as edit in, what are their underlying, often invisible, assumptions that will shape how they hear and interpret what you say. This requires a tremendous awareness and humble sensitivity of the other without losing a sense of self.'

Don't change the message; change the way you deliver it

Sir Nick Partridge is the chief executive of the Terrence Higgins Trust, a British charity that campaigns on various issues related to AIDS and HIV.

The charity aims to reduce the spread of HIV and promote good sexual health, and campaigns for greater public understanding of the impact of HIV and AIDS. It was the first charity in the UK to be set up in response to HIV, in 1982.

Sir Nicholas says: 'If people think you are not listening to them, or that you don't understand their point of view, and that all you want to do is to tell them the way it is, then you're not going to win. You are not going to bring them with you. You have to be thoughtful about your appearance, your language, your body language, your tone – everything. You have to tailor the message to their needs.'

'As HIV and sexual health are such emotive subjects, I have to be very mindful when I am talking to different audiences about the subject. If I am talking with a faith-based audience of clerics and ministers, I will be different from how I am with an audience of AIDS activists and gay men. That does not mean giving one message to one audience and a completely different message to another audience. The challenge of being focused on your audience is staying true to your values and consistent to your purpose, while also resonating with different groups of people who have a wide diversity of views on moral, sex and health issues.'

How audience centricity helped to establish Canary Wharf

Peter Levene, Baron Levene of Portsoken, is chairman of Lloyd's of London and was Lord Mayor of London from 1998 to 1999. Lloyd's is the world's leading specialist insurance market, conducting business in over 200 countries and territories worldwide – and is often the first to insure new, unusual or complex risks. He also served as chairman of London's Docklands Light Railway and then chairman and chief executive of Canary Wharf – a major London business district – in the late 1990s.

He gives a great example of tailoring a message to different audience needs. He cites the time when he took over as head of Canary Wharf, when the huge office development in east London was still regarded as 'the pits'.

'In those days we had 5,000 people at Canary Wharf. Today there are 95,000 people there. It was a huge job getting it on the road to recovery. Put simply, the place had gone bust. Newspapers were printing that they'd soon be putting the tape around the buildings, that the wind was whistling through the corridors and that the place had become a wasteland.'

'We had to really understand our audiences to make a difference. Why didn't people like Canary Wharf? What got in the way of them even being prepared to consider the place?'

Said Lord Levene: 'I used to call up the CEOs of different companies and ask them directly. Many of them simply felt that it was too far away – on the other side of the moon – and that it would be impossible to get there.

I would ask them to come and visit me there and they would say: "Well, um, I'm sort of busy at the moment." I would ask them whether they even knew where it was and it was clear they had little idea. Anyway, I drove them all nuts until they finally gave in and agreed to come. They always used to arrive at least half an hour early. The secretaries had made their travel arrangements and clearly thought it would take forever for them to get there.'

'We realized that we would have to target secretaries in order to help them better understand Canary Wharf. How do most secretaries get around? They travel on the Tube. So we bought poster space in the tube inviting them to do a quiz, for which they got prizes. We asked them how long they thought it would take them to get from their station to Canary Wharf. Or how many shops were in Canary Wharf, and what restaurants were there. They had to send in their answers and if they were correct they received a voucher. It was a huge success.'

Lord Levene continues: 'Then we found out that taxi drivers were being very unhelpful. When asked by people to take them to Canary Wharf, they would say: "Oh my goodness, you want to go there? You must be mad. Nobody wants to go to that place – it's at the end of the world." So we organized a series of huge slap-up tea parties for taxi drivers at Canary Wharf. They loved it. Then, when people got into their cabs, they would say: "Canary Wharf? Have you been there before? That place is amazing."'

'We had to target all of our audiences very closely and fully understand their perspectives in order to ensure that we not only had the right communication, but also the right way of delivering the messages.'

'After two years, I finally realized we had won when I was having my hair cut one day and the guy in the barber's chair next to me was eulogizing about Canary Wharf. He was telling the barber that when everybody had said it was going to be a disaster, he had known it was going to be amazing. I came back into the office that day and said to everybody: "We've won!"'

The story of the privy

Lord Sharman is very keen on the subject of knowing your audience. Our interview was peppered with many examples. He stresses the importance of understanding that not everyone looks at the same set of facts through the same lens.

'I grew up near Salisbury, where most people would have fish on a Friday. The man who drove the fish van was called Fishy Lane. He lived in a cottage which had a privy (an outside toilet). One day the wife of the village squire stopped her car at his cottage and told Fishy she desperately needed to use his lavatory. When she came back she thanked him profusely, but said: "I hope you don't mind me saying, Fishy, but I couldn't help noticing that you have not got a lock on your privy."'

'Fishy was mystified and said he could see no reason why he needed a lock – he explained that if you heard someone coming down the path towards you while you were in the privy, you simply yelled a warning. The squire's wife said: "But don't you think a lock would improve security?"'

'Fishy's face lit up because he suddenly understood the issue. "Ma'am, I've lived here 35 years and we've never lost a bucket of shit yet!"'

How to think about your audience

The advertising industry has long had a terrific expression to define audience focus. They use the phrase 'WIFM', which means: What's in it for me? This is the question successful copywriters constantly ask when trying to define the benefit message for a product or service. It is a phrase that leaders need to have in mind all the time.

If communication is about changing behaviours, then leaders need to ask themselves some other critical questions before preparing to talk to people. It helps when preparing to talk to an audience to have in mind a real person, said some of the leaders I interviewed:

- Who is that person, what do they do for a living, where do they live, and why are they important to you?
- What are they saying about you now and why?
- What worries them and what excites them?
- How does all of this impact on their behaviours?
- Who else is talking to them and what are those influencers saying?
- Why are their behaviours helpful or unhelpful to you? How much are their behaviours costing you?
- What would you like them to be doing instead? Why should they?
- What are their motivations and triggers, and how do you know for sure?
- What are the real benefits, to them, of behaving the way you would like them to? Why are those benefits important to them?
- Why should they even bother to pay attention?

Only when you have asked these questions will you have come close to being able to deliver messages that matter to your audience. If your communication does not address all of these issues, then you will fail to make a connection and you will fail to excite any change in attitudes or behaviour.

But even then, it might not be enough. Sometimes you have to listen first, before anyone will grant you a hearing...

KEY POINTS FROM CHAPTER 9

- In any enterprise, leadership communication is all about achieving big goals. It is about changing behaviours.

- You have *not* communicated successfully if people have not heard you, understood you and do not feel motivated to think differently and act differently as a result of your words.

- You may have stood up and talked *at* them, but communication has only taken place when your words have had an impact.

- Remember, other people will be talking to your audience as well – have you addressed what they might be saying?

- People listen from behind their own filters – filters which may be cultural or emotional, or they may be in place because of their unique perceptions or even misunderstandings.

- You have to talk to them about their concerns, their issues, before you can be understood on your own.

- You have to set out to achieve change in how they think, feel and act, but that requires you to know how they think, feel and act *now*.

- You have to think about how best to connect with people in your audience before you get in front of them.

- Be consistent with your message, but tailor it appropriately. Think about how to make your core message relevant to a group of accountants, then tailor it for human resource specialists. Same core message, different top and tail.

- Successful communication is about 'connection' – establishing an emotional link with your audience.

- Leaders rate themselves most highly for communication when they are able to engage with an audience, to make a connection.

- There is a thrill in doing this, and often it has nothing to do with a perfect presentation and everything to do with resonating with the audience.

The inspiring effect of listening leaders

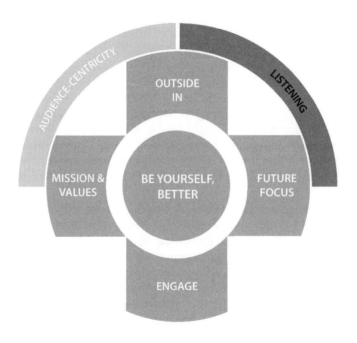

10

The average person speaks at a rate of about 150 words per minute. We can listen, with good comprehension, to something like 650 words per minute. No matter how long a speaker's message is, it appears we need less than half that time to comprehend what they are saying. The other half is ours to use as we choose.

Good leaders use that time wisely, for in that gap lies the difference between poor leadership and great leadership. Leaders who listen well are multi-tasking. They are listening to the language of the speaker while also looking at body language. They're thinking about context, they're looking into the speaker's eyes and trying to see beyond the words and into intent. They go beyond logic and into the world of emotion.

Dame Amelia Fawcett, chair of the Guardian Media Group, says: 'The ability to listen well is probably one of the most powerful tools of communication that a leader can possess. Those that listen well listen with real intent. They are hearing not only the words, but also the meaning beneath what people are saying. Also, it isn't just about hearing words and meaning; it's about whether people think you've been listening.'

'I have been in the canteen and overheard someone saying about her boss: "What a joke, I'm not going to talk to her again, she didn't pay any attention to what I was saying." If you don't bother to listen intently, then people won't bother to talk to you in the future. And when that happens, you lose your grip on the business.'

In our interview, Dame Amelia quoted Professor Nitin Nohria, dean of Harvard Business School and widely published on the subject of leadership, who says: 'Communication is the work of leadership.' Amelia expanded on the theme: 'It is the work of leadership because leadership communication is all about engaging and inspiring people. But you can't engage and inspire if you don't first listen!'

Philip Green, former CEO of United Utilities, says: 'When listening to people, it is very important to be seen to be listening. The challenge for leaders is that most of them are very bright people who understand the point very quickly and are often impatient to get on with things. The result is that they will often interrupt and finish off what the speaker is saying. That's really bad, because it is just as important to be seen to be listening as it is to actually listen.

'This requires a great deal of patience from a leader, who needs to stay in the moment and respect the speaker more. It is worth remembering that people care about the work they're doing, they care about making a contribution, and they want to give their views to leaders. They must have that platform or else they will stop giving you their ideas and perspectives. This would be really dangerous, because people on the shop floor are usually more in tune than the board is with what's really going on, and it is from them that you can get most of the really good ideas.'

Be interested, be respectful and be patient

Modern leaders have to deal with better educated, better informed and more democratically oriented employees. In the old days leadership was, in many ways, simpler. Good performance was simply demanded. Good leaders draw out the best in others and get to know what is important to them and to the enterprise. It starts with being respectful.

Sir Maurice Flanagan, executive vice-chairman of the Emirates Airline and Group, says: 'Leaders gain respect by showing respect. One way you show respect is to really listen. You get respect when people feel that you are taking their views into account. Good listening is not just about understanding what people want to tell you, it is also about the expression on your face when you are listening. People must feel you care about what they have to say. You can't fake that, so you really need to be interested.'

David Morley, senior partner at global law firm Allen & Overy, agrees that listening is a key skill, but thinks very few people do it effectively.

'For a lot of leaders, listening is about waiting for the speaker to finish, so that they can start talking. Bad idea. One of the biggest myths of leadership today is that leaders in the corporate world simply issue commands and everyone then does as they are told. But when you talk to CEOs, you find it is just not like that at all. They have senior leadership teams who don't want to be told what to do; they want to be involved and engaged and have a degree of autonomy in the way that they do things. As a leader, your job is to influence and persuade them and point them in the right direction.'

'You can only do this and be effective if you are genuinely interested in them as people, and listen very carefully to what they have to say. You have to show them that you are listening by responding to what they're saying and showing that you comprehend. It is only when you have a better sense of what's driving them, what worries them, that you can communicate in ways that are more likely to trigger the right response.'

Interrupting, then, is a deadly sin of leadership.

Sir William Osler, a Canadian physician often described as the father of modern medicine, was passionate on the subject of listening. At the dawn of the 20th century he urged his fellow physicians: 'Listen to the patient; he is telling you the diagnosis.' This admonition, delivered in 1904, is still appropriate today. Researching the subject of listening, I came across an interesting study which reported that one of the most common complaints of patients was that doctors did not listen enough. If they did, they would be likely to improve clinical outcomes.

Studies in the 1980s showed that on average, doctors interrupted patients only 18 seconds after they began to speak. Training for doctors has since laid more stress on listening to patients. A recent study in the USA showed that physicians there now listen to patients' concerns for about 23 seconds before starting to ask questions. After years of teaching, the result is an improvement of just five seconds.

When asked how long they thought they had waited before interrupting, the doctors said three minutes. Most of the patients felt they had voiced only the first of usually three concerns in the time they were allowed. When given the time to express all three concerns, the patients took an average of... yes, you guessed it... just three minutes. The doctors seemed intuitively to know how long they should listen if they wanted to get the full picture from the patient, but something kept them from listening that long.

What stops effective listening?

When the brain has time to fill that gap between spoken words and comprehension rates the urge to talk, to ask or to suggest is powerful and often irresistible. Poor leaders don't resist the urge to interrupt, and they cause dissatisfaction and disenchantment among employees.

Just as the most common complaint about doctors is that they don't listen, the same is true of managers and leaders. In countless employee surveys I have seen, the biggest cause of frustration is that employees don't feel they are being listened to, and that their views are not important to their leaders. Great leaders know how important it is to listen, and do resist the urge to interrupt.

Ian Thomas is managing director of Fluor Ltd, the UK arm of the Fluor Corporation, one of the world's leading publicly traded engineering, procurement, construction maintenance and project management companies. He says: 'I can't think of anything more important than being a good listener. The best leaders are people who are in "receive" mode more than they are in "transmit" mode. You simply cannot lead if you cannot listen.'

Christopher Garnett is a member of the board of the Olympic Delivery Authority, the statutory corporation responsible for ensuring delivery of the venues, infrastructure and legacy for the 2012 Summer Olympic and Paralympic games in London. Previously he was chief executive of Great North Eastern Railway. He believes that a failure to listen properly is the single greatest flaw of leaders. 'This is particularly so for leaders who have been in position for a long time, who stop listening and think they have already heard all they need to know. Those are the leaders on the slippery slope...'

Most leaders described to me how listening was part of the process of decision making, of developing and maintaining relationships, of problem solving and of so many other aspects of leadership. Good listeners hear the speaker's words, understand the messages and their importance to the speaker and communicate that understanding to the speaker.

Barbara Stocking of Oxfam says it is only by listening that you get a well-grounded understanding of the whole organization. 'The danger is that you wear out your ears, and you become unable to listen. You can always see the leaders who started out listening really well and then slowly stopped listening. They just don't want to know any more. They lose touch with the real issues and make the wrong decisions.'

Listen with your eyes, ears and heart

Of all the communication skills, listening is the most frequently used, but seems to be the least mastered. Great listeners use more than just their ears. Listening is not just about hearing, it is about understanding and empathizing and showing that you understand. It is about asking the right questions and getting beyond the words to the underlying messages.

David Nussbaum of WWF says that the best listening is a combination of using your ears and your eyes. 'You have to look for the subliminal message. What is the emotion behind the message? What do people really want? The worst sin of listening is finishing other people's sentences – that's when they may feel you have not bothered to understand and it can be very demotivating. Leaders often get to the point really quickly, but must learn to hang back and wait for people to finish.'

Christopher Satterthwaite, CEO of Chime Communications, says that it is only by listening that you can help people to make the most of themselves and thereby make the most of your organization. To do this requires great listening skills. 'I often tell the story of a man who used to work for us, called Rourdon Chambers. At his funeral, a friend of his stood up and said that Rourdon was one of the most "imaginative of listeners". That was such an evocative phrase. You need to listen with your heart and use your imagination if you really want to hear what people are saying. That's what I now look for in people – imaginative listening.'

Listen for solutions

Many leaders talked about how employees were simply deaf to their messages and refused to hear what they needed to know – until they had been given a chance to express their own concerns. Only then were they prepared to listen themselves. I call this 'the listening contract'. When a leader commits to listening to an employee, they deliver the first half of an implicit deal. The deal is: 'I'll listen to you, then you are obliged to listen to me.'

Rupert Gavin, CEO of Odeon and UCI Cinemas, says: 'If you don't listen, then you won't be heard. Too many organizations have a one-way communication system. That will never work. Listening is a challenge and it is the area that I have to work at hardest and train myself longest in. Every day I look at myself in the mirror and ask whether I have done enough listening. Should I have done more? Could I have done more in this meeting? Could I have done more in that meeting?'

Sir Christopher Gent says that leadership is about working with teams. It starts with the presumption that other people have skills and attributes and insights that you don't. 'If you value their contribution, then you need exceptional listening skills. You have to be able to draw people out with the right questions. Nobody has a monopoly on wisdom and when you listen wisely you can make better-informed decisions. Often you will be given insights that will help you to realize your own preferred actions might well be wrong.'

Sir Christopher tells a story of a director in one of his companies who insisted that he be given a chance to explain to the board why Sir Christopher and the management team were making a wrong decision. 'It was a significant issue involving a great deal of money, and this director disagreed with my decision. I realized how important this was to him and arranged for him to present his case to the board. After having done so, the board decided to stick with my decision. This director went away and implemented the decision brilliantly. I have made some terrible mistakes in my career, but on this occasion it turned out to be the right decision. A lot of that had to do with the commitment of the director who first resisted it. He was only committed because he had been given a chance to express his point of view, and his resolve helped us to succeed. He was only committed, though, because he knew that we respected what he had to say.'

Why leaders should be passionate about bad news

Ayman Asfari, group chief executive of Petrofac, says it is crucial to encourage people to bring you bad news. 'You must never stop the flow of bad news, because if you do that, it will be the beginning of the end. You have to create an environment where people can challenge you and you must be prepared to listen to those challenges. I know from long experience that when people have had a chance to be heard, they might then rally behind a decision even if it is not what they initially voted for.'

If you really are prepared to listen to bad news, it is often those difficult issues that enable you to make the biggest difference. Dame Fiona Reynolds of the National Trust says you have to be open to challenge and set an example to the organization you lead. 'It is only when you are prepared to surface the most difficult of issues that you can really make progress. And as a leader, you have to ensure that your whole organization is a better listening organization. Listening enables learning and every organization needs to learn in order to thrive.'

Lord Mervyn Davies says you need to go beyond being open to discussing difficult issues; you actually need to be passionate about receiving bad news. 'If you want only good news, then you won't have an open, argumentative culture. You have to show people that you really, really want to know bad news, so that they learn not to fear bringing you those difficult issues.'

Time and again, leaders spoke of the need to create a 'no-blame culture'. Without such a culture, there would simply be no quality feedback, because people would be afraid to speak up. Leaders have to become feedback junkies, who are seen to welcome bad news enthusiastically. This is a special communication skill, which requires leaders to suspend their own emotions and their own reactions to bad news. The slightest sign of anger or frustration can put employees off telling you the things that you really need to hear.

General The Lord Dannatt says that several brains are always better than one, several sets of experience are better than one, and openly debating conflicting points of view will always help you to a more robust plan. 'But the challenge is that you have to encourage people to talk without fear, which they won't do if they are wary of getting the rough side of your tongue!'

Mick Davis of Xstrata says that a leader cannot be good if they do not have an instinct to communicate. 'Listening is the most important part of communication. Being a good listener is no good if you react badly to bad news. You have to encourage an atmosphere where people can say things to you without getting an extreme reaction. It is fundamental to a constructive environment. Good leadership is about good communication and good communication is about confidence, and confidence comes from having listened well and knowing that you have made the right decision. Feeling that you have made the right decision removes any inhibition from your ability to communicate and gives you confidence. Confidence inspires people.'

'In order to make a decision, I communicate a lot. I voice my views and I listen to lots of different views, until I come to the point where I can make up my mind. Changing your mind and changing your position based on inputs you have received is all part of the process and not a weakness. It is crucial to getting people engaged because people need to feel that they have been heard. Arrogance is a killer. Too much talking at people is a killer. You simply cannot prosecute an agenda unless you have engaged your employees, your customers and society in your mission. And you can't do that unless you have understood what is important to them.'

Leaders can listen in different ways

Leaders must recognize that they have to learn to listen in a lot of different ways. Bias or predisposition can spoil the quality of information. Often leaders will listen selectively to the information that reinforces their opinions. They must have the courage to challenge their own preconceptions. They also have to listen to a wide range of people to get the best picture.

Ben Verwaayen of Alcatel-Lucent says that one of the great advantages of modern technology is that you can hear direct from all employees without the interpretation of middle management, who might filter feedback through their own agenda. 'I hate it when people say to me: "These are my people." No, they are not; they are their own people and they make life-and-death decisions all the time in their own lives. We bring them into an office and then suddenly expect that they should use corporate language and be completely politically correct all the time. What nonsense! You have to treat everybody as serious individuals and you have to allow them to express themselves freely.'

During our interview, Ben showed me the Alcatel-Lucent company intranet. He has his own blog, which he regularly updates. 'When I first started doing this, the company was in crisis and I used to tell people what I thought we should be doing and then ask them what they thought. I replied to every message within 24 hours. That sent a powerful message to everybody that I was open and I was available and that I valued their opinions.

'For example, I'm going to Malaysia this afternoon with my BlackBerry Companion, which, because I've been so open with everybody, now keeps me in touch with everything that's going on in the company. (My wife says the BlackBerry sleeps between the two of us, but I don't think that's true… well, it's almost true.)'

Graham Mackay of SABMiller says you have to sift through the information you get from a lot of different people to look for patterns and clues. Most importantly, you have to consider the motives behind the message and how those messages fit into a broader pattern. 'It is crucial to absorb and reflect on everything that comes in. You have to spend your whole life with your antennae up on all sorts of dimensions.'

Lord Levene points out that many senior leaders have ridiculously busy diaries and often find that they simply don't have enough time to listen and read. 'Listening is crucial but at times very difficult to do. You can't suddenly magic another two days a week out of thin air, so you do need to ensure that you have good people around you who will be your radar and keep you informed. I have plenty of people around me who will send flashing lights when there is something that I need to know. You must ensure you have that sort of system in place.'

When you listen, you must respond

To be effective, leaders must not only show that they're listening; they must then respond. If they have heard about a problem, then they must ensure that they do something about solving it. They must ensure that the employee who brought the problem to their attention is informed about what is happening as a result.

Equally, says Lord Sharman, there will be times when you simply don't agree with what you've heard. On those occasions, you must explain why you are not going to do what they suggest. 'People deserve a response, even if it is not what they would like to hear. I always take notes when I'm listening, in order to ensure I can take action later on. But I also use note taking as a way to send a powerful signal that I'm listening. Even if I never use the notes again, they send a signal that I'm interested in and care about what people are saying.'

Sir Anthony Bamford, chairman and managing director of JCB, says that all too often leaders don't challenge people who are outspoken and wrong. 'I believe that leaders are beholden to disagree and should have the courage to face up to their managers and employees more often. Not doing so is poor communication and is often the cause of significant problems, because employees are then not clear about what the leader really wants. Leaders must have the courage of their convictions, but I think this simply doesn't happen enough in business.'

Professor Nigel Thrift of Warwick University believes you have to carefully balance listening and talking. Leaders need to be acutely aware of the fact that they have to guide conversations and help people to discuss and decide on the right things. The danger for some leaders is that guiding can creep over into simply wanting to continually have your own say. 'Experience is both a gift and a curse. You have to give people the opportunity to speak without interrupting them but, equally, it is about judgement, and as a leader there are times when you sometimes have to put your point of view across and it is important that that happens.'

The killer questions leaders should ask

What questions do leaders ask to draw people out and get to the heart of issues? When I put this question to them, their first response was to say that the questions they asked would depend on the situation. A little relentless probing, however, brought out two key themes to their questioning.

The first was an interest they displayed in how people were feeling about matters. This was a valuable short cut to getting to the real issues quickly. Once they had surfaced issues, they were then able to demonstrate their concern and give people a commitment to taking action. Until people had given expression to their emotions, it would be difficult to have a constructive discussion about how to solve a problem. Leaders had first to give people the licence to be emotional.

Chris Satterthwaite says: 'You should always ask people how they feel about the subject you are discussing, and why they feel that way. When dealing with problems, you should then ask people what they would do about them if they were in your shoes. Often they might be reluctant to say something because they have not fully thought through the logic of their answers. The way to get beyond that would be to ask: "What does your gut instinct tell you to do?" You get some surprisingly good answers.'

Ron Sandler agrees. 'I often say this is how it feels to me; how do things feel to you? That way you are engaging at a more emotional level with people and you will find that they will be more willing to talk with you about issues. If they are feeling frustrated and they are prepared to say so in front of a group of colleagues, you can then encourage a healthy dialogue about why they are frustrated. Those sorts of conversations can illuminate ineffective processes in the business and show you what you need to fix so that people can perform better.'

The second theme involved asking questions that enabled leaders quickly to understand 'how we do things around here'.

These four questions were most helpful:

- What do we do around here that we should keep on doing?
- What should we stop doing, and why don't we?

- What should we do better or do more, and why don't we?
- What should we start doing, and why haven't we?

These questions – which I call 'the four Dos' – were valuable because they enable leaders to find out about strengths, weaknesses, opportunities and threats without sounding like a management consultant. The questions are straightforward and extremely productive. However you phrase them, they are easy to ask and get people engaged in talking about the key behaviours that impact on your business. When you ask the questions consistently at all levels of the organization, and in different parts of the organization, you can quickly build a view of key actions you need to take. They work because they reveal unknown barriers and stimulate inspiring ideas.

Good listening + a bias to action = results

How many times have you come out of a meeting with the view that it was a complete waste of time? Alarmingly, I fear that the answer to that question could be a very high number. So many leaders talked about their frustrations at the number of pointless meetings that took place in their organizations. They said the biggest problems with most meetings were the lack of a clear agenda and the lack of clear actions at the end of the meeting. Ironically, this is also a complaint of most employees, even after their managers have shown up to talk with them.

'Leaders must have a bias to action,' said a lot of the people I interviewed. Listening to understand emotions and behaviours is all about action – it is about drawing people out on the actions that need to be sustained, getting them to focus on what good things they do that should be done more often, encouraging them to try new actions that could generate better results, or stop doing things that are not productive.

Also, the questions help leaders understand why people do what they do – and uncover the beliefs, perceptions, rules and requirements that drive their behaviour. The plus for leaders is better informed decision making. Combining this with a bias to action and a continuing and constructive dialogue dramatically improves your chances of improving results.

Paul Drechsler of the Wates Group says that quality listening is tough, but stresses that the better you listen, the better you are able to communicate, because you are more likely to be in tune with the needs of the audience. 'It is a bit like being a piano tuner. If you really listen well, you can then make some really good sounds.'

KEY POINTS FROM CHAPTER 10

- Listening is a *key* communication skill, and the chances are that you are not as good at it as you should be.

- Sometimes the simple act of listening is an act of inspiration in itself.

- Listen first – it earns you the right to be heard.

- Remember 'the listening contract': when you listen to them first, they are then bound to listen to you.

- Not listening, or even appearing not to listen, demotivates and disengages people.

- When you listen *and* then respond with actions that remove barriers, or pick up on good ideas, you create enormous goodwill and demonstrate you are on their side.

- Always respond to what you've heard – with actions, or with explanations why you won't take action.

- Encourage people to open up, and create an environment where people can bring you bad news without fear of repercussions.

- You have to ask great questions and learn to unleash your curiosity and interest in people. It really shows.

- You have to show you understand, even if you don't agree.

- While you must encourage people to talk, you also need to guide and steer conversations in the right direction. Great care is needed in not then dominating the conversation.

- You have to listen beyond the words, into the motives and agendas, into the context, into the performance KPIs and the financial numbers and the mood.

- And listen beyond the words and the logic to search out emotions and intent.

- Listening is one of the most important skills of all. And there are many ways to listen. Get better at it.

11

Stand up to stand out – why you need a point of view

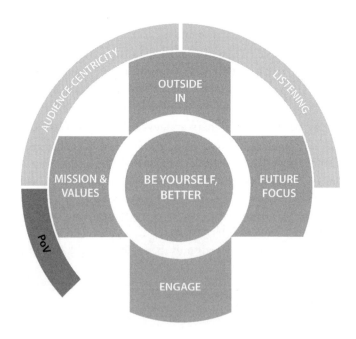

Leaders shape the future. Leaders bring change and challenge the status quo. If there is no need for change, there is no need for leadership. To change the future, leaders need to persuade others to their point of view. Which means they need to be able to articulate a compelling point of view.

Michael Eisner has been a leader in the American entertainment business for decades. For more than 10 years he was chief executive of the Walt Disney

Company, after which he founded the Tomante Company, an enterprise that invests in media and entertainment businesses. He is widely quoted as saying: 'The best leaders always have a potent point of view. What amazes me is that it's always the person with the strong point of view who influences the group, who wins the day.'

Alan Kay, the American computer scientist best known for his early pioneering work on the windowing graphical user interface, and now president of the Viewpoints Research Institute in the USA, agrees. He often makes the following point when giving presentations: 'A powerful point of view is worth at least 80 IQ points.'

Leaders, for better or worse, are opinionated and persuasive. They form strong opinions of the world around them and can sway others to their way of thinking. Having an informed, thought-out opinion on the circumstances that affect their world, combined with the ability to communicate that view, is key to influencing the attitudes and changing the behaviours of their followers.

One of the things that I was most struck by in my interviews was that all of the leaders were incredibly opinionated. They may completely disagree on things with other leaders, but they are strong in their opinion. Strong opinions, voiced with passion, are interesting, even compelling. Bland content lacking heart fails to inspire.

The dictionary defines 'point of view' as 'a manner of viewing things; an attitude; a position from which something is observed or considered; a standpoint'. A key part of that definition is the word 'attitude'. Attitude is described as 'a complex mental orientation involving beliefs and feelings and values and dispositions to act in certain ways'.

A point of view should embrace all of these things. It should be an expression of what you think and believe about the world you operate in, it should describe how you behave every day as a result of those beliefs, it should take a stand on issues that are important, and it should call on others to act and behave in the ways you believe necessary.

Leaders are strongly wedded to the persuasive capability of a well-articulated point of view. They say leaders must have strong views that enable them to capture high ground; and they say leaders need to think harder about preparing them, now...

Moya Greene is the first woman to head the Royal Mail, the national postal service of the United Kingdom. A Canadian businesswoman, previously boss of Canada Post, she is now chief executive of Royal Mail Group, an organization that employs 176,000 people and includes the brands Royal Mail, Post Office and Parcelforce Worldwide.

She believes that leaders need to have views on issues long before being called on to give them. 'Being a leader in a transparent world can be very difficult. The media can be quite cruel and can be pretty indifferent to the truth at times. Whether you are talking to the media or talking on some public platform, you have to have thought through your position on issues before you get called on to give them.

'These days, you simply don't have time to think about formulating your point of view in the heat of a discussion. You must have done it beforehand. When you were at school, you'd be very foolhardy to walk into an exam without having cracked open a book. When talking publicly, you have to make sure that you have anticipated the issues and are not in a situation in which you urgently have to search for the answers that support the position you're taking. You have to have it all mapped ahead of time.'

Using a point of view to take a stand

Philip Green, formerly of United Utilities, says that it is increasingly important for leaders to take positions on issues. When they do take a position, it should be backed up with action. You can't have a valid point of view that isn't backed up by strong beliefs and the right behaviours, he says.

'I decided five years ago that climate change was an important issue and we had to take a stand on it. I wanted to put United Utilities at the forefront of the climate change debate, so we had to think about and articulate all the reasons why. But that wasn't enough. I chaired the Prince of Wales's May Day Campaign on climate change, and I did it because this is absolutely aligned with the company's agenda. Everything the company has done has been about caring for the environment, and it has a good track record on that front. If you want to take a leadership position on an issue you have to back it up with action.'

Lady Barbara Judge, former chair of the United Kingdom Atomic Energy Authority and an experienced senior director in commercial and public sector organizations, says leaders have to learn to better articulate their points of view. 'Not everyone is going to agree with you, and that isn't the point. People need to know what you stand for and where you're coming from. They have to know what your values are and that you act on them so that they will be able to have a sense of how you are likely to react to a situation.

'When I was at the UK Atomic Energy Authority, our mission was to decommission nuclear power plants and to bring the land on which they were built back to usable quality. We also, however, gave advice on nuclear new build. We had to be very clear that our point of view was that nuclear was essential to the energy mix. We couldn't just equivocate and say: "Well, you know, maybe nuclear has problems, but then again it also has advantages." We would need to be very clear about our conclusion, which was that nuclear is essential to the energy mix and that if you're going to build a nuclear plant you should discuss with us.

'So much in life and leadership is about taking a position.'

Why you need an answer that works instantly

Dame Fiona Reynolds of the National Trust says that the 'sound bite' is one of the key characteristics of the 21st century. (In the world of the media, a sound bite is a very short part of a speech or interview, considered by those editing the speech for broadcast to be the most important point of the speech. Usually these are no more than a few seconds long, at most.)

'In this world, people want instant gratification and they have a desire for answers that work instantly. These are the drivers of the way we communicate. In our hearts we know that just is not how life really works. We live in a world where long speeches and deep arguments find little patience, so you have to both live with the phenomenon and resist it at the same time.'

Ron Sandler of Northern Rock says that because leadership is a 24/7 activity, in which so much information is coming at you all the time and things are happening so quickly, leaders have precious little time to devote to the thinking part of communication. 'A mode of communicating has been thrust upon us that makes it very difficult to get the balance right and to find the time and the space to make sure that the underlying thinking behind your communication is sound.

'In my career I seem to have ended up performing a set of roles which have become ever more visible in the public eye. In this fishbowl world, it is very easy for reputations to be quickly and completely shredded. Communication in this environment can be very immediate and very febrile. There is an ever-greater baying for blood, and balanced, sensible judgement applied in a measured way over time gets replaced by excited commentary and extreme views.

'The more extreme the view expressed, the more viral it will become. You no longer get both sides of the story or any attempt to put some real measured perspective on events. This means leaders have to respond with their own strong, short and clear points of view that communicate their position very quickly, powerfully and unambiguously.

'The danger in this febrile world is that leaders don't try and seek the upside of getting their points of view across, but rather avoid the downside and the risk, and therefore keep their voices muted. Yet it is so important that you do get over to people what your agenda is and what your motives are, or else people will not engage with your thinking or be influenced in any way by your ideas.

'What matters now is getting your ideas sensibly organized from the outset and before you need to explain them. You have to be able to express your views in ways that enable people to trust your competence, to understand your agenda, and to see that you really believe in what you say. If people don't trust you and they don't trust your agenda, you cannot be effective in your leadership.'

The corrosive effect of not taking a stand

All of the leaders I spoke with were acutely aware of the demands placed on them by the modern media environment. They commented that they seem always to be on the defensive, and want to find more ways to get on the front foot. They know that they need to find more points of resonance with customers and shareholders and stakeholders, and tell them things which help them to understand better what they are trying to do and why they should be supported.

Leadership, they said, can be boiled down to the idea that it is simply about taking a stand for what you believe, converting people to your cause and getting them to think and act differently.

Not taking a stand leads to a lack of clarity and direction, or to people not making decisions. It causes high levels of ambiguity and paralysed teams. People lose confidence in leaders who are unwilling to make a clear and decisive stand. People will spend all their time trying to second-guess what the leader really wants.

Taking a stand while withholding emotional commitment is equally confusing. Agreeing something intellectually but not committing emotionally leads to being seen as disingenuous, inauthentic or even disengaged. If you do not show the required commitment, then why should others?

When you do witness someone taking a stand, with powerfully argued logic backed up by passionately held beliefs, the result can be completely compelling. It is leadership in action.

What makes a good point of view?

Too few leaders think about developing points of view, yet well-articulated views can win friends and influence people, and give leaders a stronger voice in shaping the future. When used well, a point of view can help you develop a compelling corporate positioning and narrative, articulate a strong view on the issues that matter to your organization or your customers, and enable you to champion causes or take a position on issues of concern.

A powerful point of view is much more than simply giving expression to a random opinion. It has to be authentic and consistent, unlikely to be easily swayed by other people's views. People need to feel they are being told the truth even if they do not like what they hear.

A point of view has to help to generate trust. Trustworthy behaviour is way too complex to fake, without beliefs and values behind it. Strong points of view should therefore show how your values drive trustworthy behaviours. Key to creating trust is a willingness to bring an uncomfortable subject into the open where it can be understood and debated and resolved.

A point of view should also show personality. It should give insights into the emotional, temperamental and behavioural attributes that characterize you as a unique individual. The result will be a more compellingly articulated point of view and a powerful tool that can help you to win support.

Points of view are liberating; once you have them, you can find many opportunities to use them. They come in most useful when faced with the urgent need to respond. Having a point of view is like having a loaded six-gun that you can draw and shoot when under fire. If you have one, you won't be looking around for the ammunition you need to defend yourself.

Everything I heard from leaders boiled down to the idea that framing a point of view needs four key ingredients. The first is giving clarity to what you think and believe. The second is explaining how you behave as a result of your beliefs. The third is about articulating the benefits you gain (and give) as a result of your behaviours. And the fourth is how you think others should behave as a result.

Sir Christopher Gent of GSK says that leadership is often about taking a stand. 'This means you have to have a strong point of view on the issues that matter to your business. We live in a world of increasing scrutiny and ever-greater transparency, so leaders have to be very clear about their viewpoints. Those viewpoints have to be values based and they also have to be based on substance. Leaders must understand and be clear about the things that really matter to them.

'Quite a few leaders I have seen are uncomfortable and feel inhibited talking publicly about their values and the things they care passionately about. You have to come to terms with the fact that if you're going to give leadership to a business, clarity of viewpoint is critical if you want to thrive rather than just survive in the fishbowl.'

KEY POINTS FROM CHAPTER 11

- Leadership is often about taking a stand.
- This means being courageous and speaking up about what you believe in, and persuading people to your cause to get them to act differently.
- Speaking out on what you believe in shows your followers that you have a moral compass and are worthy of their trust. It gives them the confidence to follow you.
- As a leader, you are going to have to stand up and give your point of view, time and time again.
- The best leaders have a potent point of view.
- It is always the person with the strong point of view who influences the group, who wins the day.
- A powerful point of view generates trust: it shows people where you are coming from and allows them to align with you.

- Not taking a stand leads to a lack of clarity and paralysed teams.
- Not showing emotional connection to your cause sends a message that you are disingenuous or inauthentic.
- Too few leaders think about developing points of view, yet when well articulated, a point of view can help you win friends and influence people, and gain a stronger voice in shaping the future.
- Prepare points of view on issues important to you – before you might need them.
- Once you have them, they are liberating: you will be able to use them on all sorts of occasions and you will look for occasions to use them.
- People trust the motives, judgement and competence of business leaders less now than just five years ago.
- Leaders should be talking to important issues more often, with more transparency, more conviction and, yes, passion.
- To do this, your point of view should always make clear what you believe in, how you behave and what benefits are derived from your actions. It should always call for people to support your cause. Powerful stuff.

The power of stories

12

In July 1973, I was escorted into the newsroom of *The Star* newspaper in Johannesburg, South Africa. It was my first day of work and I was dressed in a brand-new suit, shining with enthusiasm and naivety. The veteran newsroom chief who showed me to my desk guided me with a firm hand and a gruff voice. I was overawed at the sight and sound of 50 journalists at work in an open office that seemed to be nothing but noise – telephones, typewriters and talking. How could anyone actually work in here?

My new boss pointed to the journalists shouting on the telephone and taking notes, and said: 'They're gathering information for the next deadline.'

He pointed to the ones hammering away at their typewriters and said: 'They're trying to meet the current deadline.'

Then he pointed to the journalists who looked idle, staring into space with their hands behind their heads, or looking intently out of a window, and I thought he was going to tell me those were the ones on a break. He didn't. He said: 'They're working hardest of all – they're working out how best to tell their stories.'

I've been looking for the best way to tell stories ever since. Telling stories is in my blood, and encouraging people to tell me their stories is a way of life. Telling a good story well is hard work, but pays enormous dividends. Why?

It is because when you listen to a story, you become an active participant in the tale. A story requires you to activate your imagination to see the detail. Equally, you can hear the sounds and feel the emotions being conveyed. Research has shown that it is only when people listen with their hearts and minds, when they actively engage with a story and use their imagination to co-create the story they are hearing, that ideas take root and lodge in their memories.

Did you hear the cacophony of the newsroom? Did you feel my sense of awe? Did you see the journalists staring out the window? If you did, you were engaged in the story, co-creating it by using your imagination to see what I was describing. This is why stories are so powerful.

These days there are so many distractions in our lives – television, mobile phones, e-mail, internet, newspapers, posters, radio – it isn't easy getting cut-through and grabbing someone's attention. But stories can get instant access.

On the other hand, the first slide of a PowerPoint presentation is like a klaxon sounding a warning to the cynic in you. You may be interested in what is to come, but as you prepare to deal with the charts and data and logic about to unfold, the warning horn has called into action your critical faculties. The way that you listen changes. Even though you pay close attention, and even though your brain has been fully engaged, you can sometimes find it hard to remember much about the presentation, just a day later. You have been so busy judging it that you have little capacity left to retain it.

A good story is like a Stealth fighter plane; it can slip beneath your cynic's radar and fire its message straight into your heart. Most likely, the next day, you'll remember the story. If something about the story engaged you, you'll even retell it. You may even change your behaviour as a result. This is why leaders love stories.

Stories are the Superglue of messages, and stories *move* people. If you get to their hearts, their minds will follow.

Stories tell us great truths

There is a crucial difference between the stories you are likely to use in business and the stories you tell at dinner parties. At dinner parties, you want to entertain. In business, you want to achieve a result. Achieving a result requires discipline, an understanding of the audience, a clear view of your desired outcome and a good story with two key attributes.

The best stories either deliver a powerful lesson or highlight a great and resonating truth. Through stories, people identify with tragedy or triumph, with hopes and fears, with values they value or behaviours they loathe. In this way, storytelling leaders become truth tellers to their people, and enable them to bring meaning to their listeners.

As you have already read, the leaders I interviewed told me dozens of stories. Many of them were uncomfortable with the idea of 'storytelling', and preferred to talk about using 'anecdotes' instead, but all of them used stories to illustrate a concept or demonstrate a point. My interviews were the richer for it, and I can remember pretty much every story I was told.

At first, each leader logically and rationally answered every question I put to them. But it didn't take very long before the first story appeared. Then they began to talk in stories, and more from the heart. When they told stories, their body language changed. Their eyes seemed to light up, they would lean ever so slightly closer towards me and they would become more animated.

Many of the things leaders have to convey – from setting direction, managing expectations, setting and reinforcing values, revealing the authentic person they are – are not easily done through key messages. These more intangible things are better relayed in stories.

Logic gets to the brain, stories get to the heart

Sir Nicholas Young of the Red Cross says a storytelling organization is a healthy organization. 'I just love stories. They are incredibly powerful and potent ways of getting messages across, far more powerful than statistics or analysis, the death-by-PowerPoint approach. Stories move me and they move people in the organization.

'Wherever I travel in the world, I'm always on the lookout for stories, particularly stories that move people. To tears, if necessary. For a charity, getting people to give money is a real humanitarian act, and to encourage people to do that you need to move them emotionally.

'Inside the Red Cross, stories are incredibly powerful change catalysts. People love to hear about the really heroic things that we do and those stories are very necessary and we tell them a lot, but the stories that work hardest are the ones that demonstrate what we still have to do, how much better we need to be. When I come back from a trip to places like Haiti, I can probably get more out of the organization by inspiring people with stories that illustrate what we still need to do than by telling them about things we have already done.'

Dame Amelia Fawcett of the Guardian Media Group says stories are the oldest communication tool known to man – 'and still the most effective'. She cautions that good stories are authentic stories. 'You can't just make up stories – they have to be based on actual experience. And you have to use stories with discretion. People who use stories all the time, without backing them up with data, will fall flat. Stories can help people understand your values, or who you are, and draw lessons that influence the way they behave.'

Sir Maurice Flanagan of Emirates Group uses stories to fortify the points he's trying to make. 'A good story combined with strong logic and supporting statistics can go a very long way. Logic gets to the brain and stories get to the heart.'

Rupert Gavin of Odeon and UCI Cinemas says that great stories have the power to permeate through the whole organization. 'The best stories have the power of myth. They become embedded in your organization and the more people pick up on those stories the more they become the embodiment of the organization. Those stories sometimes can have the power to help people decide why they prefer working in your company rather than any other, or how to behave in difficult situations.

'In our world, the world of cinema, the story is central to our DNA. If we can't get stories, then who can? It is the power of stories that can differentiate success from failure.

'You have to have a strategic vision for the enterprise you lead, but it only becomes powerful when you've converted it into a story – a story about where you have been, about where you're going, about how you will behave along the way. And you have to persuade everybody in the organization that they are part of the story. Your story has to describe how people are going to feel when they reach your destination, so that they feel it is going to be worth the journey getting there.'

Barbara Cassani, formerly of Go Fly airline and the 2012 Olympics, says stories are everywhere and you don't have to work too hard to find them. 'We all know the leaders who stick to a few stories and repeat them endlessly. You need someone close to you to tell you that you're becoming boring with the stories you tell. The great thing is that it isn't hard to find them. When people know you want stories they bring them to you. The best stories are the ones which shine a light on exemplary performance by employees. When leaders tell those stories, they send powerful signals into the organization about the behaviours everyone should adopt.'

The four types of business stories

Looking through the dozens of stories in my interviews, and reflecting on the stories I have heard from leaders and have coached leaders to tell, it seems to me there are basically four kinds of business story to look for and tell:

- the 'who you are' story (be yourself better);
- the context or future story (future focus);

- the values at work story (mission and values);
- the customer or needs story (outside in).

The 'who you are' story, which gives people an insight into you as a leader, is often delivered with a self-deprecating style and a touch of humour. A close cousin is the 'connection' story, designed to create empathy with an audience or to break down barriers, and show people that you can identify with how they think and feel. The 'future' story typically focuses people on what it is that needs to be achieved. The 'values at work' story shines a light on employees doing exactly the right thing. (Of course, sometimes, leaders will use 'bad values at work' stories to show where things need to improve.) The 'customer' story highlights a customer need, or provides an example of great or bad customer service.

Here are some examples of each of these different kinds of stories.

The who you are story

Many leaders also told me that it was useful to reveal past mistakes in order to show your human side. One such story came from Lady Barbara Judge.

'This is a story that illustrates a big mistake I made when I didn't ask for advice. I was asked to be chairman of William Hill, a large chain of betting shops, when it floated. I'm American, and to Americans, gambling is not seen as savoury. I thought of a working man with a small pay cheque walking into a betting shop on the way home, and when he walked out again there was no pay cheque left. I thought, I don't want to do this, because I really do not believe in gambling, so I turned it down.

'Almost as soon as I turned it down, I started talking to people about the job, whereas before I turned it down, I hadn't spoken to anybody. They all said I was crazy, that in Britain everybody bets, including the Queen. I was totally in the wrong, because I didn't think to get other people's perspectives. In fact it would have been a nice job. Ever since then, when I've had a hard decision to make, I always consult a number of people to make sure my perspectives are relevant.

'Good stories always have a lesson in them. When a leader is prepared to talk about their mistakes, it helps people to identify with you. People can identify with you and build trust.'

Barbara Stocking of Oxfam says that stories can also help you to establish an emotional relationship with the public.

'Yesterday I was on a visit to Wales. I went to a Young People's Centre where they are working with disadvantaged 16- to 25-year-olds. I found myself explaining why Oxfam had come to visit the centre and telling them about the work we do. I told the story about our experience with cholera in Haiti.

'We were trying to build latrines for people who never actually use latrines. They go home and use plastic bags which are called flying toilets. Once we discovered this, we had these biodegradable bags made, which can go into a big pit and be environmentally friendly. Now they are called pee-pooh bags. The youngsters thought this was absolutely horrendous but really funny. It was a great story to break down the barrier between me, as a visiting 'chief executive' and these young kids. Telling stories about the realities of life can enable you to engage better with people.'

The future story

Sir Anthony Bamford of JCB says a recent trip to China provided him with huge insight and motivation. He is now telling the story of his trip to all of his teams to invigorate them to the possibilities that exist there.

'While I was in China I was told about their system of five-year development plans. I went to visit various places and found that these plans cascade from the very top right down to the smallest village in China. From what I saw, most of these plans actually work to at least 90 per cent. The incredible thing is that they do what they say they'll do. They have hugely ambitious plans in place now. A large part of this planning is to do with the development of infrastructure. Of course, for building roads and infrastructure, they require a lot of heavy machinery. The big question is: how will we respond?'

Sir Anthony now tells this story widely inside the company to keep people focused on a key opportunity for the business.

The values at work story

Christopher Garnett, formerly chief executive of Great North Eastern Railway, remembers a time when he was trying to get employees to be prepared to take more initiative, especially when dealing with customers.

'We often had problems when overhead wires would blow down on the tracks and stop our trains. On one occasion there was a train that got stuck at Berwick-upon-Tweed. After being held up for hours, the train ran out of food. The manager of the train called a taxi and went into Berwick and bought all the fish and chips he could find. He came back and gave the fish and chips to all the passengers. The reaction inside the company was to question why he did that. I not only backed him but went around telling that story everywhere as an example of how our values should work when put to the test.

'That story helped to drive significant changes to people's attitudes as they began to understand the scope they had when showing initiative. Most importantly, it told them that I would back them when they did.'

The customer story

We saw in Chapter 7 how Paul Polman of Unilever used the story of his visit to a home in Egypt to explain to people what his company does for customers.

Phil Bentley of British Gas tells a similar story about an old lady, Mrs Crampton, living in a home on a post-war housing estate in Leeds.

'Some of the housing stock in Britain is incredibly poor. After the war many houses were made with concrete, no bricks and no insulation. We got to hear about one lady living in such a house, where she had no gas and had to rely on electric storage heaters that loaded up overnight. They gave out heat during the day but by three o'clock she would be sitting with a coat and gloves on because there was no heat left. By five o'clock she would go to bed because it was so cold.

'We went in and we put in new windows for better insulation and we put in a special pump which is a very efficient heating system. I went to visit her after this and she was complaining again. Now it was too hot, but her heating bill had more than halved.'

Phil says he tells the story inside the company because it is a great example of showing employees how his company can bring quality to people's lives. 'It is a bit like the janitor telling the president he's there to put a man on the moon – I want my people to know that we're here to improve the lives of our customers in whatever way we can. If I talk about the importance of our community energy savings programme and how we're spending £100 million a year, it gets lost on people. But if the story about Mrs Crampton doesn't tug on their heartstrings, they shouldn't be working for British Gas.'

Rupert Gavin of Odeon and UCI Cinemas tells a story about kettles in order to explain how important the consumer confidence index is in his industry.

'As a cinema group, we probably sit in a slightly different place from a lot of other organizations who are struggling in the recession. We are selling dreams, and relatively affordable dreams. In times of austerity it is all about confidence.

'When I worked at Dixons, we were one of the biggest sellers of kettles in the world. We wanted to know what drove kettle sales. A kettle isn't hugely expensive, and they don't break down very often, and they are not driven by fashion or technological trends. Yet we could see the sales changing – some weeks we would be selling 8,000 kettles and at other times of the year the sales were down. We spent forever trying to correlate what was driving kettle purchases. We tried to correlate them with new home purchases, anything that would help us to make some sense of sales.

'Finally we found that there was one very important factor – the consumer confidence index. This determined the movement in kettle sales, and not just kettle sales but other things as well. The confidence index was completely different from pay and discretionary spending power – it had everything to do with how people felt. We discovered it was one of the most telling indexes that the country has.

'Do I feel good? Do I feel optimistic? I may have the money but if I'm worried that things are going to get worse I'm not going to spend on big ticket items if I am concerned. But I will spend on small luxuries. This is why the cinema market has actually done quite well during the recession. Going to the cinema is a small amount of enjoyment with relatively little commitment. As a result the cinema has done well, theatre has done well – and condoms, of course, have done well.'

Good stories are easy to find and easy to tell

Good stories will have characters with personality. They will have a conflict or challenge. They will have vivid images. They will have a key turning point. They will 'show', not 'tell'.

Chris Satterthwaite of Chime Communications advises that even people who are not skilled at storytelling can tell a good story if they stick to the simple formula of 'Problem. Solution. Benefit'.

He says every story contains that basic formula. 'Problem? The princess is stuck in a tower where no one can reach her. She sings at night to overcome loneliness. Solution? A brave prince hears her magical voice and is moved to fight his way to the top of the tower to free her. Benefit? After overcoming a series of challenges, they ride away into a happy future together.'

Craig Tegel was managing director of Adobe Systems in Northern Europe when I worked with him. Now he is president and representative director of Adobe in Japan. He had always been concerned about communicating with large groups of people. 'When you work for a multinational it can be hard to convey the corporate message in a way you can put into your own voice and get over with authenticity.'

When I first met him, Craig faced a crucial presentation in front of 300 customers. He had to engage these people, be truly authoritative and spark change. He was armed with a battery of communication materials – slides, video clips and a carefully crafted script – yet he was still worried. Something felt wrong. I told him to use just four stories. No slides, no script, and just four stories he enjoyed telling. He should use those four stories as the four pillars of his talk, and build what he had to say on those stories. Obviously, he was reluctant, looking back at all the work in his mountain of close-written slides. After a little nudging, he agreed.

We quickly identified the things he wanted people to be thinking and saying after his speech, which in turn helped to identify four stories that we knew had the right takeouts. We found those stories in his experience inside 30 minutes, and articulated them in minutes flat. We rehearsed them several times, with me subtly refining the way he told them, but he was a natural. (We are all natural storytellers; the art is in our DNA.) Afterwards, I sent him home to practise in front of a mirror. In less than 24 hours, he was ready.

Craig threw away his graphs and stood before his people armed with only a microphone. He told the stories well. They all came from his experience, reflected his values, cut to the core of what needed to be done and powerfully, emotionally demonstrated why clients needed a new relationship with his company. Afterwards, he was jubilant. The feedback was incredible.

One member of the audience said: 'You really knew what you were talking about... authoritative, clear – and with no damn slides to distract, people really heard what you had to say!'

Craig's relief was immense, his clients were engaged and his confidence redoubled. Now he is a strong advocate for the real bottom-line business benefit of stories. 'The right use of stories opens up new leads and new possibilities. After presentations, clients come up to me and say, "I relate to what you were saying, I believe you understand what we're going through, I would like to talk to you about what Adobe can do for me." Inside and outside the company, stories work. The best is that more customers come to us from listening to my stories and I have the pleasure of knowing that what I get out of it overlaps completely with what the company needs.'

A key point of this story is that practice makes perfect. You should never tell a story if you don't love the story. Of course, you have to judge whether the audience is in the mood for one, or whether analysis actually is better – and there will be those times. However good the story, it can still fall flat if badly told. I believe that you have to tell a story to yourself at least 10 times before you become comfortable with it.

Choosing the right story

So, storytelling in business can give leaders an 'emotional edge' that leads to real competitive advantage. This is why I collect them, relish their structure, characters and colour. I admire their ability to hook the imagination and their versatility to fulfil varying needs at different times.

What stories should we choose? The key principle, as always, must be to change behaviours and achieve results. The first step is to define your purpose. Since stories in business are designed to provoke action, be clear what your stories are for. Remember: it is the takeout that is key, not the message. Ask yourself who you need to influence and what you want them to do. Give particular attention to 'What's in it for him?' – ie what benefit accrues to the people whose behaviours you want to change, what will persuade them that acting differently is in their interest too? Finally, know what you want them to take out of the story, but don't make this your message.

Let people come to that conclusion themselves.

David Morley of Allen & Overy says messages sink in better when people work things out for themselves. 'There's something about the discovery process which helps people to remember better. When they conclude things from your story, it is so much more powerful than if you try to tell them in a series of dry points.'

You may believe your organization must embrace change. Look for a 'future story' that talks so vividly about your vision of a typical day in the future that it will make everyone else want to get to this inspiring place. You might want your people to have a different value. Then look for a great story about a principled decision. But be warned: you had better be someone who really aspires to that future or makes those principled decisions, otherwise all the story shows is the fatal gap between the storyteller and the story. The storyteller has to be authentic.

One simple story can achieve more than a volume of rules

There is a great truth in the fact that we sometimes find ourselves having to communicate on millions of trivial issues when we fail to get over just one simple profound point.

Some years ago, I was asked to counsel the safety director of a home construction company. He was passionate about health and safety but his staff knew 'Steve' as angry, controlling and adversarial; they had no sense of what drove him or why he pushed so furiously for every last detail to be checked. Steve fumed that his people 'weren't paying attention', hated that they merely responded to crises and never sought active ways to tackle problems or bolt the fine points down.

We dug into his beliefs and values to find what really drove him. Steve told me how, at a previous company, a boy had strayed onto one of his sites. He had managed to get through a gap in the fence after everyone had gone home, fallen into a deep pit excavated for foundations and had been severely injured. In pain, bleeding profusely, he died alone in the night.

Steve took on the agonizing responsibility of telling the boy's mother himself. It was his duty, but it was the most harrowing experience of his life. It was made all the more bitter when he learned the gap in the fence had not been secured by one person in his crew. The pit had not been protected properly by a different member of his crew; by themselves, minor omissions, but a confluence of details which proved fatal.

Steve's credo became that no detail was too small when it came to health and safety. No one could have mistaken the strength of his feeling when he told me, 'I never want to have to tell another mother that her child has been in an accident on one of our sites.'

I advised Steve to go and tell that story everywhere in the organization. Every chance he got, he was to tell that story without making any other points. 'Just tell that story and then get out,' I told him. His story, when told, had a profound and positive impact on his business.

Steve's entire workforce saw why attending to such details of health and safety practice was important and responded wholeheartedly. His story moved them in a way that rules and regulations never could. Authentic, based on his strong point of view and entirely appropriate to his organization, it changed behaviours and raised the benchmark for safety. His people did what was right whether he was there or not and were happier doing it.

Initially, Steve had acted rationally in pursuing a strategy of active health and safety for his company but this alone left him frustrated and his people cold. His story channelled his passion and produced a win–win for all the stakeholders – especially Steve, who now knew what his integrity could achieve.

Once you understand the power of stories, finding the right ones for your business is just a matter of looking and listening. Stories have the potential to encourage the heroes around you. 'Listen with intent' and you will find stories everywhere. Think about your stakeholders – your customers, employees and shareholders. Look for strategy stories, product benefit stories, brand stories, stories about history, quality and image.

Armed with these stories you can challenge, enable, inspire and encourage the behaviours the organization needs. Use them to celebrate the everyday heroes around you and they may even make a hero of you in return.

This is not to banish logic – use analysis when analysis is better, sense when a story is wanted and when one is not. Never use a story you don't love or one that is half-baked. But a story you believe in, when used well, offers a route to the heart. That's where we go to get people to take action with energy and enthusiasm.

KEY POINTS FROM CHAPTER 12

- Stories are the Superglue of messages.
- Great stories have legs and travel far: they can define you or your organization.
- Every leader uses stories, knowing that we are wired to listen, imaginatively, when we are told stories.
- Good stories get under the cynical radar and touch hearts.
- Backed up by facts to cover off the mind, stories have the power to move people.
- The best stories tell us about customer experiences, good and bad;
  - or make heroes out of employees delivering the values of the organization;
  - or show up the frustrations of workers unable to do their best because of the system;
  - or vividly portray the future;
  - or reveal aspects of the leader to the audience.
- Let people conclude the message or lesson in the story – that will make it more memorable.

- The best stories have in them a resonating truth, and must be authentic.
- Use the problem–solution–benefit (or disbenefit) method to tell your stories, as this is the basis of pretty much any story you care to think of.
- Tell only stories you love, and make sure you practise.
- Repetition is key. Only when you've told a story 10 times do people start 'getting it'.

Watch out for the undermining signals beyond the words

13

Leaders are being watched all the time. You might use English or French or Spanish or Chinese for your words, but your body language can overpower everything you have to say. Every gesture or facial expression sends a powerful signal that can reinforce or completely undermine your message.

Everything you do is an example, and everything communicates. Decisions you make, policies you put in place, things you do or don't do, issues you fail to act on – all of these communicate more clearly than your words. As uncomfortable as that is, leaders have to recognize that they send signals beyond the words they use. A truly adept leader uses this to their advantage.

Beverley Aspinall of Fortnum & Mason says being a leader is like being on a stage. 'You are in a position where people are going to watch what you do all the time, and you can't hide from that. Everything you do comes under scrutiny. That is simply the way it is and the way it should be.'

This means that leaders must be cognizant of the fact that they need to look, act and sound like a leader, 24 hours a day.

Richard Gnodde of Goldman Sachs International says that leadership communication can be defined very broadly as everything we say, everything we do, how we conduct ourselves, and what body language we display. 'Good leaders instinctively know when to talk, when to shut up, how to hold themselves and how to behave. People have always looked to the top for signals and leaders have always been in a fishbowl. The bowl is more transparent than ever today with the internet and 24/7 scrutiny.'

Fields Wicker-Miurin of Leaders' Quest says that instinctively, often without knowing it, we react to people every day based on what we see when we look at a person, their facial expressions and reactions, whether they smile or frown, their body language. 'Leadership is not just what we say, or what we communicate with words, it is how we say it, and more importantly, always, it is what we do and how we are who we are. If we say things we don't really believe, it will be obvious (even if no one tells us!). This is why it is impossible to lead well if we are pretending to be someone we are not. It shows. We can't hide who we really are. So we need to know and be comfortable with who we are, and lead from that space. We must wake up to the fact that we are in the spotlight all the time.'

Consider the negative messages that leaders can send to followers when they are not conscious of their facial and body language:

- a sense of a lack of confidence or trust in an employee;
- the degree to which the leader accepts the feelings of employees;
- implicit acceptance of inappropriate behaviours;
- their own negative feelings about an issue;
- or their own lack of commitment to a course of action.

These are powerful messages that no leader would want consciously to fire into an organization.

It's written on your face

Your face and eyes are a major source of expression when communicating with others. Your eyes are often the first piece of body language that others see or notice. With your eyes you can make visual contact, avoid visual contact or show interest or lack of interest. With facial expressions you can show anger, disgust or frustration. You can mask emotions or show emotions both positive and negative.

Barbara Cassani says leaders need to be told that they can turn off their teams by their demeanour. 'They should be told that it's the way their face looks when they walk around the office that is putting people off. If they could just fake a smile, then people wouldn't think they were in crisis all the time. When you tell people that, they are shocked, because they haven't realized that they look down in the dumps. Self-awareness is the first step to good communication.'

'I know that when I'm thinking really hard about something, I look angry and upset. To other people that can be scary. Knowing this is incredibly valuable in helping me to avoid sending the wrong signals to people, which can have very negative consequences.'

So what should leaders focus on? Making eye contact and smiling are two powerful facial signals that can do wonders. Eye contact encourages communication and conveys interest and warmth. It helps to establish credibility. Smiling helps you to be perceived as likeable, warm and approachable. It helps make people comfortable and encourages them to listen to you more.

Gestures help to animate what you're saying, and a lack of gestures may be perceived as boring and stiff. The way you speak sends signals too. Dull speakers use a monotone voice, without any variation in tone, loudness or inflection.

People watch your body language too

John Heaps is chairman of Eversheds, an international law firm headquartered in London. He highly recommends a leadership book called *Shackleton's Way – Leadership Lessons from the Great Antarctic Explorer*, by Margot Morrell and Stephanie Capparell (Penguin, 2001).

The book is about Sir Ernest Shackleton, a British explorer who died in 1922 after several expeditions to the South Pole. He was knighted for a march which took him and his crew to the southernmost point ever reached in Antarctica at the time, but he is more famous for a disastrous expedition between 1914 and 1917. His ship, *Endurance*, was crushed in pack ice before the expedition had even really started, stranding him and his crew. He successfully led all 27 members of his crew to safety after a two-year fight for their lives, and his method of leadership during that struggle has been studied ever since.

'The section in the book that impressed me the most,' says John Heaps, 'is a part about non-verbal communication. On many occasions when the prospects looked bleak, Shackleton rallied his men by his cheerful and positive disposition, never once allowing their predicament to reflect in anger, frustration or bad temper. When at sea in an open boat for days on end in freezing conditions with limited food and water, the crew would be encouraged by seeing their leader with the tiller under his arm, whistling a tune to himself as if he was on a trip around the lighthouse. His spirit and his positivity never wavered regardless of the seriousness of their position.

'This really resonated because it reminded me of a time when, in a situation that bore no resemblance whatsoever to the risks Shackleton and his crew faced, I fell well short of Shackleton's standard. One morning after I had taken responsibility for the litigation team in our Leeds office, a young lawyer came into my room to explain that the department was hugely concerned that something serious had happened because I had walked in my office that morning totally preoccupied without, as usual, wishing everyone "Good morning" with a cheerful smile. They expected me to impart some terrible news.

'Until that point it had simply not occurred to me how significant an impact my demeanour and attitude could have, particularly in my newly acquired leadership role. Leaders need to understand the crucial importance of the way they appear as well as what they say.'

Leaders must always remember everything that is expected of them, including that they should always be positive in their appearance and in the way they behave towards people.

How we are feeling reflects in how we stand and walk. Non-verbal communication reveals to the world how we feel inside, so it is critical to achieve emotional mastery if we are to prevent our body from sending signals that may be at odds with the messages we wish to communicate.

Antony Jenkins of Barclays Global Retail Bank says that he always counsels new leaders to remember that they are now going to be observed all the time. 'If I walk the floors in Barclays and I'm frowning the whole time, hunched over with my hands in my pockets, concern will pass through the building like wildfire. People will be asking why the boss is so cross. Sometimes, it will be fine that people know you're angry about something – you might want them to understand that you're upset. But you have to be very sensitive to how you present at all times. Managing your emotions and channelling them in the right way, as opposed to just letting them run wild, are really important.'

How you hold your head, where you put your hands, whether you fold your arms – all of these send signals. Posture is important. Leaning into somebody when they're talking to you sends a signal of interest, but standing too close can invade space.

My personal pet hate is when leaders clasp their hands behind their heads and lean back in their chairs, exposing their armpits. Apart from the danger of putting sweaty armpits on show, it sends signals of arrogance, superiority and disrespect.

Leaders also need to be very conscious of their appearance. The clothes they wear, cleanliness, grooming – all send signals.

Asked what he looks for in people when interviewing them for leadership positions, Sir Stuart Rose says he looks at their shoes to see if they're clean, their fingernails to see if they are trimmed and their hair to see if it is washed and parted.

'Appearance matters,' he says. 'How you speak and what you say are important but, if someone doesn't look me in the eye when they are talking to me, they won't get the job, because that is part of communication and interacting with people, getting people to trust you. While business is all about delivering hard numbers, it is the soft people skills that enable good results, so leaders must be self-aware and recognize that everything they do is communication.'

When being visible is the message

Many of the leaders I talked to spoke of the need to be visible. Showing up was a powerful signal all by itself.

James Hogan of Etihad Airways says being visible helps to establish a connection. 'Every day I leave my office and walk the campus. I will go to the operations room, I'll go to the marketing area, I have lunch in the canteen. It's really important that I am visible. It sends a signal that I am around and I am accessible.'

Lord Sharman of Aviva says that leaders must not only show up, but they must send visible signals to people about the things they believe in. 'Whenever I leave my room, I switch the lights off. It can be such simple things, but they send powerful signals about what you believe in and what you are committed to. For instance, I never frown when I'm talking to someone, I always try to show that I'm happy.'

He says that when he became UK Senior Partner of global accounting firm KPMG, he used to walk every floor of the buildings they occupied in London every Friday. 'The first time I did it there was an almighty uproar from the management team. They said I was disturbing the troops. I had to tell them that it wasn't a chicken house. I just want to go around and have a chat to people. After a period, I happened to be away one Friday and people started ringing my office and asking if I was all right. They really noticed. That was me simply saying: "Look, I'm around, I'm available."'

Barbara Stocking of Oxfam tells the story of when she worked in the UK's National Health Service and had to lead the merger of two regional offices with a total of 800 people. Only 150 were being kept in the NHS and the rest were either moving into the private sector or being made redundant.

The problem was that she was very often awaiting approval or instructions from above and had no news to give people who were desperately uncertain and worried about their jobs and the future.

'I turned up to talk with them even when I had nothing to say. It wasn't easy standing there week after week, being grilled without being able to respond. I took the view that if I didn't show up there would be rumours and gossip everywhere and people would prefer me turning up, even with nothing to say. Then at least I would be showing them I had integrity.'

Model the behaviours you want

Dame Fiona Reynolds of the National Trust says: 'Leadership is absolutely the most watched thing, particularly when you're trying to introduce and lead change. A very tiny example was when the Trust decided to move everybody out of London to a new office in Swindon, in Wiltshire. At the time it was an incredibly unpopular thing to do. When I got the job as chief executive I was living in London and people asked me what I was going to do. I absolutely knew that if I had said you are going to move to Swindon and I'm going to stay in London, it would have been an absolute disaster. You have to model the behaviours you want and you cannot demand things of people that you aren't prepared to do yourself.'

Lord Mervyn Davies says everything you do communicates. 'How you react to the death of a member of staff, or what you do to support victims of a tsunami: these actions send powerful messages. If your eyes and ears are working properly, then you will know what to do, and what you do will be a powerful piece of communication.'

Sir Stuart Rose says that being the leader of a business means that you have to be an exemplar of everything that business stands for. 'For example, I happen to fly a light aircraft as a hobby. It is a little single-engine aeroplane, but we had debates about whether that was appropriate for me to do as it causes pollution. That is quite an imposition on my life because it is my hobby. But you have to be scrupulous and so I have done some carbon offsetting as a result. You can't do things that seem hypocritical when compared with the things you say. That's very dangerous.'

The meaning between the lines

Colin Matthews of BAA, operators of Heathrow Airport, says the big danger is saying that you want one thing but inadvertently sending a message that says you really don't. 'Say, for example, that you line up a telephone conference call and tell people that you want a robust discussion, but wind up lecturing someone in front of everybody else. The overriding message will be that you don't want challenge and that will kill off any discussion, achieving exactly the opposite of what you want.'

What Colin is referring to is a communication phenomenon called meta-messaging. A meta-message is an unspoken, implied message that we unknowingly deliver when we are communicating. The meaning of the meta-message is so strong that it overwhelms your message and leads to people interpreting what you say very differently. For example, many people will start a sentence with: 'With great respect...' and then proceed to criticize, implying that they have absolutely no respect for you whatsoever. Many of us use these phrases and forget that an astute person will quickly spot that our choice of words differs from what we really mean.

Meta-messages can kill trust and openness in the workplace. For instance, the word 'but' is a strong meta-messenger. If you tell somebody that you think their idea is great, but..., you have negated the praise and the listener will only hear the words after the 'but'. The real signal is that you didn't think their idea was very good at all. Try instead to say: 'That's a great idea and here's something we can add to it.' That sends a very different message.

Symbolic acts send lasting messages

Sometimes leaders have to do something that either shakes people out of their complacency or gives them a reminder of what is expected of them.

Lord Sharman tells of the time he was leading cultural change in KPMG and, with his leadership team, was trying to reduce bureaucracy and empower teams more. 'One of our high-earning partners came to see me and said he did not believe in our concept of teamwork and empowerment. He said he was the boss and that his team would do only what he told them to do or else they would be fired. I told him that he had the choice of either accepting the change or he could go. He went. But when he went, we subtly communicated that he had gone because he wasn't prepared to buy into the new ideas. That signal from the leadership team of a very serious intent worked wonders in the firm. After that people really got the message.'

When I am coaching leaders, I often ask them to rank themselves on a scale of 0 to 10 on five key areas of leadership communication. I ask them about how much they talk about finding new and better ways of doing things, how well they articulate the future, how well they model the behaviours they require, and how much and how well they thank people. I then ask if I can get their direct reports to judge them on the same criteria. Usually there is a remarkable similarity between the marks, indicating great self-awareness. The one area where there is usually a significant gap is in the area of how well leaders thank their followers.

Most leaders I have spoken to recognize that they probably don't spend enough time celebrating success and thanking people for their efforts. Their direct reports will inevitably rate them even lower than they rate themselves.

As Barbara Cassani says, it is crucial to shine a light on people who have done well and who are behaving in exactly the way you would like. 'Recognition can often be more important than money,' she says. Taking time out to recognize great deeds and send clear signals of appreciation is something most appreciated by employees and least often delivered by leaders.

Speaking off the cuff

Simon Calver of LOVEFiLM says that any male leader doubting that his followers take cues from his non-verbal communication should try the French double cuff test.

'There are huge amounts of non-verbal communication that go on day in and day out in any organization. For example, if a male leader changed all of his shirts for a month to what the Americans call a French double cuff and used cufflinks, and then observed what other men in his team were wearing, he would be staggered. I once advised a colleague of mine to do this when he complained that his team weren't really listening to what was going on. He was amazed at how many people had copied him. But it isn't that amazing. People try to conform to the standards and behaviours that a leader sets, and will often subconsciously emulate what the leader does.

'If you can't understand the behaviours of your team, perhaps you should first be taking a look at your own.'

If everything you do is an example, and you are being watched closely all the time, then your actions are also being assessed by people who will be coming to their own conclusions about the right way to behave, the acceptable ways of getting things done around here, or what really matters to the leader, and they will shape their behaviours accordingly.

Being in the fishbowl means you have to behave with integrity all the time and do the right thing, even when you don't feel like it.

KEY POINTS FROM CHAPTER 13

- Actions speak louder than words. A cliché, but nevertheless one of the hardest truths for a leader to grasp.
- Leaders often forget they are in a fishbowl and are being watched all the time.
- A look of frustration here, a preoccupied walk through an office without speaking to anyone, a frown of frustration when someone is talking – all of these send powerful signals that staff take away and dissect for meaning.
- Your facial expression and body language can reinforce or undermine everything you say: be aware of this and make it work for you.
- Being a leader means looking, acting, walking and talking like a leader.
- What you act on, what questions you ask, what you don't act on, and how you act are all acts of communication too.
- There is nothing more corrosive than the conflict between saying one thing and doing another.
- For example, saying that bullying is offensive but then doing nothing about a high-earning bullying manager really says money matters more than staff welfare.
- Go out of your way to model the behaviours you want.

- Leaders who clearly love what they are doing, who show it in everything they do, in every expression, are hugely infectious.
- Great leaders communicate positivity and optimism, and they often do it through a smile, or by walking with energy, or by standing straight and tall.
- You have to learn to channel your emotions in order to use body language to reinforce your messages.
- Being visible and available is a powerful signal of integrity.
- Beware of the destructive power of meta-messages.

14

Prepare properly for public platforms

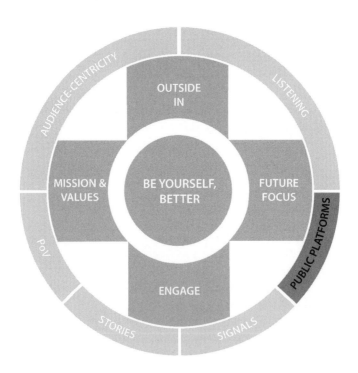

Leaders lay their reputations on the line every time they get up on a public platform to speak, especially if it is to the media. Many a CEO has had their reputation shattered because they have not taken sufficient care over what they say in public. All of the leaders I interviewed spoke of the dangers of media interviews, but all recognized that these are a crucial part of the role.

The more senior a leader gets, they say, the wider the number of audiences they will need to communicate with, and the more they will need training to develop the right skill sets. Not only will they need to be taught the skills, but they will then have to learn to give sufficient time to rehearsing before each public appearance.

Imagine the following scenario. Our fictional leader is enjoying huge success, his share price is rising, a new and innovative product is in huge demand, and he is about to make a key speech to an influential audience, with media in attendance. He is feeling confident. But confidence quickly tips over into overconfidence, and the leader feels able to make jokes and give spontaneous views on a wide variety of subjects.

I have witnessed this scenario so many times. The danger is that it is in those moments that one thoughtless comment can result in catastrophe.

It has happened. Ask Gerald Ratner. Mr Ratner is a British businessman who was formerly chief executive of the British jewellery company Ratners Group. Jewellery in Mr Ratner's stores was cheap and very popular. Giving a speech at the Institute of Directors in 1991, he commented that his products were 'crap' and that some of his earrings were 'cheaper than an M&S prawn sandwich, but probably wouldn't last as long'. His comments were widely reported in the media. After this, the value of his group plummeted by about half a billion sterling, which very nearly resulted in the collapse of the company. In his defence, he said he thought it was a private gathering and that he didn't mean to be taken seriously. But he was, and it resulted in serious damage to his and his company's reputation.

Tony Hayward is the immediate past chief executive of the global oil and energy company BP. In 2010 his company was engulfed by the problems of the Deepwater Horizon oil spill, when an explosion on one of the company's oil rigs resulted in the deaths of 11 people and an oil leak into the Gulf of Mexico which poured tens of thousands of barrels of oil into the Gulf every day. At a time when estimates were suggesting that the spill had deposited up to 44 million gallons of oil in the sea, Tony described the spill as 'tiny' compared to the size of the ocean, angering many people. He further angered people by saying that the environmental impact of America's biggest oil spill, and of the almost 1,000,000,000 gallons of toxic dispersant used to treat it, would be 'very, very modest'.

The moment that everyone remembers occurred when he visited Venice, Louisiana, to apologize for the disaster. 'The first thing to say is I'm sorry,' he told reporters, when asked what he would like to tell locals whose livelihoods had been affected. 'We're sorry for the massive disruption it's caused their lives. There is no one who wants this over more than I do. I would like my life back,' he said.

Telling struggling residents that he would like his life back is now, unfortunately, what he will be most remembered for. Soon after, he was replaced as chief executive by Bob Dudley.

More than half the leaders I interviewed volunteered this 'Tony Hayward' moment as an example of the pitfalls that await a leader who doesn't recognize that every word he says will be scrutinized. As every leader I spoke to said, reputations have always been important, but these days they can be ruined in an instant, and a life's work can be undone in one unguarded moment.

Ian Thomas, managing director of Fluor UK, tells a story of how he was being interviewed for the *Today* programme on Radio 4. 'They sent a radio car to my house, which was good for my reputation with my neighbours. I was in the car talking live on air on the subject of a financial crisis in Asia, with particular reference to Malaysia. I was on for just a few minutes, and right at the end, the interviewer threw in a 'By the way' question: "And what about Indonesia?" Without hesitation, I replied that Indonesia was a total basket case. By the time I got into the office the Indonesian ambassador had been on the phone three times – I nearly caused an international incident by speaking without thinking. Thankfully, I eventually recovered from this self-inflicted crisis and now I am even chairman of the Indonesia British Business Council.'

Get the right training and do the right preparation

To cope with this challenge, leaders must get the right training and must put the right preparation into their public appearances. After every appearance, they must seek honest and critical feedback in order to keep getting better at what is a demanding art.

Every time a leader appears on a public platform, they are not only representing themselves but also the organization they lead. What they say can have a huge positive or negative impact on reputation, on share price, and on perceptions.

Lord Tim Bell, chairman of Chime Communications, has told his clients for decades: 'Perceptions are real. If you are playing to win they have to be favourable. Your ability to persuade people to listen to you, understand what you're saying and support you will determine whether you win or lose.'

Ben Verwaayen of Alcatel-Lucent says the world is ruled by perception. 'Perception is reality with a time lag, and it's my job to make sure that the time lag is as short as possible. But perception is a truly important element of people's buying behaviours and general attitudes, and if you want to influence people's perceptions then you have to master communications.'

The more senior a leader gets, the more likely they are going to have to deal with the media, give speeches, talk to investors and deal with government ministers or NGOs. Says Kevin Beeston of Taylor Wimpey: 'You have to get specialist training in these areas if you want to be able to handle them well. If it is well managed, it can positively influence your reputation and help to establish a significant competitive advantage. This area of the leader's job is a critical driver of business value – you simply have to get it right.'

General Sir Mike Jackson says most emphasis should be placed on media training. 'Particularly as one gets more senior, the need to handle and communicate with the media is increasingly part of the job. In the army, media training is taken very seriously. The world of 24/7 media is here and that genie is not going to go back in the bottle, so leaders have to learn to live with it. Living with it is one thing, but you have to become competent enough to turn it to your advantage. That requires training and practice.'

Sir Stuart Rose believes leaders have to become competent in all forms of media. 'You have to be able to do radio, you have got to be able to do TV, you've got to be able to do a pre-record, or handle being on a location, or on a studio set – they are all quite different approaches and senior people must know how to handle all of them. And it can't just be the CEO; the top team needs to be trained.'

Remember, every word counts

Barbara Cassani says that once you step outside the organization you lead, you need a completely different set of skills. 'Sadly, many good leaders simply do not have that external skills set. The openness and informality that make you a good internal communicator need to be contained and tempered when you go external.

'Leaders should always avoid accepting a public platform if it is simply about flattering their ego. When accepting a public appearance you have to ask yourself whether it will serve your business interests, rather than your ego. At all costs avoid allowing yourself to be put on a pedestal for reasons that do not have to do with your business objectives. You always need to be clinical in your assessment of why you are appearing on a public platform. If you completely understand the reason you are appearing, who you are talking to and what you're trying to achieve, you'll be more focused and on message and less likely to fall off the pedestal.'

John Stevens, Baron Stevens of Kirkwhelpington, was commissioner for the London Metropolitan Police from 2000 until 2005. He is now executive chairman of Monitor Quest Ltd, a strategic intelligence and risk-mitigation company based in London. He says leaders in high-profile positions need to assess every word they utter.

'When I was leading the Northern Ireland collusion enquiry, which lasted two decades and led to the conviction of 90 people, it was the highest-profile criminal enquiry of its time. I soon came to realize that every word mattered and echoed throughout Northern Ireland. You don't want to appear to be wooden, but at the same time you do have to be very careful.'

Graham Mackay of SABMiller says leading a business is more difficult now than it was 30 years ago. 'The modern world places much greater demands on leaders to be all-round communicators. You have to explain yourself all the time to regulators, global NGOs, politicians and the media, so you have to learn how to handle very structured and formal communications that abound at the top of the business. You simply cannot get by, talking off some scrappy notes.'

Philip Green, formerly of United Utilities, says the more senior you become, the more weight people give to your words. 'Whether you like it or not people hang on your every word and the words have more impact than you realize, arguably more impact than they should have, but it takes great skill to talk with passion and still be on message and careful. Not only great skill but a great deal of rehearsal and practice.'

Simple messages repeated often

Legend has it that American author Mark Twain once received a telegram from his publisher that said: 'Need two-page short story two days.' Apparently Twain replied: 'No do two pages two days. Can do 30 pages two days. Need 30 days do two pages.' His observation about brevity, time and quality of writing is good advice for all leaders.

You have to be very discriminating about your messages, says Barbara Stocking of Oxfam. 'You simply can't have too many messages and those that you do have, you have to repeat constantly. It is all the more important that you make those messages simple and memorable. Never fire off too many messages at people at the same time.'

Whenever I coach leaders today, I replicate a graphic lesson I was taught years ago. On one training course I attended, I noticed the instructor had a waste-paper basket full of tennis balls. She picked up one of the tennis balls and threw it to me, and I caught it easily. Then she threw two more in quick succession. I managed to catch both of those as well, but only just. Then she threw the remainder of the bucket at me, and I failed to catch a single ball.

The point was well made, though. The more messages you send at one time, the less likely people will hang on to any of them.

Tom Hughes-Hallett of Marie Curie Cancer Care says that in more than 10 years at the helm he has only had three messages that he has wanted to deliver into the organization. 'You have to repeat and repeat and repeat before people will get even just one message, so you have to be very discriminating. After years of hammering home the point, I now feel confident most people will know that my key message is that everything we do in this organization has to be about improving cancer care for patients. They know I will always ask them to ask the question about any proposed activity – is it likely to be able to help us improve the way we give care? If not, then why are we doing it? You have to focus down on the most important messages and deliver them and then find new ways of delivering them, to ensure that people hear and understand.'

General the Lord Guthrie agrees. 'I think one of the most important things about leadership communication is to keep it simple. Then you must have confidence in what you're saying and not be knocked off course. You have to give the same message time and time again. The danger is we get bored with our messages before people have really begun to hear what we want them to hear. You have to be persistent.'

General The Lord Dannatt says the ideal is to explain things clearly and have them understood easily. 'To do this you have to almost oversimplify to make sure that things are understood. Then you have to be aware that once you have said something you can't take it back, so you must be careful in your choice of words and metaphor.'

Sir Clive Woodward, former English rugby union player and head coach of the 2003 Rugby World Cup winning side, is now director of sport for the British Olympic Association. He believes preparing properly is the key to getting your message across. 'My whole experience tells me that the more thought I have given to my message, the better I will communicate it. It is like any aspect of sport: if you prepare well you will communicate well. And, always think about what questions you might get, and prepare for those as well.'

Top tips for dealing with the media

Shelves of books have been written on the subject of handling the media, and media training companies abound, offering courses that are several days long. I simply could not do credit to the subject in a short chapter in this book. However, the leaders I interviewed did make a few key points about dealing with the media.

Helen Alexander of the CBI says that the media present an opportunity to get your message over and leaders must not shy away from this. If you have a strong message and you are confident and know your subject matter, you will do well. However, woe betide the person who does not do adequate preparation. 'If ever you appear on the British Radio 4 programme, *The Bottom Line*, Evan Davis the presenter will welcome you and assure you that they are not there to make you look stupid. "But," he says, "I can't stop you from looking stupid."

'Speaking off the cuff is dangerous. You need to be clear about the points you want to get across, and have rehearsed them. The media can help you in your communications, but you need to understand what they want too.'

Working for a public relations business as I do, I know that dealing with the media is an opportunity sometimes simply too good to pass up. Just one free minute on TV can do wonders for sales. One thoughtful article in a national newspaper can change the way people perceive your business. The key is to remember that the media want a good story, relevant to their audience.

In that regard, your interests are the same as the journalists'. You too want to reach that audience with something of interest to them. Sir Nick Partridge of the Terrence Higgins Trust says the key to dealing with the media is to remember who you are actually talking to. The danger is that you fall into the trap of thinking you're speaking to the journalist, when really your audience is out there and you need to be focused on them.

'For example, when I first needed to get to the parents and grandparents of young men suffering from HIV and AIDS, I would go on the Jimmy Young show on BBC Radio 2, because I knew that he had a huge following among that target audience. I could then tailor my messages for that audience – mothers and fathers of those affected – in every response I gave to questions from the host. All the time I was thinking about the right message for the right audience through the right channel and with the right tone,' said Sir Nick.

You have to know the format and audience of the show or publication that you are dealing with. It helps to know the journalist and what approach they take to stories. And it certainly helps not to feel on the defensive, but to recognize that good preparation enables positive outcomes. In the age of sound bites, it helps to have thought through your quotable quotes before appearing in front of a microphone. You don't need notes if you have thought about the three key points you want to make. Speak in layman's terms, be enthusiastic about your topic and at all costs avoid corporate jargon.

Barbara Cassani cautions: 'If, during an interview, you find yourself having fun, you'd better stop and check whether you are going off message. You are not there to have fun; you're there to deliver messages that support your organization, and if you're having fun you might be getting into some dangerous waters.'

The essence of good presentations and speeches

Nobody, but nobody, thanks you for a long presentation, says Sir Stuart Rose. 'The one thing I have learned in the last decade of communicating is that short is better. You have to take the time to distil what you want to say down to its essence. Keep it short and simple and it is amazing how people will thank you and retain what you have said.'

Graham Mackay advises never to try and show off how clever you are when making a presentation. 'PowerPoint is the invention of the devil and it encourages disjointed thought. Great communication is about real clarity, and clarity has many enemies. One is business jargon, one is PowerPoint and another is length. You have to avoid being abstract or conceptual, because this doesn't grab people's attention. You need story and you need anecdote to fix the message in people's minds. People relate to hard concrete examples.'

Both Philip Green and John Connolly stress that you have to own your speech if you are to deliver it well. Senior leaders often have speeches and presentations written for them. They then give little time to rehearsing them and their delivery can be dull and inauthentic. If you edit the speech and rewrite in your own words the key parts of it, including the introduction and the close, you will be more confident and able to give a better performance.

In my coaching, I always say that confidence is the key. We have already discussed how people can give a technically poor delivery but get a great reception, if the messages are delivered with passion and self-belief, and especially when the points resonate with the audience. Often, when rehearsing leaders, I know that my job is simply to give them confidence rather than pick apart their technique. As we saw in Chapter 12 about storytelling, real confidence comes from telling stories you know and love and using those as the pillars of any talk, drawing on the stories to make the points you want. Avoid drowning the audience in facts. When you have a powerful point of view, about which you feel passionately, you will deliver your speech well.

Ideally, you should speak without notes. Lord Sharman and Simon Calver are both advocates of standing up and speaking in a conversational style to the audience.

Says Lord Sharman: 'If you want them to believe that you believe in something, then don't speak from notes. I always remember the first speech I ever made to the KPMG assembled partners, when I was the senior partner designate. The previous speaker had performed from behind the lectern and I decided to walk to the front of the stage and said: "When you elected me I think you knew what you were doing, so now I want to tell you what I think we need to do." I had been thinking about these issues for quite some time and was very clear about the key things we needed to tackle. I spoke for 40 minutes about the issues facing us and the reaction was quite amazing. The feedback was that 80 per cent of the people said I absolutely knew what needed to be done and they were persuaded by my conviction. About 20 per cent were trying to figure out how I did it without an autocue. When you speak without notes what comes across is the strength of your conviction.'

Simon Calver says: 'You should always speak to audiences like you're speaking to people across the dinner table. Keep it simple, speak with conviction and never use jargon. This is how you get your own personality and your own feelings across. You have to learn to use all the same conversational cues that you would normally use – facial expressions and gestures and body language. The danger is standing up behind a lectern and looking wooden and therefore being unconvincing.'

Lady Barbara Judge says that professional training is invaluable for giving speeches and presentations. 'You get so little time to make a positive impression, and some techniques are very simple and effective. Always remember to smile when you start. Look people in the eyes. Always write your own material and know it very well. Write it for the ear and not for the page. Little things like that can make a difference.'

I once coached a senior executive who, in spite of the best efforts of his staff and my urging, remained stubbornly wooden during his presentations. In the feedback from staff, they always commented on this and it was undermining his credibility. However, we found a glimmer of hope in the fact that people really enjoyed his performance during the short question-and-answer session. Over the next few town hall meetings, we gradually shortened his speech from half an hour to just 10 minutes, and allowed between 50 and 80 minutes for questions. When he answered questions, he became much more animated and passionate, and spoke without any notes.

It was not surprising that his rating increased dramatically when we shortened the formal part of his speech. It is good advice – if possible, always allow more time for questions and answers, and bring a few of your own questions along to get the session going. ('If I was you I would have asked about...'). If you make that the question about the 'elephant in the room' that everyone wants to ask about but is too afraid to, you are sure to provoke a lively debate.

The final tip is always to remember what is called 'the rule of threes'. People usually can only remember three points. Organize your speech around three key points and use the rule of threes when you make points. Some of the most memorable political points and corporate slogans come in threes. For example:

- Location, location, location.
- Veni, vidi, vici (I came, I saw, I conquered).
- Vorsprung durch technik (Audi).
- Never knowingly undersold (John Lewis, department store chain).
- Every little helps (Tesco, grocery chain).
- Just do it (Nike).
- Government of the people, by the people, for the people.
- Friends, Romans, countrymen.
- Blood, sweat and tears.

All are memorable and all are effective. Good advice is to craft a really good finishing line, the one that people remember long after you've sat down. You might even consider using the rule of threes in a finishing line.

In summary, then, perhaps the best advice on speech giving comes from US president Franklin D Roosevelt, who said: 'Be sincere, be brief, be seated.'

Communicating in a crisis

The first thing you are hit with in a crisis is a great paradox: at a time when you probably least want to have to say something, the greatest danger is in saying nothing at all.

Having worked with clients experiencing crises in a number of highly controversial and sensitive industries, including chemicals, nuclear and airlines, the one thing I know is that you will be deluged when a crisis first hits. The media will probably know about it before you do, and will be clamouring for information. The problem will be that, usually, you are still trying to find out what happened and are unable to comment. If you do that, then you will be chasing the agenda and always on the defensive.

To cope with these situations, you have to have planned ahead, you have to have considered all possibilities and worked out beforehand what you would do in each dreadful scenario. Many crises are simply issues that have got out of hand and could easily have been foretold. Some, however, do strike you suddenly, without a chance to anticipate. Effective communication before, during and after a crisis can significantly alter the outcome of the crisis.

Lord Stevens of Monitor Quest says it is essential to get ahead of the game. 'Crisis management and risk management are the most important things for a leader to consider in this transparent and fast-paced world. It is essential that you work out strategically what you will do in a crisis and how you're going to behave when things go very wrong – and they will go wrong, whatever kind of business you're in. You have to have a course of action, and in that you have to have every detail worked out.

'For example, when I was police commissioner, I used to have a spare set of uniforms in my flat in case Scotland Yard was blown up. That way I would be able to come out in front of the television cameras with my uniform on and say "Calm down, we're in control and we will do what is necessary." So attention to detail is critical. You also need people around you who have been through this kind of thing before, who can keep calm and help you to survive.'

The golden rule of crisis communications

Even with the best planning, in the early stages of a crisis the simple rule is to tell people what you know and only what you know. You have to recognize how emotional people will be, especially when there are fatalities or life-threatening circumstances, and the golden rule is that emotional people do not respond well to factual argument or rational reasoning.

I believe this to be one of the big mistakes that Tony Hayward made. Even though he may have been correct about the size and impact of the oil spill, it was a fatal error of judgement in regard to people's emotional response. Saying it was a drop in the ocean may have been right, but for residents looking at their oil-soaked beaches it was staggeringly insensitive. Then, when he put his own needs ahead of others by saying he wanted his life back, he sealed his fate. He was not forgiven.

He was right to take ownership of the problem. Leaders must get in front of the cameras and microphones and take accountability for the incident, and responsibility for fixing it. They must talk to their concerns for everybody involved; they must talk about their commitment to solving the problem, and they must talk about the benefits that will be derived when the problem is solved. Finally, they must promise that the underlying causes will be corrected so that mistakes like this can never be made again in the future.

You will notice that none of this requires facts – all of it requires emotional empathy from a leader and the ability to recognize how all of those affected will be feeling, and what they will want to hear. This is the time when the manual doesn't help. Sifting your way through a huge book of procedures will slow everything down at a time when you need to be working fastest. The best companies run crisis simulations that cause participants to sweat and suffer palpitations because they are so realistic. By doing this, when an actual crisis hits, you don't have to think, you just respond. And you don't have to dig out the manual because how to react has been ingrained in you.

Lord Mervyn Davies says that in a world where news can move across continents in milliseconds, the nature of crisis management has changed. Every leader is obliged to thoroughly examine their own operations and try to imagine the worst that could happen. They also need to consider things that are beyond their control.

'I give a speech in which I say to people that they should try to imagine me standing up a decade earlier and telling them that a great wave is going to come and kill hundreds of thousands of people, that the Royal Bank of Scotland will go bust, that New Orleans will disappear, that jet aircraft will fly into the World Trade Center, that a chicken with a virus in the Far East will infect a human being and cause a global panic, that an incredible volcano will cause devastation in Japan.

'If I'd given that speech 10 years ago people would have said that I was nuts, but what you learn in business is that you have to be prepared for uncertainty and constant change. The more prepared you are for uncertainty and unlikely events, the better you will handle them. A key part of that is how you will set context and communicate through those periods.'

In a crisis, go to your values for guidance

When a crisis hits, it is the most important time for a leader to go to their heart. Fields Wicker-Miurin of Leaders' Quest says that it is in a crisis that your values matter most. 'At these times leaders must draw on their values to decide on the right thing to do, and recognize the human needs that must be addressed.'

My experience tells me that it is only by doing the right thing in the immediate aftermath of a crisis that you avoid turning it into a catastrophe. It is not the crisis itself but the aftermath that can destroy your enterprise. People understand that mistakes happen in everyday life. They will be less forgiving of negligent mistakes, but they will want to hear you admit mistakes, and they will want to see you doing everything in your power to fix the problem and ensure it won't happen again. And they want you to do what is right by those who've been hurt or had their lives disrupted by the incident.

Communication without action can lead to allegations of spin and be more damaging in the long run. Lawyers will argue that you need to constrain what you say to avoid the legal consequences that will cost a huge price in the courts. I believe that if you lose in the court of public opinion, the damage can be much deeper and much longer lasting. If your licence to operate is removed, then you have no business and you have no future.

The best leaders take full responsibility during a crisis and stand up for their organization. Sir Christopher Gent of GSK says every leader should ensure that their organization is set up to cope with the crisis. Furthermore, they should recognize that they will be the one in the spotlight when it occurs.

'I once had a candidate to be chief executive who was very unsure about this aspect of the role,' says Sir Christopher. 'I could tell that in the back of his mind it was a big concern. He didn't get the job, because standing up and taking the full brunt of a crisis and handling the media are very much part of the leader's role and you have to be up for it. You have to be prepared to get up there and set the agenda, and be seen to be taking control. You have to have all of your media channels and lines of communication sorted out, you have to have your more discreet, specialized communication channels ready, and you have to be able to be on the front foot within 24 hours, or else you will be chasing the game and that can be disastrous.'

A marathon run at full speed

Many a CEO has fallen foul of a crisis by believing that it will be a sprint, when usually they are marathons. However, it is a marathon run at full speed.

Social websites, tweeting, ubiquitous mobile telephones with cameras and video capability have forced companies in crisis to have to respond with lightning-fast reactions. If you are still having to set up the channels at the beginning of the crisis, you will never get on top of the situation. You have to have thought through all the channels that you're going to use in the event that the crisis hits you, and that will need to include all the modern channels of communication as well.

Christopher Garnett of the Olympic Delivery Authority was one of the two leaders of the Eurostar independent review into a pre-Christmas crisis in which 2,000 passengers were stranded when trains came through heavy snow into the Eurotunnel between Britain and France. Among the many criticisms, one had to do with the lack of information provided to people during the crisis. Both Eurostar and Eurotunnel took some sharp words over the confusion and lack of information. Christopher called for better information equipment at the terminals, fit for purpose in the event of major disruptions, including variable message boards.

'One of the things we had to look at while writing the report was the speed at which they had to respond because of the internet. Afterwards, British Airways was keen to see Eurostar, to try and learn lessons about the internet and instant blogs. The real lesson was that you have to be even faster getting your story out and your information up to date during a crisis these days, because people involved in the crisis will be able to communicate and you will be found wanting if you can't.'

Equally, says Christopher, if you are the leader appearing as a spokesperson, you might not always have the information to hand. In that case you need to tell people when you will have something for them so that you can start managing expectations. 'You don't have to be totally driven by the deadlines of the media, and you also have to remember to pace yourself. You've got to get some sleep sometime, otherwise your judgement goes, you may get short-tempered when giving answers and you will come over very badly in an interview – and that's the one that they will show over and over again.'

Christopher, who had to communicate during two serious train accidents, says that even when the story is all over the news, it is amazing how many people don't see it. 'We have to be careful about managing the situation through the filter of newspaper and television headlines. The newspapers and TV and radio broadcasters feed off each other and report on each other's headlines and you have to be very careful that you don't slant your decision making through the prism of the media and miss listening to the far more important groups that you depend on for your survival.'

You have to stay in touch with all of the audiences affected, and you have to find ways of understanding what they are saying and how they are feeling. Using market researchers, web analysts and your own network of influences is critical at this stage in order to understand what the people who really matter to you are really thinking.

And what about the web and social media and Twitter and...?

The leaders I interviewed were split in their views about modern communication technology. Some felt that the radical transparency that came with modern channels made leadership much more difficult and was an unwelcome imposition, because it could give undue weight to insignificant audiences, who would always have an anti-point of view, and who did not represent the mainstream stakeholder views that the organization depended on.

Others, like Phil Bentley at British Gas, embraced new media channels as a way to build better and deeper relationships with key stakeholder groups, especially customers. All of them, however, recognized the need to engage in using the new media, even if leaders didn't understand these themselves. There was simply no choice.

Rupert Gavin of Odeon and UCI Cinemas says that his company has decided to take a much more active presence in social networks. 'We have to manage that presence very carefully, otherwise it could cause us significant problems. We have empowered a lot more people inside the company to speak on behalf of the company, and to express views on behalf of the company. It is impossible to control that, so we have had to sharpen our values framework, in order to ensure that the people representing the company online, and having to respond to queries and issues within seconds, can do so within the company ethos.

'When one of our cinema managers has to respond to an angry customer on a Saturday afternoon and doesn't have the time to go to his manager for advice on how to handle a situation, the values framework will help them to make the right decision. The difference is that the angry customer at a cinema can be heard by about 10 people within earshot. On social networks, you've got potentially tens of millions of people who can jump on any inappropriate or confrontational response that one of our staff may post.

'These sorts of things can become a national issue with a degree of rapidity that is scary. But you just have to have a more interactive presence online these days, and you have to ensure your own people understand the values so that they don't say anything inappropriate. It's just one of the pressures of the modern world – and the advantages far outweigh the disadvantages.'

KEY POINTS FROM CHAPTER 14

- Always prepare properly for any appearance on a public platform – and never make glib comments off script; too many rocks await you in those dangerous waters.

- In public, every word counts, and can count against you, so weigh every word carefully.

- The essence of good public speaking is to keep it short and simple, and use the rule of threes.

- You should always 'own' any speech you give, and speak about things you care about.

- It is not just about technique; it is about passion.

- Brevity matters. It really, really matters.

- Always allow time for questions. You'll probably be better in those.

- Handling the media requires special training: you have to be comfortable with all forms of media.

- When talking to journalists, remember the journalist is not your audience. Be clear about who you are talking to and why.

- Prepare for the inevitable crisis, and ensure you have put in place all the necessary channels of communication before a crisis occurs.

- In a crisis, it is critical to do the right thing and communicate those actions, always empathizing with people who have been affected, or else you could turn a crisis into a catastrophe.

- Breathtaking speed will be the issue, and at those times only your corporate values and sense of true north can help you stay on track. Emphasize these to everyone involved in helping to sort out the crisis.

- Embrace modern media channels; and if you don't get it, get someone who does.
- Speaking on public platforms requires a great deal of practice.
- Always remember that rehearsing makes a good speaker a great speaker.
- Never stop pursuing perfection – always ask trusted advisers for tough feedback after every performance.
- Embrace the digital age of transparency. The risks are higher but the rewards are greater.
- If you don't know how to, make sure you hire someone who does.

PART FOUR
Conclusion

Learn, rehearse, review, improve; become fluent in the language of leaders

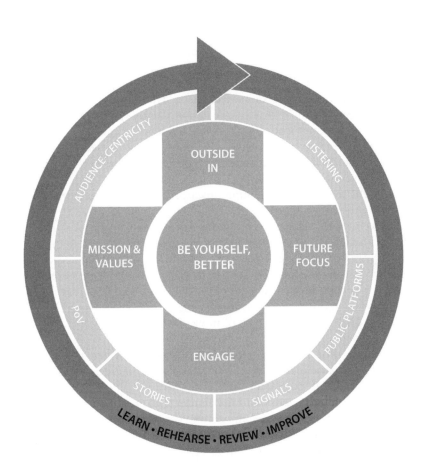

15

After years of coaching senior leaders on communication, I am still impressed with the amount of effort most of them put into trying to be a better communicator. Not one of the leaders in this book was prepared to give themselves a mark of 10/10 as a communicator, in spite of decades of experience. They all believed they had to keep striving to get better.

Moya Greene of the Royal Mail says that every leader needs to devote time and effort to improving their communication skills. 'You have to prepare, and you have to practise. As a leader you have to appear in front of so many publics and you only have a few seconds to make a good impression – to make your board feel comfortable, your employees feel proud or enhance the reputation of the business you lead.'

Antony Jenkins of Barclays says that he probably spends about 80 per cent of his time on communications activities. 'I would define my job as being the chief advocate for Barclays Global Retail Banking, so it's terribly important I get it right. I am quite used to adapting my style for different situations with employees, but leaders also have to do more external and internal communications and big set-piece events. These set-piece events are much more formal and you have to stick to the script. I work hard to keep improving in this area. You can never stop getting better.'

Sir Christopher Gent believes there is far too little emphasis placed on communications training in business. 'Not only does a leader have to make sure that they personally are capable when it comes to all forms of communication, but they should also make sure that senior people around them are also getting the right professional assistance. They should also be ensuring that they are making their whole organization a better-communicating organization. Good communication is crucial to success.'

Even when leaders have received the best training in media handling or speech making, there is no substitute for rehearsal. The problem is that most leaders' diaries are so busy that rehearsal often feels like an optional extra. However, the most successful communicators, in the most senior positions, never leave things to chance.

Lord Mervyn Davies says there is no substitute for being properly prepared. 'After a lifetime of giving presentations and speeches around the world, nothing prepared me for the nerves that I felt for my maiden speech in the House of Lords. You always face new situations and you have to give the time to being prepared. The way I describe it to people is that if you are a professional footballer, you train during the week, you practise taking penalties, you practise every type of movement within the game. You never stop practising in order to get better.

'Communication is so important to business leaders that they can't just play the game without learning the right skills and having the right coaching. Too often chief executives and leaders are unwilling to set aside the time, but they need to get better at communication and be prepared to be taken out of their comfort zone in order to get better.'

Sir Clive Woodward has a saying he calls 'T-CUP' – thinking correctly under pressure. 'It applies to sport or business, to communication, to everything you do. It is the best definition of a champion – someone who thinks correctly when pressure is at its greatest.

'When you are communicating, if you are hit with something you have never thought about before, you can choke, freeze, bottle it – all those terrible words. You can't experience every possible circumstance, but you can think through every scenario. Then, when asked, you will deliver your message, and answer questions as you would want to. It is vital to spend time thinking things through beforehand.'

Lord Stevens says that even after decades of communicating on public platforms, on behalf of the police, on behalf of national criminal inquiries or as chancellor of Northumbria University, he is still seeking to improve his capability.

'After every interview with the media or every appearance on stage, I ask people whom I trust what I did wrong and what I could do better next time. You have to keep assessing how you've performed and you have to be prepared to take a fair bit of criticism, otherwise you're not going to improve. Always, always, always make sure you have prepared adequately for every public platform, and then make sure you get feedback on your performance. Communicating to the public is just too important to leave to chance.'

A top-three skill of leadership, yet sadly neglected

Few leaders that I have met in my career have had well-rounded communications training. The leaders I interviewed for this book mostly learned through a process of osmosis, supplemented by occasional specialist training in media handling or speech making. They all recognized the vital role that communication has to play in enabling great performance, and increasingly seek good 'people skills' in the leaders they hire or promote. Yet I did not find evidence of widespread leadership communication training. It is almost as if aspiring leaders should be naturally good at communicating, or else.

I kept hearing that the job of leaders is to create more leaders. Ralph Nader, a renowned American attorney and political activist, says that the function of leadership is 'to produce more leaders, not more followers'. This is where we face our biggest challenge. How do we enable all those new leaders to be motivational and inspirational, emotionally intelligent and trustworthy communicators?

In a recent feature in *The Times* of London on MBA courses, the newspaper reported that MBA students were frequently weak in communication skills. At best, the courses they attended gave a nod towards presentation skills, but whether they were trained to get their messages across effectively was a matter of some controversy. Headhunters, it said, found that even students hired from the best schools could not communicate. University deans were equally scathing. Communication, along with other supposedly soft management skills, has too long been neglected in many schools.

It is an issue which not only affects the fortunes of businesses, but also the prosperity of nations.

Peter Cheese, chairman of the Institute of Leadership and Management, Europe's leading management organization, says that good leadership in business is the key to organizational effectiveness and social and economic prosperity. He continues: 'Our challenge is that the traditional model for what constitutes a good leader is changing. How we develop our leaders must change too. The institute recently conducted a survey of HR professionals from global businesses. First and foremost, the senior HR professionals we approached emphasized a distinct set of personal characteristics that future leaders need to possess. These were principally in the relationship and interpersonal domain – they sought visionary, motivational and inspirational people who are emotionally intelligent, trustworthy, natural leaders and communicators, and who are also driven and ambitious.

'HR professionals want leaders who can understand, inspire and motivate people. The ability to motivate and inspire others was the characteristic most commonly cited as important when recruiting senior leaders.

'Many of the most desirable personal characteristics, such as the ability to motivate others, emotional intelligence and being a good communicator can be learnt. While there is a general acceptance that many aspects of leadership can be taught, how can we equip aspiring leaders and managers with an all-round leadership perspective? The research shows that there is certainly a training and development need.'

As I have said already, all but a few leaders interviewed for this book identified communication as a top-three skill of leadership. Strategic ability was inevitably placed at number one. However, they cautioned, the best strategy was useless if people could not be inspired to help deliver it.

Strive to be an excellent communicator, and you will improve results

Good leaders steer organizations to success by inspiring and motivating followers, by providing a moral compass for employees to set direction and by communicating a compelling vision for the future. For this reason, I believe that leaders should place communication and people skills at the top of their training agendas if they are to unlock the real potential in their organizations.

I also believe that striving to be an excellent communicator should be just as important to every leader as striving to improve performance. You simply can't achieve the one without the other. Leaders who communicate with courage and clarity, with passion, with authenticity, who listen as well as talk can significantly improve the performance of the teams or organizations they lead.

The difference between competent communication and inspiring communication can be the difference between poor performance and outstanding results. The ability to inspire and motivate people is now one of the most needed attributes of leaders.

In my interviews and research, I found little evidence of a model for leadership communication, embracing all of the lessons in this book. Undoubtedly, the leaders I know devote time to, and understand the value of, communication, but have no schema for thinking about it. (A schema is a mental model structured in such a way as to make things easy to recognize or remember. It is often presented as a diagrammatic representation, an outline or model.)

This book has been about presenting you with a model for leadership communications. I urge you to use the model as a catalyst for your leadership communication. It doesn't have all the answers, but it will focus you on the things you need to think about.

I believe it will be just as useful to experienced leaders as to aspiring leaders.

I hope it will become your favourite schema, and that you will use it often. Most of all, I hope it will help you to become fluent in the language of leaders.

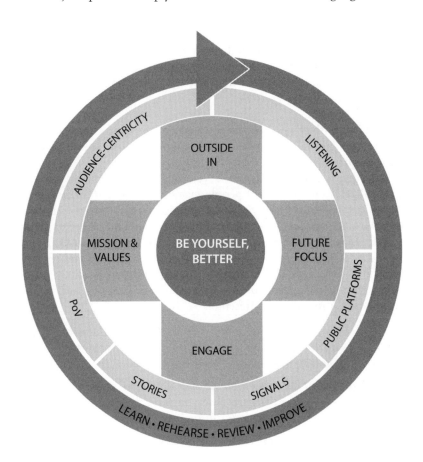

16 If you remember nothing else...

At the end of every interview I asked each leader the following question: 'If there is only one point that you would have me take away from everything that you have said today, what would that be?'

The idea was that I would be able to compile a list of the points most frequently brought up, as a useful summary with which to end the book. I anticipated finishing with around 10 key points to report. I was surprised at the uniformity of responses to this question. But then again, in hindsight, it makes absolute sense.

In fifth place, with 9 per cent of the vote, is the idea that leaders must recognize how critical it is to be a good communicator, and never give up trying to improve.

As a leader, you will always be developing your communication skills. When you're leading groups of people inside an organization, you need to become a better listener, and you need to become more effective at holding productive meetings, and coaching and mentoring people to better performance. The more senior you become, the more likely you are to have to deal with the media, give speeches, speak to government ministers and regulators, or present to investors. These require specialist training, constant practice, and your guiding principle should be that only rehearsal will turn you from a good presenter into a great presenter.

'I believe passionately in the power of communication and its importance as a skill for all leaders within an organization. Without it, you cannot build trust, nor can you inspire people.' – Nicholas Young

'The most important thing to remember is how critical it is to be a good communicator and to make sure that you have a good communications capability within your whole organization.' – Christopher Gent

'As a leader, communication is the job and you should always be trying to get better at it.' – Antony Jenkins

'Always prepare properly and you will communicate well.'
– Clive Woodward

Equal third, with 12 per cent of the vote, is the need for leaders to be visible, constantly on the road, engaging with people in an ongoing conversation.

Leaders have to find ways of making themselves more visible, and ensuring that everyone across the organization hears what they've got to say. Communicating is the job of leadership, and people who aren't out there, communicating every day, should question their own performance. An adjunct to this point is the need to keep repeating and repeating and repeating, to ensure that everyone hears and understands the message.

'Communicate, communicate, communicate. You've just got to keep on communicating. But that can't work on its own; you also need a good strategy.' – Phil Bentley

'The only way you can lead is by being visible. If you're visible you will be out and about. If you are out and about you will be listening to your customers, to people in the business, and to all the people who matter to your organization. In order to tune in with the right communication, you have to have listened.' – Paul Drechsler

'The best communication, no matter how complex the message is, is about simple language repeated over and over and over and over again. The danger is that we tire of hearing our own message when many people haven't heard it at all. You've got to find ways to make your message sound as fresh on the 157,000th time as it was on day one.' – Amelia Fawcett

'You have to be visible. For people to trust the CEO, they have to be exposed to him or her.' – John Gildersleeve

'You can never do enough communication. At the end of every week I look at my diary and ask myself whether I spent enough time communicating. You have to be tough on yourself and if you think you haven't, then you've got to do a better job the following week.' – Moya Greene

'Just keep showing up, even when times are bad. That's the most powerful act of communication of all.' – Barbara Stocking

Joint third is the need to be focused on your audience, both in terms of listening to people and in crafting the right messages.

A total of 12 per cent of leaders said that it is impossible to communicate effectively unless you had your audience clearly in mind. That means you have to listen carefully to their concerns and issues, and you have to learn to ensure your communication resonates. Listening is itself often an inspiring act of leadership.

'Good communication starts with putting yourself in the shoes of the people you're going to talk to. If everybody started from that point, they would be much more effective communicators.' – Barbara Cassani

'It's all about understanding your audience and crafting your message in a way that is appropriate for that audience.' – Philip Green

'Always remember who your audience is.' – Charles Guthrie

'Good communication is two-way communication. It is about mutual trust, confidence and respect between the leader and the led.' – Mike Jackson

'"Grant me, O Lord, a listening heart" is what King Solomon asked of the Lord, when offered anything he desired.' – Chris Satterthwaite

The second most often raised point, cited by 20 per cent of the leaders, is the importance of effectively communicating your vision, your values and your mission.

The military concept of 'commander's intent' – clearly articulating exactly what it is you're trying to achieve – is crucial, in order to help everybody in the business understand your goals and their role in achieving them. This vision of success has to be united with a powerful mission and a liberating set of values, all of which create a framework for action and decision making throughout the organization. It has to be easy to understand, memorable, motivating and unambiguous. Only then will everyone in the organization be able to take action, and act with greater speed and creativity in pursuit of the goals.

'It's all about ensuring everybody in the organization – from top to bottom – knows exactly what you're trying to achieve and is involved in achieving it.'
– Maurice Flanagan

'The most important communication issue is the primacy of the values and the cultural framework, which ensure everyone in the organization can operate to the best of their ability.' – Rupert Gavin

'Having listened to your customers to get the strategy as tightly focused as you dare make it, the most important thing is being remorseless about communicating it. There is absolutely no substitute for shoe leather.'
– Tom Hughes-Hallett

'Your vision and your values are the most important thing, and you have to devote huge amounts of time to communicating them.' – Nick Partridge

'It is the crucial nature of formulating and communicating your intent.'
– Richard Dannatt

'You have to have a really clear vision. But there's no point in having a vision unless you communicate it to everyone.' – Ron Dennis

The single most important idea, raised by 45 per cent of the leaders – more than twice as many times as the next most often raised point – is the need to look first to yourself before you can become a truly great communicator.

You have to learn to show your passion if you are to inspire others to great performance. You have to be authentic and to act at all times with integrity. Communication, they said, is not about technically perfect delivery, it is all about whether you are able to move people to change their behaviour and achieve the result you desire. How can you persuade people to a cause if you are only half convinced yourself? The passion must come from truly understanding what it is you want to do, why it is important, how you want to do it, and what values are most important to you. Most of all, it comes from the absolute belief that what you want to do can be done.

'You have to believe in what you are saying. You can never communicate well if you don't – you'd have to be a professional actor. But if you are a business leader you have to have that conviction to convey the conviction.'
– Ayman Asfari

'Self-belief and conviction are the most important things. You have to have conviction about principles, conviction about decisions and the conviction to prosecute an agenda.' – Mick Davis

'It all comes down to honesty, integrity, values and respect. People see that.'
– Christopher Garnett

'To communicate effectively, you have to do so with integrity and you have to believe what you are saying. You have to understand the audience and tell them as you mean it.' – John Heaps

'What matters most is your integrity and how you show it in everything you do. Your success as a leader hinges on whether you can build trust. The integrity underpinning your communication will help people decide whether to trust you, how much to trust you, and what to trust you about.'
– Graham Mackay

'The most important thing is authenticity and sincerity and walking the talk. You can get away with a lot of shortcomings in your communication style if you have high levels of authenticity and integrity.' – Paul Polman

'You have to communicate honestly and openly or else you will be in peril.'
– Stuart Rose

'If you are a person who finds showmanship difficult, a key thought is that sincerity is powerful and crucial in communications. Authenticity can count for more than a flash and fluent delivery.' – Colin Matthews

'If you don't have passion, go home, for goodness sake, because you'll be going nowhere.' – Frank Williams

'The single most important thing about communication is to remember that as a leader your job is to inspire, and you cannot inspire unless people feel your passion.' – John Connolly

'Good communication is passionate communication.' – Ron Sandler

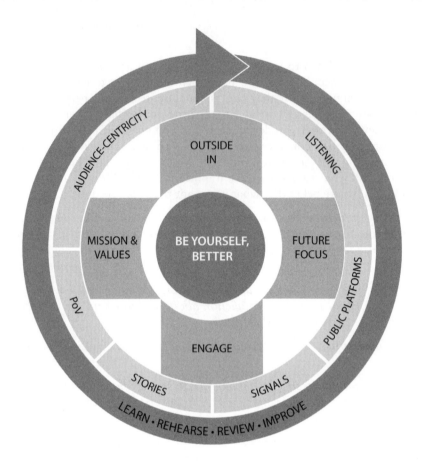

The fundamentals

1 Learn to be yourself, better.
2 Provide a framework for leadership and action, through mission and values.
3 Communicate the future to drive the present.
4 Bring the outside in and focus on relationships and trust.
5 Engage and align through potent conversations.

Communicate, communicate, communicate.

Receiving

6 Remember it's all about them – the need for audience centricity.
7 Give them a damn good listening to – the inspiring effect of listening leaders.

Sending

8 Stand up to stand out – why you need a point of view.
9 Use the power of stories as the superglue of messages.
10 Watch out for the signals beyond the words.
11 Prepare properly for public platforms – speeches, media and crisis handling.

Continuous improvement

12 Learn, rehearse, review, improve – become fluent in the language of leaders.

Meet the leaders interviewed for this book

Dame Helen Alexander

Dame Helen Alexander is the immediate past president of the Confederation of British Industry (CBI), the premier lobbying organization for UK business on national and international issues. She is also chair of Incisive Media and of the Port of London Authority (PLA).

She is currently non-executive director and chair of the remuneration committee at Centrica plc (2003) and Rolls-Royce Group plc (2007), and senior adviser to Bain Capital.

Helen is a trustee of the WWW (World Wide Web) Foundation, deputy chair of the Governors and chair of the Education Committee at St Paul's Girls' School, and chair of the Business Advisory Council of the Said Business School, Oxford University.

She was chief executive of the Economist Group until 2008, having joined the company in 1985 and been managing director of the Economist Intelligence Unit from 1993 to 1997. In addition to her experience at the helm of an international business, Helen also has board experience across a range of sectors. She was a non-executive director at Northern Foods plc (1994–2002) and at BT plc (1998–2002). She has an MBA from INSEAD and is an Honorary Fellow of Hertford College, Oxford.

Ayman Asfari

Ayman Asfari is group chief executive of Petrofac Ltd, an international provider of facilities solutions to the oil and gas production and processing industries. Petrofac has around 14,000 employees, with 26 offices worldwide.

Ayman studied engineering in the United States and then got a construction job in Oman to fund an MBA at Wharton, Pennsylvania, but made so much money building infrastructure for the oil industry that he never went back to business school. He joined Petrofac in 1991, bought out Petrofac in 2001 and the company was listed in 2005, making him a rich man.

Ayman has more than 30 years' experience in the oil and gas industry. He is a member of the board of trustees of the American University of Beirut. He funds scholarships in the Middle East and a Centre for Syrian Studies at St Andrews, and in 2010 he gave £10 million to his sister to fund other charitable works.

Beverley Aspinall

Beverley Aspinall is managing director of Fortnum & Mason, a world-famous department store and royal warrant holder (the Queen's grocer), situated in central London, with two other branches in Japan. Fortnum's headquarters are located at 181 Piccadilly in London, where it was established in 1707 by William Fortnum and Hugh Mason.

She joined the John Lewis Partnership straight from university and worked both as a buyer and within store management. In 1995 she became managing director of John Lewis Peterborough and was then appointed managing director of Peter Jones, Sloane Square in 1997, heading the £100 million refurbishment of the store.

She became managing director of Fortnum & Mason in 2005, and soon oversaw a £24 million refurbishment of the store. Before joining John Lewis, Beverley gained a linguistics degree from the University of York. She is married and lives in Norfolk with her husband and two children.

Sir Anthony Bamford

Sir Anthony Bamford is chairman and managing director of JCB. He succeeded his father in 1975. His father, Joseph Cyril Bamford, founded the company on the day his son was born, 23 October 1945. Sir Anthony's career began with a two-year engineering apprenticeship at Massey Ferguson in France before he started at the JCB world headquarters in Rocester, Staffordshire, in 1964.

Under Sir Anthony's leadership, JCB has grown to become one of the world's largest and most successful construction equipment manufacturers. JCB now exports more than 75 per cent of its machines to 150 countries around the world. The company has eight plants in Staffordshire, two in Wrexham, one in Derbyshire, a factory in Savannah, Georgia, one in Brazil, three in India, one in China and one in Germany.

Sir Anthony has a lifelong interest in both classic and modern cars and it was his idea to make an attempt on the world diesel land-speed record with a car powered by JCB engines. In 2006 his vision saw the JCB Dieselmax car set a new diesel land-speed record of 350.092 mph on the Bonneville Salt Flats, USA. The record remains unbroken.

Kevin Beeston

Kevin Beeston is chairman of housebuilder Taylor Wimpey plc and holds a number of non-executive roles, having stood down as chairman of Serco Group plc in May 2010 following a 25-year career with the company.

An accountant by training, Kevin joined Serco in 1985, since which time the company has developed from a small UK technical services business to become a leading FTSE 100 international service company. He was previously both chief executive and finance director before becoming chairman in 2002.

Kevin was appointed chairman of Taylor Wimpey plc in July 2010 and is also chairman of Partnerships in Care Ltd (owned by Cinven), the UK's leading independent provider of secure mental health services, and chairman of Domestic and

General, the leading provider of post point-of-sale extended warranty services. D&G is owned by private equity company Advent International.

He also served as a director of Ipswich Town Football Club from 2003 to 2008.

He is married to Jayne and they live in Shepperton, Middlesex with their three teenage children, a cat and a dog.

Phil Bentley

Phil Bentley has been the managing director of British Gas since March 2007. Employing 28,000 people in the UK, British Gas is the number-one energy and services provider to British homes and businesses. Previously he was group finance director and managing director Europe of Centrica plc. Phil joined Centrica in November 2000 from Diageo, where he was global finance director for Guinness-UDV. Prior to that he was group treasurer and director of risk management of Diageo plc.

Phil was previously at BP, where he spent 15 years in senior finance roles, six of which were spent in BP's exploration businesses in China, the United States and Egypt.

He holds a master's degree from Pembroke College, Oxford University and has an MBA from INSEAD in France. Phil is a fellow of the Chartered Institute of Management Accountants and is a member of the Association of Corporate Treasurers. Until March 2010 he was also a non-executive director and chairman of the audit committee of Kingfisher plc, the international home improvement retailer.

He is married with two teenage children and his interests include rugby, sailing, golf and horse riding.

Nick Buckles

Nick Buckles is chief executive of G4S plc, (formerly Group 4 Securicor) a global security services company headquartered in Crawley, in the United Kingdom. G4S is the world's largest security company. It has operations in

more than 125 countries, and employs more than 625,000 people. (It is the world's second-largest private sector employer, after Walmart.) G4S was formed from the merger of Group 4 and Securicor in 2004.

Nick was appointed to the board in May 2004 and was the company's deputy chief executive and chief operating officer. He became chief executive in July 2005. Nick joined Securicor in 1985 as a projects accountant. In 1996 he was appointed managing director of Securicor Cash Services (UK) and became chief executive of the security division of Securicor in 1999.

He was appointed to the board of Securicor plc in 2000 and became its chief executive in January 2002. Nick is a non-executive director of Arriva plc. He grew up in Essex, son of a local policeman. He is a West Ham fan.

Damon Buffini

Damon Buffini is a founding partner of private equity firm Permira and was chairman and managing partner from 1997 to 2010. Since 2000, Permira has helped to build numerous successful businesses across Europe including: Travelodge, one of Europe's largest hotel groups; global aviation services group Jet Aviation, which created approximately 2,400 new jobs while backed by Permira funds; and Inmarsat, the global satellite operator, which invested US$2 billion in new technology while in the Permira portfolio.

Damon is also co-founder of Breakthrough, a joint initiative between Permira and CAN that seeks to grow charities and social enterprises by utilizing the knowledge, skills and capital of the private equity industry.

Damon has a keen interest in education and social exclusion. He is president of Fairbridge, a nationwide charity that works to support over 4,000 young people per year, and Cambridge University Endowment Fund advisory board. He is a board member of the Royal Shakespeare Company. He was educated at the University of Cambridge, where he read law, and at Harvard Business School, where he gained an MBA.

Simon Calver

Simon Calver is CEO of LOVEFiLM, a leading European film and TV subscription service delivering films and TV shows online to people's PCs and to their TVs and PlayStation 3 consoles, as well as through its traditional postal DVD rental service. In 2011 it was acquired by Amazon.

Previously Simon has held leadership roles in both private growth companies and large multinationals including president of River-deep, the interactive digital education and productivity software company, and general manager and VP of Dell's UK and Ireland Consumer and Small Business operations.

Before that he was international VP of sales operations for Pepsi-Cola, based in the United States, and general manager and VP of Pepsi-Cola UK where he launched Pepsi Max, Pepsi Blue and the development of the Pepsi Music activity. He started his career as a graduate in Unilever and as a strategy consultant at Deloitte.

Barbara Cassani

Barbara Cassani was the founding chairman of the successful London 2012 Olympic bid. She recently joined the board of directors at Air Berlin. She gained public prominence as a corporate entrepreneur in 1998 when she founded a low-cost airline for parent British Airways. After three years, she led a high-profile management buyout, then sold the airline, Go Fly, to easyJet. She was named UK Businesswoman of the Year and co-authored the bestselling book *Go: an Airline Adventure*.

Barbara started her career in management consulting, then held a variety of strategic and management roles at British Airways, including general manager USA.

In 2003, she was appointed the founding chairman of the London Olympic Bid. When Lord Sebastian Coe took over as chairman, she served in a voluntary capacity as vice-chairman until the bid was won in 2005. In 2006, she joined the Spanish low-cost airline, Vueling, as a board director, and later became chairman. From 2008 until

2010, Barbara was executive chairman of Jurys Inn – a private equity-owned, fast-growing hotel group in the UK and Ireland.

Barbara splits her time between London and the Boston area with her husband, Guy Davis, and teenage children, Lauren and James. She is an avid rider and competes in amateur eventing competitions.

John Connolly

John Connolly has spent his whole professional career with Deloitte and is the immediate past senior partner and chief executive of the UK firm and a member of the board of partners. John was also global managing director of Deloitte Touche Tohmatsu and has been involved in important global roles with the firm for over 15 years. He served as chairman of the global management committee and a member of both the global executive and the global board of partners. Deloitte is the largest private professional services organization in the world, with about 170,000 staff at work in more than 150 countries, delivering audit, tax, consulting, enterprise risk and financial advisory services.

By background, John is a corporate finance partner, and has significant experience on a wide range of corporate transactions. He continues to have significant involvement with a wide range of clients and is the advisory partner on a number of the firm's major clients including The Royal Bank of Scotland, Vodafone and KKR.

He is a Manchester United fan and season ticket holder, and also loves horse racing. He owns four horses and is a keen opera fan.

General The Lord Dannatt

General The Lord Dannatt is the constable of the Tower of London and is a former Chief of The General Staff of the British Army. He started his career at the Royal Military Academy, Sandhurst, and was commissioned into the Green Howards as a second lieutenant on 30 July 1971. He served with the 1st Battalion in

Northern Ireland where he was awarded the Military Cross. He commanded 4th Armoured Brigade from 1989 to 1991 and served in Kosovo as Commander-in-Chief, Land Command in Bosnia.

He assumed the appointment of Chief of the General Staff in 2006, taking over from General Sir Mike Jackson. He was appointed constable of the Tower of London in 2009 after handing over his role to General Sir David Richards.

General Dannatt was created a cross-bench peer in 2010 and chose the title Baron Dannatt of Keswick. He enjoys cricket, tennis, rugby, football, skiing, fishing, shooting and reading. He is churchwarden of Keswick and Intwood, Norfolk.

Jeremy Darroch

Jeremy Darroch is chief executive of BSkyB, the largest pay-TV broadcaster in the United Kingdom, with more than 10 million subscribers.

Jeremy was appointed a director of the company in August 2004. He was appointed CEO in December 2007, having previously been chief financial officer since 2004. Prior to joining the company, Jeremy was group finance director of DSG International plc, formerly Dixons Group plc. Prior to DSG, Jeremy spent 12 years at Procter and Gamble in a variety of roles in the UK and Europe.

He is a non-executive director and the chairman of the audit committee of Marks & Spencer plc. He is also a board member of the charity Youth Sport Trust and a council member of the Council for Industry and Higher Education.

Jeremy was born in 1964, and is married to Karen, a GP, with three children. He is a Newcastle United fan.

Lord Mervyn Davies

Lord Mervyn Davies is a partner and vice-chairman of Corsair Capital, a private equity firm specializing in financial services. He is also non-executive chairman of PineBridge Investments Ltd and chair of the advisory board of Moelis and Co. He holds a non-executive director role at Diageo plc and is a non-executive independent director at Bharti Airtel Ltd.

Lord Davies was Minister for Trade, Investment and Small Business from January 2009 until May 2010, a joint role between the Department for Business, Innovation and Skills and the Foreign and Commonwealth Office, also with responsibility for Infrastructure UK.

Prior to that, he was chairman of Standard Chartered plc from November 2006. He joined the board of Standard Chartered plc in December 1997 and was group chief executive from November 2001 until 2006. He was a non-executive director at Tesco plc from 2003 to 2008.

Lord Davies is married with two children and is a fluent Welsh speaker.

Mick Davis

Mick Davis is chief executive of Xstrata plc, a global diversified mining and metals company, listed on the London Stock Exchange and headquartered in Zug, Switzerland. Xstrata has operations and projects in 20 countries and is the world's largest producer of export thermal coal, zinc and ferrochrome.

Mick was appointed chief executive, Xstrata AG in October 2001 and became chief executive and a member of the board of the newly-created Xstrata plc in February 2002. Previously, he was an executive director and chief financial officer of Billiton plc and chairman of Billiton Coal. Prior to joining Billiton, Mick was an executive director of South African state-owned Eskom, one of the world's largest electricity utilities.

In a personal capacity, Mick is chairman of the United Jewish Israel Appeal (UJIA,) and a member of the Jewish Leadership Council (JLC) and chairman of the JLC Executive Committee. In 2009, Mick and his wife Barbara, a solicitor, were appointed to the board of trustees for the Kew Foundation, which supports the work of the Royal Botanic Gardens, Kew.

Mick and Barbara live in London and have three children – Sarah, Ronit and Eita.

Ron Dennis

Ron Dennis is executive chairman of the McLaren Group, which encompasses McLaren Racing, McLaren Marketing, McLaren Electronic Systems, McLaren Applied Technologies and Absolute Taste. He is also executive chairman of McLaren Automotive.

Ron began his career in motor racing in 1966 with the Cooper Racing Car Company. He moved to join the Brabham Racing team and by 1968 he had been appointed to the position of chief mechanic to Sir Jack Brabham. Three years later he launched his own company, Rondel Racing.

In 1980, his company Project Four merged with Team McLaren Ltd to form McLaren International, which has won eight Constructors' World Championships. The team has also claimed the Drivers' World Championship on 12 occasions, most recently in 2008 with Lewis Hamilton.

In 1989 Ron co-founded McLaren Cars, which designed and manufactured the revolutionary F1 road car and then worked in collaboration with DaimlerChrysler on the Mercedes-Benz SLR McLaren high-performance sports car. The SLR was manufactured at the award-winning McLaren Technology Centre. McLaren Cars has since then been renamed McLaren Automotive, and began production of the McLaren MP4-12C high-performance sports car in 2011.

Paul Drechsler

Paul Drechsler is chairman and chief executive of the Wates Group, the largest family-owned construction services and development company, established by Edward Wates in 1897. Paul joined the Wates Group board in September 2004 as chief executive and was appointed chairman and chief executive in April 2006.

He was previously an executive director of ICI plc, chairman of ICI Pension Trustees Ltd, and a member of the World Business Council for Sustainable Development. He is the senior independent director of Filtrona plc, a member of the Trinity College Dublin Business School advisory board, chairman of the CBI energy policy committee and chair of the BITC education leadership team.

Thomas Enders

Thomas Enders is chief executive of Airbus, makers of the modern icon of the skies, the giant A380, as well as a range of other civil and military aircraft. Airbus employs 52,000 people around the world and recently sold its 10,000th aircraft.

Tom studied economics, political science and history at the University of Bonn and at the University of California in Los Angeles.

Prior to joining the aerospace industry in 1991 he worked as a member of the planning staff of the German Minister of Defence and subsequently held various positions, including chief of staff, director corporate development and technology, and head of defence systems, at DASA.

Following the creation of EADS in 2000, he was appointed CEO of the EADS Defence and Security Systems Division, holding this position until 2005 when he was appointed co-CEO of EADS. He took over as CEO of Airbus in 2007. Tom Enders became president of BDLI (German Aerospace Industry Association) in 2005.

He was born in 1958, and is married with four sons. He enjoys mountaineering, skiing and skydiving.

Dame Amelia Fawcett

Dame Amelia Fawcett is the chairman of Guardian Media Group (GMG) plc in London and a non-executive director of State Street Corporation in Boston, Massachusetts. Until June 2010 she was also chairman of Pensions First LLP, a financial services and systems solutions business, based in London,

Prior to joining the boards of GMG, Pensions First and State Street, Amelia worked for Morgan Stanley, first as an executive and then in a non-executive role. She started her career at the US law firm of Sullivan and Cromwell, first in New York and then in Paris. She joined Morgan Stanley in London in 1987, was appointed vice-president in 1990, an executive director in 1992 and managing director and the chief administrative officer for the firm's European operations in 1996. In 2002 she was appointed vice-chairman reporting to the chairman. As vice-chairman and chief operating officer, she was a member of the European management committee and the boards of directors of the firm's major European operating companies. She stepped down from her executive role in October 2006 and was a senior adviser to the firm until April 2007.

Dame Amelia, a British and American citizen, was born in Boston, Massachusetts, USA in 1956. She has a degree in history from Wellesley (1978) and a law degree from the University of Virginia (1983).

Her interests include fly fishing, sailing, hill walking and history.

Sir Maurice Flanagan

Sir Maurice Flanagan is executive vice-chairman, Emirates Airline and Group. Emirates is the national airline of Dubai, in the United Arab Emirates. It is the largest airline in the Middle East, and flies to 105 cities in 62 countries across six continents. The Emirates Group, which has over 50,000 employees, is wholly owned by the government of Dubai.

In 1953, Maurice joined BOAC, the forerunner of British Airways, as a graduate trainee, after serving in the Royal Air Force as a navigation officer.

In 1978, he left British Airways to become director and general manager of Dnata, the forerunner of Emirates and now its sister company. He became managing director of Emirates in 1985, when the airline began operations, and was appointed group managing director of the Emirates Group in 1990. He became vice-chairman and group president in July 2003 and was appointed executive vice-chairman in 2006.

Maurice received the Official Airline Guide (OAG) Lifetime Achievement Award during the 23rd annual OAG Airline of the Year Awards 2005 ceremony. It was presented both for his part in developing the Dubai-based international carrier into a major global airline, and also for his more than 50 years of dedicated service to the aviation industry. He is only the second recipient of the award.

Christopher Garnett

Christopher Garnett is a member of the board of the Olympic Delivery Authority and chair of the Olympic and Paralympics transport board. The Olympic Delivery Authority is the statutory corporation responsible for ensuring delivery of the venues, infrastructure and legacy for the 2012 Summer Olympic and Paralympic Games in London. It was established in 2006 and is the responsibility of the Department for Culture, Media and Sport.

Previously he was chief executive officer of Great North Eastern Railway (GNER) and simultaneously senior vice-president and chief executive of the Rail Division of Sea Containers, GNER's parent company. Before that he was commercial director of Eurotunnel.

He is non-executive director of Aggregate Industries Ltd, a supplier and manufacturer of concrete and aggregate products, and non-executive director of Anglian Water Services Ltd.

His main hobby is sailing.

Rupert Gavin

Rupert Gavin is chief executive of Odeon and UCI Cinemas Group, the largest European cinema chain, with 210 cinemas and 1,900 screens in the UK, Spain, Italy, Germany, Austria, Portugal and Ireland. From 1998 to 2004 he was chief executive of BBC Worldwide.

From 1994 to 1998 he was at British Telecom, latterly managing director of BT's UK consumer operation. From 1987 to 1994 he was at Dixons, latterly as deputy managing director of Dixons Stores Group in the UK. Prior to 1987, he held various positions in the marketing and advertising industry.

He started life as a writer in radio, theatre, film and music. He is an advisory director and shareholder of Ambassador Theatre Group, the largest theatre group in the UK, as well as chairman of his own West End production company.

Sir Christopher Gent

Sir Christopher Gent became chairman of GlaxoSmithKline plc (GSK) in January 2005. Sir Christopher is the former chief executive officer of Vodafone Group plc. Prior to his retirement from Vodafone in July 2003, he had been a member of its board since August 1985 and its chief executive officer since January 1997. He was also chairman of the supervisory board of Mannesmann AG, a non-executive director of China Mobile (Hong Kong) Ltd, and on the board of Verizon Wireless.

Prior to joining Vodafone in 1985, Sir Christopher was director of Network Services at ICL. In this role, he was managing director of Baric, a computer services company owned jointly by Barclays and ICL, and was responsible for ICL's computer bureau services worldwide.

Sir Christopher served as the national chairman of the Young Conservatives from 1977 to 1979, and was vice-president of the Computer Services Association Council at the time he left ICL.

He is a non-executive director of Ferrari SpA and Lehman Brothers Holdings Inc; a member of KPMG's Chairman Advisory Group; a senior adviser at Bain and Co; and a member of the Advisory Board of Reform.

John Gildersleeve

John Gildersleeve is deputy chairman of Carphone Warehouse, and is the immediate past chairman of New Look, the fashion retail group with more than 1,000 stores in Europe, the Middle East and the UK.

John joined the Carphone Warehouse board in June 2000 and became non-executive chairman in July 2005. He was appointed a non-executive director of the British Land Company plc in September 2008. Previously, he was an executive director of Tesco plc until he retired in February 2004. He was chairman of Gallaher Group plc until April 2007 and chairman of EMI Group plc until September 2007. Prior to this he was a non-executive director of Vodafone Group plc from 1998 to 2000. He will also become non-executive deputy chairman of

New Carphone Warehouse. John has been a TalkTalk director since 20 January 2010.

He worked at Tesco from 1965 until 2004, and ultimately became director of commercial and trading, having joined as a trainee manager.

Richard Gnodde

Richard Gnodde is co-chief executive officer of Goldman Sachs International. He has been a member of the management committee since 2003 and also serves on the client and business standards committee, the public policy committee and the steering committee on regulatory reform. He served on the firm's partnership committee from 1999 to 2004.

Richard joined Goldman Sachs in London in 1987 and helped build the firm's European merger and acquisition franchise, eventually leading the investment banking effort in the United Kingdom. He was appointed co-head of the firm's investment banking division in Japan in 1997.

Richard became president of Goldman Sachs (Singapore) Pte. and co-head of investment banking in Asia in 1999 before moving to Hong Kong that same year to become president of Goldman Sachs (Asia) LLC. In 2005, Richard returned to London as vice-chairman and assumed his current role in 2006.

Richard earned a bachelor's degree from the University of Cape Town and a master's degree from Cambridge University.

Philip Green

Philip Green was chief executive of United Utilities plc from February 2006 until 31 March 2011. United Utilities is one of the largest utility companies in the UK, ranked midway in the FTSE 100, with a market cap of approximately £4 billion after recently returning £1.5 billion to shareholders.

In 2003 Philip was appointed CEO of P&O Nedlloyd, one of the largest container shipping companies in the world, and a joint venture between P&O and Royal Nedlloyd. He led the company to its successful listing as Royal P&O Nedlloyd BV in Amsterdam in April 2004.

He was previously chief operating officer at Reuters Group plc, which he joined in 1999. His responsibilities included the design and implementation of a global change management programme. From 1990 to 1999 he was at DHL, the global market leader for cross-border express delivery, becoming chief operating officer for Europe and Africa.

He holds an MBA from the London Business School and a BA (Hons) from the University of Wales.

Philip is chairman of Sentebale, a charity set up by Prince Harry to focus on disadvantaged young people in Lesotho, and is personally involved in several philanthropic projects in southern Africa. He is also chairman of the BITC environment leadership team.

He was born in 1953 and is married with two daughters.

Moya Greene

Moya Greene was appointed chief executive of Royal Mail Group in July 2010, previously having been president and chief executive officer of Canada Post Corporation since 2005. While there she led a wide-ranging transformation programme to increase quality of service and efficiency across the organization.

Prior to joining Canada Post she held senior roles at companies including Bombardier Inc and TD Bank.

Royal Mail is the national postal service of the United Kingdom, employs 176,000 people and includes the brands Royal Mail, Post Office and Parcelforce.

Moya was named among the 100 most influential women in Canada by the National Post and in 2004 as one of the top 40 female corporate executives in Canada by the Ivey School of Business. She is also a member of the board of directors for coffee shop chain Tim Hortons.

General The Lord Guthrie

Lord Guthrie joined the Welsh Guards in 1959 and in the 1960s served with them and the SAS in the United Kingdom, Germany, Libya, the Middle East, Malaysia and East Africa. He spent 1972 as a student at the Army Staff College and then held a number of appointments in Whitehall and with his regiment in London, Northern Ireland and Cyprus.

From 1977 to 1980 he commanded the Welsh Guards in Berlin and Northern Ireland. In 1980 he served briefly in the South Pacific and as the Commander British Forces, New Hebrides, recaptured the island of Espirito Santo which had been seized by insurgents.

Apart from holding a number of senior staff appointments, he commanded an armoured brigade, an infantry division, 1st British Corps, the British Army of the Rhine, and the Northern Army Group before becoming Chief of the General Staff (head of the army) in 1994. From 1997 to 2001 he was Chief of the Defence Staff and the Principal Military Adviser to two prime ministers and three secretaries of state for defence.

He was for ten years Colonel Commandant of the Intelligence Corps and is currently Colonel of the Life Guards, Gold Stick to the Queen and a former Colonel Commandant of the SAS. He retired from the army in February 2001.

He was a director of N M Rothschild & Sons Ltd, is now a director of Cold Defence and Petropavlovsk, a council member of the International Institute of Strategic Studies and a visiting professor at King's College London University.

General The Lord Guthrie is married with two grown-up sons. He is a keen sportsman. He played rugby for the army, regularly rides and plays tennis. He attends the opera as often as he can.

John Heaps

John Heaps is the chairman of Eversheds LLP and a partner in the commercial dispute resolution team based in London. He is an elected member of the firm's board and its constitutional committee. Eversheds is an international law firm headquartered in London.

John represents European and US multinational companies in relation to their commercial disputes, often involving cross-border issues. He introduced to Eversheds the concept of dispute management which uses as its key analytical tool early case assessment (ECA). This approach has now been adopted by many of the firm's clients including the UK government, in connection with the defence of claims arising from the foot and mouth epidemic.

John is a Fellow of the Chartered Institute of Arbitrators and is recognized as an expert in the field of commercial litigation. He lectures widely and has spoken at the Federalist Society in Washington, DC on law reform, at many International Bar Association meetings and at conferences throughout Europe. He is the co-author of the UK chapter of *Privilege and Confidentiality: An International Handbook*.

John was elected chairman of Eversheds with effect from 1 May 2010 for a four-year term.

James Hogan

James Hogan was appointed CEO of Etihad Airways in September 2006, bringing more than 30 years of travel industry expertise to the Abu Dhabi-based airline.

He has overseen rapid growth of the UAE's national airline over the past four years, adding 33 new destinations and 35 new aircraft, and increasing the number of passengers carried each year from 2.7 million to 7.2 million.

In July 2008, he signed one of the largest aircraft orders in history for up to 205 aircraft worth approximately US $43 billion at list prices, to meet the airline's ambitious long-term growth plans.

James started his career in 1975 at Ansett Airlines, and subsequently held senior positions with bmi, Hertz, Forte Hotels and Gulf Air. He moved back to his native Australia in 2001, where he was appointed chief executive of the Tesna consortium, which was created with the aim of acquiring Ansett Airlines from administration, before joining Gulf Air in 2002, where he served as chief executive for four years.

James is a fellow of the Royal Aeronautical Society and a former non-executive director and member of the board's audit committee of Gallaher plc.

Baroness Sarah Hogg

Baroness Sarah Hogg has been chairman of the Financial Reporting Council, the regulator and standard setter responsible for corporate governance and financial reporting as well as the audit, accounting and actuarial profes-sions, since May 2010.

She is senior independent director of BG Group plc, lead independent director of HM Treasury, a director of the John Lewis Partnership and chairman of Frontier Economics Ltd, a consultancy founded in 1999 to specialize in the provision of strategic competition advice and the economics of regulation. She is also a member of the Takeover Panel, senior adviser to the Financial Services Authority and a member of the prime minister's Business Ambassador Network.

With extensive experience of business, government and the media, Sarah has worked at a high level in all three. She was chairman of 3i Group plc from 2002 to 2010. As head of the prime minister's policy unit, with the rank of second permanent secretary, from 1990 to 1995, she was closely involved in the programmes of privatization and private finance, performance measurement in public services and international economic issues.

Before that Sarah was responsible for the economics coverage of a number of Britain's most respected publications, including the *Economist*, *The Times* and the *Daily Telegraph*. She was created a life peer in the 1995 New Year's honours list.

Thomas Hughes-Hallett

Thomas Hughes-Hallett became chief executive of Marie Curie Cancer Care in 2000 after 22 years in the international investment banking sector. Marie Curie is a charitable organization with more than 2,700 nurses, doctors and other healthcare professionals, and provides care for terminally ill patients in the community and in its own hospices, along with support for their families. This year, Marie Curie expects to provide care to more than 31,000 people with cancer and other terminal illnesses.

Tom is chairing the Philanthropy Review – a fresh look at reshaping philanthropy to encourage more people to give and people to give more. He is also a member of The King's Fund general advisory council, chairman of the End of Life Care Implementation advisory board, review chair for the Palliative Care funding review for adults and children in England and a trustee of Esmee Fairbairn Foundation.

Tom has formerly been chairman of English Churches Housing Group and the Michael Palin Centre for Stammering Children, a director of the National Council for Palliative Care and a special trustee of Great Ormond Street Hospital.

General Sir Mike Jackson

General Sir Mike Jackson is a senior adviser at PA Consulting Group and former Chief of the General Staff of the British Army.

He served as Chief of the General Staff (CGS) from February 2003 to August 2006, after a highly distinguished career in the British army spanning more than four decades.

Prior to his appointment as CGS, General Sir Mike Jackson served most recently as Commander in Chief Land Command (from 2000), Commander Kosovo Force (in 1999), Commander ACE Rapid Reaction Corps (from 1997) and director general development and doctrine.

General Sir Mike Jackson has seen considerable active service: he commanded at company and brigade level in Northern Ireland, as a divisional commander in Bosnia, and as a corps commander in Macedonia and Kosovo.

Antony Jenkins

Antony Jenkins was appointed chief executive of Barclays Global Retail Banking and joined the Barclays executive committee in November 2009. Prior to that he had been chief executive of Barclaycard since January 2006.

Antony is the executive responsible for diversity and inclusion at Barclays and in February 2009 he additionally became a Barclays-appointed non-executive director of ABSA, the South African banking group. Since October 2008, Antony has been on the board of Visa Europe Ltd.

Barclays is where Antony started his career in finance in 1983, when he completed the Barclays management development programme before going on to hold various roles in retail and corporate banking. He moved to Citigroup in 1989, working in both London and New York. Antony was educated at Oxford University and has a master's in philosophy, politics and economics. He also has an MBA from the Cranfield Institute of Technology.

Antony is married and a father of two children.

Lady Barbara Judge

Lady Barbara Judge, a trained commercial lawyer with both British and American citizenship, has a broad international career as a senior executive, chairman and non-executive director in both the private and public sectors.

In 1980 she was appointed by the US president as a commissioner of the US Securities and Exchange Commission. Thereafter she was appointed as the first woman executive director of both Samuel Montagu and subsequently News International, among others.

She was appointed a director of the United Kingdom Atomic Energy Authority in 2002 and became its chairman in 2004 and was reappointed in 2007. In 2010, upon completion of her two terms, she was appointed chairman emeritus. In addition she is chairman of the business advisory board of the UK National Nuclear Centre of Excellence, and a member of the UK Nuclear Development Forum. She is also chairman of the Energy Institute of University College London.

Lady Judge is a non-executive director of Statoil ASA (Norway), NV Bekaert SA (Belgium) and Magna International Inc (Canada). Previously she was deputy chairman of the UK Financial Reporting Council as well as a public member of the International Ethics Standards Board for Accountants, among others.

She is also chairman of the International Advisory Board of SOAS and its London Middle East Institute.

Lord Peter Levene

Lord Peter Levene was elected chairman of Lloyd's, the world's leading specialist insurance and reinsurance market, in November 2002. In this role, he chairs the council of Lloyd's and Lloyd's franchise board.

Peter started his career in the defence industry with United Scientific Holdings. Subsequently, he was asked by defence secretary Michael Heseltine to act as personal adviser in the Ministry of Defence, and subsequently as permanent secretary in the role of chief of defence procurement, a position which he held for six years. He thereafter held a number of government posts, as adviser to the secretary of state for the environment; to the president of the board of trade; and to the chancellor of the exchequer. He was appointed as adviser to the prime minister on efficiency and effectiveness from 1992 to 1997. During this period, he also served as chairman of the Docklands Light Railway and then chairman and chief executive of Canary Wharf Ltd.

Later he became vice-chairman of Deutsche Bank in the UK, having also been at Wasserstein Perella and Morgan Stanley. Peter Levene currently holds four non-executive directorships, as chairman of General Dynamics UK Ltd and on the boards of Haymarket Group Ltd, Total SA and China Construction Bank. He is also the chairman of NBNK Investments plc and is a member of the House of Lords Select Committee for Economic Affairs.

Graham Mackay

Graham Mackay is the chief executive of SABMiller plc, one of the world's largest brewers, with brewing interests and distribution agreements across six continents. He was appointed chief executive of South African Breweries plc upon its listing on the London Stock Exchange in 1999. The company became SABMiller plc following its acquisition of Miller Brewing Company in 2005. He is based at SABMiller's head office in London.

Following positions with BTR (South Africa) Ltd and its subsidiary Sarmcol, Graham joined South African Breweries Ltd (SAB Ltd) in 1978 as a systems manager. In 1987 he was appointed managing director of SAB Ltd and in 1992 he became chairman.

He holds a number of directorships and is the senior independent non-executive director of Reckitt Benckiser Group plc and a director of Philip Morris International Inc.

Born in 1949, Graham was brought up in Swaziland, Natal and Rhodesia (now Zimbabwe). He graduated from the University of the Witwatersrand in 1972 with a BSc in Engineering and gained a BCom from the University of South Africa in 1977.

He is married with six sons and enjoys squash, music and literature.

Colin Matthews

Colin Matthews is the chief executive of BAA Ltd. He was appointed to the role in April 2008, and is also a non-executive director of Mondi plc, the British and South African paper business. BAA operates six airports in the UK, which are Heathrow, Stansted, Edinburgh, Glasgow, Aberdeen and Southampton.

After graduating in engineering from Cambridge, he started his career in a number of technical roles in the automotive industry with Lucas Industries in the UK and Japan. He then took an MBA at INSEAD in France and joined Bain as a strategy consultant. From Bain, he joined the (US) General Electric Company, taking roles in

London in strategy, then Paris in medical systems and finally in Montreal where he led GE's worldwide business in hydro turbines and generators.

Returning to the UK, he joined British Airways, first as director of engineering and then as director of technical operations, responsible for aircraft maintenance, IT and procurement. Subsequently, Colin was group managing director of Transco, the national gas transmission and distribution company, and then the CEO of the business services company Hays plc. More recently he was group CEO of the water and waste company Trent from 2004 to 2007.

David Morley

David Morley is worldwide senior partner of Allen & Overy LLP, a global law firm. He joined Allen & Overy as a trainee in 1980 after studying law at St John's College, Cambridge. He qualified as a solicitor in 1982. He spent a year on secondment at a US investment bank and became a partner in 1988. In 1998 he became the global head of the banking practice. In May 2003 he was elected to the position of worldwide managing partner and was elected to his current position in May 2008.

David practised for 25 years as a banking lawyer advising major banks and corporate borrowers on a wide variety of debt and structured finance transactions.

He is married to Sue, also a lawyer, and they have four grown-up children, none of whom wants to be a lawyer. He is a member of the Mayor of London's International Business Advisory Council. He enjoys cycling, skiing and sailing.

Heidi Mottram

Heidi Mottram is chief executive officer of Northumbrian Water. She was appointed to the NWG and NWL boards as an executive director, on 1 March 2010, and became chief executive that year.

Northumbrian Water operates in the North East (good water supply) and also in Essex and Suffolk (driest parts of the UK). The company has 4.5 million customers and about 3,000 employees. There are 10 regulated water and sewage companies in the UK. Only four are listed on the London Stock Exchange – Northumbrian Water Group, Pennon, Severn Trent and United Utilities.

Heidi began her career with British Rail as a general management trainee in the mid 1980s. Her first senior position was that of station manager in Harrogate in 1986 and she then held a number of roles before joining Midland Mainline in 1999 as operations director, where she was fully accountable for the operations team. Heidi was commercial director for Arriva Trains Northern from January 2004, before joining Serco-NedRailways in November 2004 as managing director, Northern Rail Ltd.

She is in her mid forties and is married with two children.

David Nussbaum

David Nussbaum joined WWF-UK as chief executive in May 2007. WWF is an international, non-governmental organization working on issues regarding the conservation, research and restoration of the environment.

Prior to joining WWF, David was the chief executive of Transparency International ('TI'), based at the international secretariat in Berlin. TI is the leading global NGO focused on curbing corruption, with national chapters in around 100 countries.

David is also a non-executive director of the quoted private equity fund Low Carbon Accelerator and of the leading fair trade finance company Shared Interest. Until 2006, he was the (non-executive) chair of Traidcraft, the leading UK fair trade company.

Previously, David was the director of finance, information and planning and a deputy chief executive of Oxfam, the international relief and development organization.

After qualifying as a chartered accountant, David went to work in venture capital with 3i plc as an investment controller. From there he moved into the manufacturing industry with the European packaging company Field Group plc, where he was its finance director, through the company's management buyout and subsequent flotation on the London Stock Exchange.

David holds degrees in theology from Cambridge and Edinburgh universities and an MSc in finance from London Business School. He was born in 1958, and he and his wife have four children.

Sir Nick Partridge

Sir Nick Partridge is chief executive of the Terrence Higgins Trust. Sir Nick has worked for Terrence Higgins Trust since 1985 and was appointed its chief executive in 1991. Over the past 25 years, his has been a consistent voice in the media coverage of AIDS and sexual health in all its aspects from health promotion, social care and advocacy through to research and treatment issues.

Terrence Higgins Trust has negotiated 36 mergers with other charities over the past 10 years and now mobilizes over 1,000 volunteers and 330 staff, providing a wide range of sexual health and HIV services. Sir Nick is deputy chair of the expert advisory group on AIDS (EAGA), which advises ministers and the chief medical officers.

In health research, Sir Nick is chair of INVOLVE, which promotes patient and public involvement in NHS, public health and social care research. He is also deputy chair of the UK Clinical Research Collaboration, which aims to establish the UK as a world leader in clinical research.

Paul Polman

Paul Polman became an executive director of Unilever in October 2008, and assumed the role of global chief executive officer on 1 January 2009. He began his career at Procter and Gamble in 1979, and was group president Europe of the Procter and Gamble Company until 2006.

Prior to joining Unilever, Paul was chief financial officer of Nestlé SA from January 2006 as well as executive vice-president for the Americas from February 2008. Paul serves as president of the Kilimanjaro Blind Trust and chairman of Perkins international advisory board. He is a member of the executive committee of the World Business Council for Sustainable Development.

He is also on the board of the Consumer Goods Forum where he co-chairs the board strategy and also the sustainability committees. He is a trustee of both the Leverhulme Trust and Asia House, a former board member of Alcon and, since February 2010, a non-executive director of the Dow Chemical Company.

Married with three children, Paul's interests include reading, marathon running and mountaineering, but his main passion is for his role in running the Kilimanjaro Blind Trust.

Dame Fiona Reynolds

Dame Fiona Reynolds has been director-general of the National Trust for England, Wales and Northern Ireland since 1 January 2001. The Trust is one of the world's most successful charities, fulfilling its responsibilities to 'look after special places for ever, for everyone' through the ownership of 650,000 acres of land, 700+ miles of coastline, c250 great houses and their gardens and parks, tens of thousands of smaller vernacular buildings and many sites of nature conservation, archaeological and historic importance.

Dame Fiona has a first class honours degree in geography/land economy and an examined master's in land economy from Cambridge University. Before the Trust, Fiona spent 18 years in the voluntary conservation movement (as chief executive of the Council for National Parks and CPRE) and a short spell in the cabinet office as director of the women's unit from 1998 to 2000.

Fiona has been married to Bob Merrill since 1981 and they have three teenage daughters. They live in Coates, near Cirencester. Fiona loves walking, landscape history, classical music and opera.

Sir Stuart Rose

Sir Stuart Rose has worked in retail for over 30 years, starting at Marks & Spencer plc in 1972 and joining the Burton Group in 1989. Following the group's demerger in 1997 he became chief executive of Argos plc. In 1998 he became chief executive of Booker plc, which was merged with the Iceland Group in 2000.

He became chief executive of Arcadia Group plc in November 2000 and left in December 2002 following its acquisition. He was named chief executive of Marks & Spencer plc in May 2004 and became chairman in 2008. He stood down as chairman in January 2011.

He was chairman of Business in the Community from 2008 to 2010, is a non-executive director of Land Securities plc, Woolworths (South Africa) and No Exclusions; is on the advisory committee of Bridgepoint and is a member of the Measuring National Well-being advisory panel.

Stuart was knighted in 2008 for services to the retail industry and corporate social responsibility.

Ron Sandler

Ron Sandler is the chairman of Northern Rock, the publicly owned UK bank, and also chairs the Phoenix Group, the largest UK consolidator of closed life assurance funds. He was born in Zimbabwe in 1952. He has an MA from Queens' College, Cambridge and an MBA from Stanford University.

He was previously chief executive of Lloyd's of London and played a key role in the Lloyd's reconstruction and renewal programme. Subsequently, he was chief operating officer of NatWest Group. In 2002, at the request of the chancellor of the exchequer, he led an independent review of the UK long-term savings industry. He is a recent past president of the Chartered Institute of Bankers.

Christopher Satterthwaite

Christopher Satterthwaite is chief executive of Chime Communications, the holding company for a portfolio of 52 companies which include public relations, advertising, digital, marketing, sports marketing, market research, corporate responsibility and design businesses.

He began his commercial career as a graduate trainee at H J Heinz. Since his grounding on the client side, he has been part of three different marketing communication agencies: IMP (1983–93), then the UK's largest sales promotion and direct marketing agency; HHCL and Partners (1993–2003), *Campaign* magazine's Advertising Agency of the Decade; Bell Pottinger (2000–2), the UK's leading public relations agency.

He is senior independent director of Centaur Media, chairman of the Roundhouse, a Trustee of the Watts Gallery and a member of the government's professional and business services group. He is a former chairman of the Marketing Society.

Lord Colin Sharman

Lord Colin Sharman joined the KPMG partnership in 1966 and spent most of the 1970s in Europe, latterly with responsibility for the Benelux and Scandinavian countries. KPMG is one of the largest professional services firms in the world, and one of the Big Four auditors.

A specialist in financial and economic aspects of large scale investment, he was also responsible for KPMG's national marketing from 1987 to 1990 and in 1990 took over the responsibility for KPMG's operations in London and the southeast. From 1991 to 1994 he was chairman of KPMG Management Consulting worldwide. He was also a member of the KPMG international executive committee and KPMG European board. In 1994 he took over as the UK senior partner. On 1 February 1997 he assumed responsibilities as chairman of KPMG International and retired as international chairman and from the partnership on 30 September 1999. On 27 October 1999 he was sworn into the House of Lords.

Lord Sharman is now chairman of Aviva plc, the sixth largest insurance company in the world, created by the merger of Norwich Union and Commercial Union and employing 46,000 people.

He is a non-executive director of BG International plc and Reed Elsevier plc, and a former chairman of Aegis Group, member of the supervisory board of ABN Amro NV, the board of Young's Brewery plc, AEA Technology plc and Group 4 Securicor plc.

He was born in 1943 and educated in Salisbury before qualifying as a chartered accountant.

Lord John Stevens

Lord John Stevens of Kirkwhelpington is chairman of Monitor Quest, a global specialist risk consultancy. In this role, he led the inquiry for the Premier League into alleged irregular payments in football player transfers and chaired the Fédération Équestre Internationale ethics panel on behalf of HRH Princess Haya Bint Al Hussein. He is a former commissioner of the London Metropolitan Police.

During his career with the police, he led the inquiry into the alleged collusion between the security forces and paramilitaries in Northern Ireland; he continues to advise the historical enquiries team of the Police Service of Northern Ireland. Lord Stevens later headed the Metropolitan Police investigation into the allegation of conspiracy to murder Diana, Princess of Wales and Dodi Al-Fayed.

From June 2007 to May 2010, he was appointed by the then prime minister Gordon Brown to the position of senior adviser on international security issues. David Cameron appointed him as chair of the borders policing committee in 2007. He continues as an adviser for the committee.

In addition to being chairman at Monitor Quest, he holds a number of non-executive directorships. He is a non-executive director of Travelex and was appointed in 2007 a board member of BAA. He also sits on the board of LGC, the UK's leading analytical laboratory providing chemical, biochemical and DNA-based analysis.

Lord Stevens is the chancellor of Northumbria University.

Dame Barbara Stocking

Dame Barbara Stocking joined Oxfam GB as chief executive in May 2001. Oxfam GB is a major international non-government organization whose mission is 'to work with others to overcome poverty and suffering'.

Barbara is a member of the Steering Committee for

Humanitarian Response (SCHR), an alliance for voluntary action of currently nine major international humanitarian organizations, and was chair from 2008 to 2010. She was also a member of the UN Inter-Agency Standing Committee for Humanitarian Action (IASC) from 2006 to 2010.

Barbara is a member of the Food and Agriculture Organization (FAO) High-Level External Committee on Millennium Development Goals. In 2007, she was a member of the BBC's impartiality panel on business coverage, led by Sir Alan Budd.

Previously a member of the top management team of the National Health Service, in her eight years with the NHS Barbara worked as regional director and then as the founding director of the NHS Modernisation Agency. Barbara has a master's degree in physiology, and has broad experience of healthcare systems, policy and practice, including periods at the National Academy of Sciences in the USA and with the World Health Organization in West Africa.

Barbara is married and has two sons.

Ian Thomas

Ian Thomas was appointed senior vice-president of Fluor's corporate strategy and emerging markets group in July 2007 and managing director of Fluor Ltd, the company's operations in the United Kingdom, in January 2008. Fluor Corporation provides services on a global basis in the fields of engineering, procurement, construction, operations, maintenance and project management. Headquartered in Irving, Texas, Fluor is a Fortune 500 company with revenues of $20.8 billion in 2010.

In his roles Ian has specific responsibility for business development in emerging markets. In his role as managing director of Fluor Ltd UK he leads the company's pursuit of projects in Europe, the Middle East and Africa.

He joined Fluor in mid 2007 from international project management and engineering group AMEC plc, where for more than 10 years he was business development director and a member of the senior management committee reporting directly to the chief executive officer.

He is co-chairman of the Indonesian British Business Council and sits on the UK government's Nuclear Development Forum and Carbon Capture Forum.

Professor Nigel Thrift

Professor Nigel Thrift is vice-chancellor of the University of Warwick. He joined Warwick from the University of Oxford where he was pro vice-chancellor for research.

Since becoming vice-chancellor in 2006, Professor Thrift has established high-profile partnerships and research collaborations with leading universities in the USA, Australia, India, Asia and Europe; and has increased Warwick's international profile through initiatives such as the Warwick Commission and the International Gateway for Gifted Youth.

He was born in Bath, educated at Aberystwyth and Bristol, and is an international research figure in the field of geography. He continues to maintain an active research career alongside his role as vice-chancellor and has been the recipient of a number of distinguished academic awards including the Royal Geographical Society Victoria Medal for contributions to geographic research in 2003, Distinguished Scholarship Honors from the Association of American Geographers in 2007 and the Royal Scottish Geographical Society Gold Medal in 2008.

He writes a regular blog for the Worldwise series in *The Chronicle of Higher Education*. His current research spans a broad range of interests, including international finance; cities and political life; non-representational theory; affective politics; and the history of time.

Ben Verwaayen

Ben Verwaayen is CEO of Alcatel-Lucent, the global telecommunications corporation, headquartered in Paris, France. It provides voice, data and video hardware and software to service providers, enterprises, and governments around the world. It holds Bell Labs, one of the largest R&D houses in the communications industry, and operates in more than 130 countries. In 2010, Alcatel reported revenues of almost €16 billion.

Previously, Ben Verwaayen was appointed to the board of directors of BT on 14 January 2002 and became chief executive on 1 February 2002. He left BT Group on 1 June 2008 as chairman of the board's operating committee.

Before joining BT Group, he was at Lucent Technologies, starting September 1997, holding various positions. He left Lucent as vice-chairman of the management board. Other positions that Ben held at Lucent were executive vice-president and chief operating officer, and executive vice-president, international.

Prior to joining Lucent, he worked for KPN in the Netherlands for nine years as president and managing director of its subsidiary PTT Telecom. From 1975 to 1988, he worked at ITT in Europe.

Ben is a Dutch national and graduated with a master's degree in law and international politics from the State University of Utrecht, Holland.

Fields Wicker-Miurin

Fields Wicker-Miurin is co-founder and partner of Leaders' Quest, an international social enterprise whose purpose is to be a catalyst for positive change through its work with leaders from different sectors and from around the world. Through experiential learning quests to China, India, Brazil, parts of Africa, Russia, Turkey, the UK and the United States, Leaders' Quest creates programmes that foster insights and reflection for senior people to learn both about how the world is changing and to consider their own roles and responsibilities as leaders.

Fields's own interest in leadership has developed over an international business career spanning different industries and countries. She is also a non-executive director of BNP Paribas, of Ballarpur International Graphic Paper (the largest writing paper company in India), and of the CDC Group plc, the UK's development finance institution, where she chairs the Best Practice and Development Committee that evaluates the impact of CDC's investments on development.

An active supporter of the arts and of education, she is a governor of King's College London, where she also chairs the audit committee. Over a career spanning some 20 years, she is perhaps best known for her time at the London Stock Exchange as chief financial officer and director of strategy.

Fields has degrees from the University of Virginia, l'Institut d'Études Politiques (Paris), and the Johns Hopkins School of Advanced International Studies. She speaks French and Italian fluently. She loves learning, competing in dressage, and cooking and discussing world affairs and ideas with her husband, Paolo.

Sir Frank Williams

Sir Frank Williams is founder of the Williams F1 Formula One racing team. He recently handed over his role as chairman to Adam Parr. Sir Frank remains as team principal and will have the final say on all decisions, but Adam now looks after the day-to-day running of the company.

Patrick Head, Sir Frank's long-time partner, continues as director of engineering, taking charge of the technical side of the company.

Sir Frank established Frank Williams Racing Cars in 1966, after deciding he was not good enough to continue racing as a driver. With Patrick Head, his team went on to win the Grand Prix Manufacturers' World Championships in the 1980s and 1990s. His drivers included Alan Jones, Nelson Piquet, Nigel Mansell, Ayrton Senna and Damon Hill.

Sir Frank, 68, recently floated his company on the Frankfurt Stock Exchange.

He has been confined to a wheelchair since 1986, as a result of injuries sustained in a road accident.

Sir Clive Woodward

Sir Clive Woodward is the coach who led England's rugby players to World Cup glory in Australia in 2003. He is now the full-time director of sport for the British Olympic Association. On 6 March 2008, he had the privilege of running with the Olympic torch through Russell Square, London. At the Beijing 2008 Summer Olympic Games he acted as deputy chef de mission and undertook a review of practices at the games for preparation for London 2012.

Clive enjoyed a successful career with Rank Xerox that included a spell in Australia while playing his club rugby down under. On his return to the UK he ran his own IT leasing company and has hands-on experience of business at the sharp end.

His distinguished playing career included 21 England caps and touring with the British Lions in 1981 and 1983. His coaching career prior to England included Henley and London Irish.

Sir Nicholas Young

Sir Nicholas Young is chief executive of the British Red Cross, the country's leading voluntary disaster response organization, and part of the worldwide Red Cross Red Crescent Movement. The British Red Cross has 3,000 staff, around 40,000 volunteers and an annual income/expenditure of over £200 million.

Internationally, Nick plays an active part in the work of the Red Cross Movement. In the UK, he is actively involved in the work of the voluntary sector as a whole and its interface with government. He has undertaken various high-level strategic and operational reviews, both nationally and internationally.

Prior to rejoining the Red Cross in 2001, Nick was chief executive of Macmillan Cancer Relief. Before that he was director of UK Operations at the British Red Cross, following five years with the Sue Ryder Foundation, setting up new Sue Ryder Homes.

He started his career as a commercial solicitor in the City of London and then as a partner in a firm in East Anglia. He was educated at Wimbledon College Grammar School and at Birmingham University.

Nick is married with three sons and lives in the City of London.

THANKS

*T*he Language of Leaders *was my idea and is all my work and nobody else deserves any credit.*

At least, this was how I felt, alone in my study, usually after midnight, as I struggled to get all the ideas and stories out of my head and onto the page. It was solitary work. But that was the only lonely part of this project. It has been, overall, such a social enterprise, and there are actually many to thank.

First, I want to thank the leaders who gave their time and were so generous and open when discussing their views on communication. Without your words, this book would not be. I hope you enjoyed the experience.

Thank you also to the colleagues at Chime Communications who approached many of these leaders on my behalf, and encouraged them to see me. Lord Tim Bell, Chris Satterthwaite, Sue Farr, Patsy Baker, Elizabeth Buchanan, and Celia Dunstone – your help was invaluable.

Credit must also go to Matthew Smith, Sara Marchington and Abby Coften at Kogan Page, publishers of this book, and freelance copy-editor Kevin Doherty. You have obviously done this many times before, and your guidance was invaluable.

Most of the people in this book were photographed by Stewart Goldstein and Ben Fitzpatrick of Newscast Limited, who have done a great job in coaxing these leaders to reveal something of their personalities. While on the subject of illustrations, thank you also to Debbie Macey White for the diagram at the heart of this book. Thanks also to Louisa Knox for her eagle eye when correcting the proofs of this book.

Special recognition is due to my Council of Critics, a band of conscripts who read my early efforts and provided precious advice on what was, and wasn't, working. Thank you to Rick Huckstep, Andrew Sherville, Roger Bateson, Vic Hawker, Geoff Smith, Tricia Moon, Stefan and Kirstin Kaszubowski, Jason Murray and Bill Whalley. You provided the fuel of encouragement, and that kept me going.

To my wife, Liz, who made this all possible by shielding me from everything else, I express deep appreciation. The sight of you late at night, loyally reading my drafts, pencil to lip, is one of the many images from our marriage that I will always treasure.

Special recognition must go to my tireless, patient, gracious, dedicated and detail-obsessed PA, Vicky Swales. It has been a joy working with you on this.

Finally, thanks to my friend the late Phil Duncombe. I miss him still, and it was his words that got me going. Just as he inspired so many others, he inspired me with what was his constant response to any good idea: 'Well, what are you waiting for?!'

INDEX